Harold Bindloss

In the Niger Country

Harold Bindloss

In the Niger Country

ISBN/EAN: 9783743317437

Manufactured in Europe, USA, Canada, Australia, Japa

Cover: Foto ©ninafisch / pixelio.de

Manufactured and distributed by brebook publishing software (www.brebook.com)

Harold Bindloss

In the Niger Country

IN THE NIGER COUNTRY

BY

HAROLD BINDLOSS

WITH TWO MAPS

WILLIAM BLACKWOOD AND SONS
EDINBURGH AND LONDON
MDCCCXCVIII

All Rights reserved

CONTENTS.

CHAPTER I.

IN EARLY DAYS.

General characteristics of the Niger region and its inhabitants—The fever belt—Moslem influence—The Sahara—Early eastern explorers—The advent of the European—Mungo Park, his forerunners and successors 1

CHAPTER II.

ON THE WAY TO THE NIGER—TENERIFFE AND SIERRA LEONE.

Santa Cruz, Teneriffe—Repulse of Nelson—N.E. trades—Young factory assistants — Freetown, Sierra Leone — Influence of missionaries—Types of population 15

CHAPTER III.

THE BATTLE OF WEIMA.

Emir Samadu—Konno and Sofa raiders—March of the West Indias—Attack on Weima—Fatal mistake—Defeat of the raiders 29

CHAPTER IV.

LIBERIA AND THE BEACHES OF THE KROO COUNTRY.

A tornado—Monrovia—The black republic—Kroo labourers—Kroo villages—Means of transport—Want of harbours . 41

CHAPTER V.

THE GOLD COAST COLONY AND DAHOMEY.

Early settlements—Fantis and Shantis—Haussa constabulary—Elmina and Cape Coast Castle, Accra—African surf—The French in Dahomey 54

CHAPTER VI.

LAGOS AND THE NIGER MOUTHS.

Lagos roads and town—Colour-caste—Trade of Lagos, and its bar—First glimpse of Niger delta—Crossing the bar—Early traders and establishment of Royal Niger Company . 66

CHAPTER VII.

AKASSA.

General aspect of Akassa—Salt and gin—Arab traders—European dwelling—The Chartered Company 78

CHAPTER VIII.

THE RAIDING OF AKASSA.

The Nimbi tribe—Cause of hostilities—Attack on the factory—Murder of Krooboys—Unexpected help—Cannibalism—Destruction of Nimbi 91

CHAPTER IX.

A BURNT VILLAGE.

African bush—Native village—Down an African stream—The mantle of Ananias—Sunday evening on the Niger . . 104

CHAPTER X.

THE INLAND REACHES OF THE NIGER.

Lower reaches—French policy—Moslem industries—Timbuktu—The Sahara—Turning back of trading expeditions—Rise and fall of Songhay—The advent of the Fulah—Emir Othman and the rise of Sokoto 115

CHAPTER XI.

IN FORCADOS RIVER.

Commercial importance of this water-way—A negro pilot—Tragic story of French survey vessel—Forcados post-office—Her Majesty's mail on the Niger—Propitiating the powers of darkness 126

CHAPTER XII.

ON THE WAY TO WARRI.

Mangrove swamps—Characteristic accident—Ramming the forest —Trade canoes—Warri and its Consulate—How justice is administered on the Niger—Major Crawford . . 138

CHAPTER XIII.

WARRI.

Yoruba troops—Palm-oil—How the trading agents live—Importation of fire-arms—Influence of the forest—End of Major Crawford—Red tape 150

CHAPTER XIV.

THE SLAVE-TRADE AND THE JU-JU SYSTEM.

Heathen mythology—The Ju-Ju—Superstitious white traders— The first of the slave trade—Bristol and Liverpool—Palm-oil ruffians—Domestic slavery 163

CHAPTER XV.

AT NEW BENIN.

Benin river—New Benin—The building of a factory—Young trading clerks—The man who struck 179

CHAPTER XVI.

NEW BENIN.

Seamen traders—A Niger headman—The Consulate and Government policy—Old Benin—Fetiche treasure—Early Latin explorers—Unfortunate expedition—Characteristic episode—A few climatic evils 193

CHAPTER XVII.

THE RISE AND FALL OF NANA.

The evolution of a bush potentate—How Nana defied the Government—Sapelli palaver—The impregnable stockade—Futile attack on Brohemie—Destruction of Brohemie—Nana's expiation 205

CHAPTER XVIII.

SAPELLI.

Mosquitoes—Early morning in a Niger factory—Silk hat and gun-case—General aspect of Sapelli—How trade is carried on—The fascination of the forest—The ways of the bush traders—Aggri beads 217

CHAPTER XIX.

DOWN THE SAPELLI RIVER.

Government headquarters—The banks of an African river—The power of the Ju-Ju—The home of the fever—In chase of an alligator—Jack's diversions ashore 231

CHAPTER XX.

ON THE BRASS RIVER.

An unsuccessful venture—A refractory oil-launch—The police of the seas 243

CHAPTER XXI.

A FUNERAL IN THE DELTA.

The last journey—Englishmen in the tropics—A faithful minister
—The ways of the fever—An incident at sea . . . 254

CHAPTER XXII.

MISSIONARY INFLUENCE.

Why some missionaries fail—Trading preachers—The power of
faith—The Jesuits—Modern martyrs—Need of medical skill—
Missionary women 264

CHAPTER XXIII.

BONNY AND OPOBO.

Bonny bar—Native squalor—How the Opobo men kept their guns
—Beneficent missionary influence—The black man's bishop . 277

CHAPTER XXIV.

THE OPPOSITE ENDS OF THE NIGER.

The Protectorate of Sierra Leone—Source of the Niger—Native
races—Moslem conquest—Northwards from the delta—Onitsha
slave market—Lokoja camp—Our black soldiers . . 288

CHAPTER XXV.

THE EVOLUTION OF THE BLACK TRADER AND HIS MERCHANDISE.

The seaboard negro—How the bush trader begins—Negro method
of dealing with competition—Chopping oil, a new method of
collecting accounts—Products of the Niger basin . . 300

CHAPTER XXVI.

RUBBER-GATHERING.

Expansion of the rubber trade—Rapid development of West African commerce—A rubber forest—How rubber is gathered—Devious ways of native traders—A field for the adventurer—How Johnson searched for rubber 311

CHAPTER XXVII.

FAREWELL TO THE NIGER.

Hauling out from Warri—Good-bye—Vanquished by malaria—Funerals at sea—Training of Englishmen—A necessary sacrifice—What we look for 324

INDEX 337

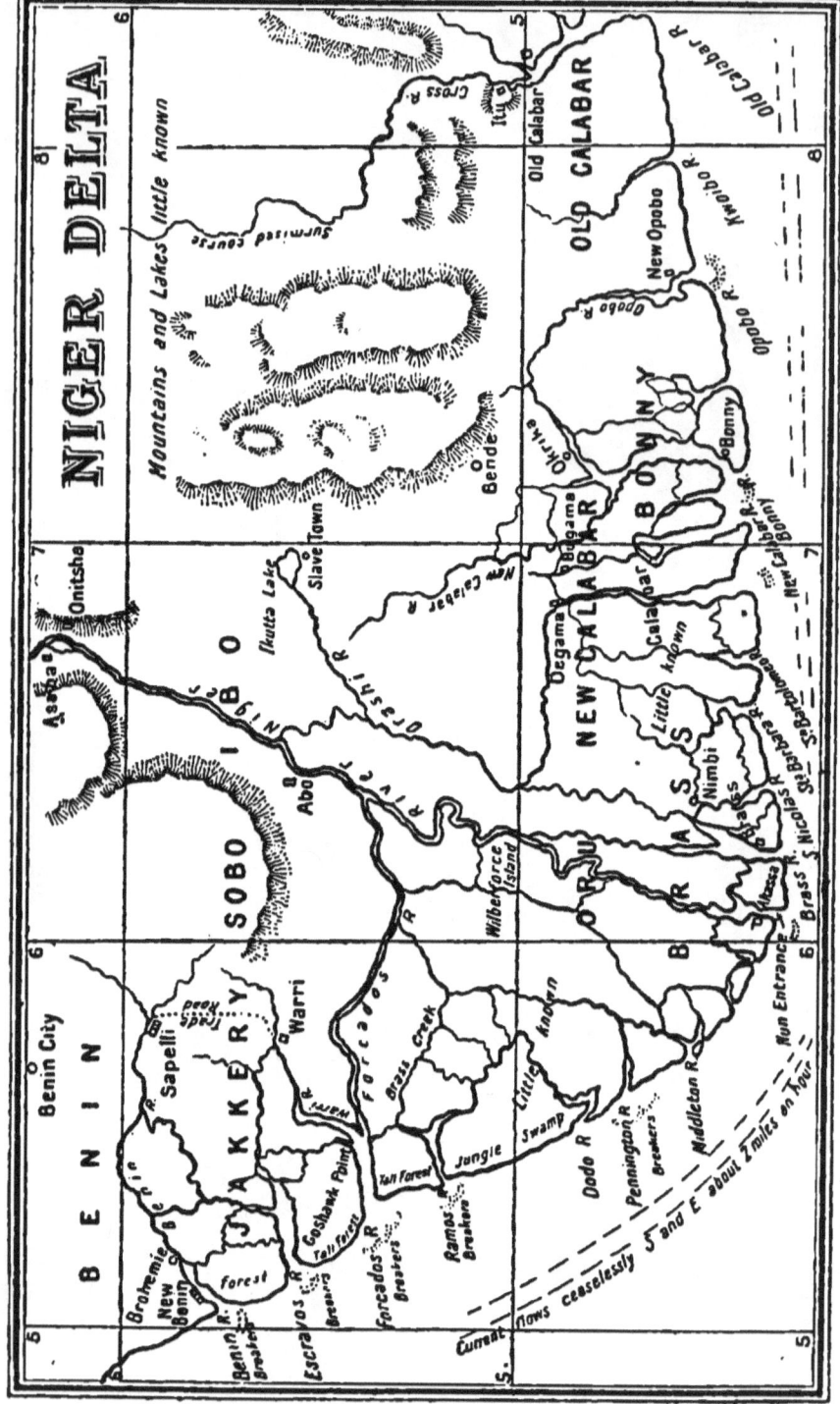

IN THE NIGER COUNTRY.

CHAPTER I.

IN EARLY DAYS.

BETWEEN two lines drawn roughly north and south from Sierra Leone to Bojador, and the Bight of Biafra to Fezzan, there lies a vast quadrangular tract of northern Africa, through the heart of which the Niger flows. The story of this region is more or less bound up with that of the great river, for throughout the greater portion of a thousand years rumours of the fertility and wealth of the Niger basin led adventurous explorers, first from the ancient East and then from the young West, onwards into the wilds of the Sudan. Many races, differing widely in origin, character, and mode of life, dwell there, and for the clearer understanding of its aspect and history it may be divided into three zones.

Starting at a point some two hundred miles from

the mouth of the Gambia, a line running approximately parallel to the sweep of surf-fringed beach as far as Lokoja on the Lower Niger would enclose what may be termed the coastwise strip. This is the tract with which Europeans are best acquainted, though even now, after trading there for four hundred years, portions of it still lie beyond their knowledge. It is a land of heat and steam, dense forests of cotton-trees and oil-palms, muddy rivers and wastes of quaking swamp. The shadow of the pestilence hangs heavily above it, and throughout the greater portion Ju-Ju superstition reigns supreme. White men suffer many climatic ills, or die by scores of malarial fever, while the native tribes are decimated by infectious sicknesses. Its inhabitants are generally of pure negro type, and, with the exception of Sierra Leone, Liberia, the Gold Coast, and Lagos, where some have been civilised with a vengeance, are for the most part degraded savages, worshippers of devils, and participators in horrible fetiche rites. There are exceptions; but, generally speaking, the classification holds good, for contact with Europeans has done little after all to change the character of its swarming peoples, neither has Christianity touched more than the fringe of this mass of dark humanity.

North of this line, and in places south of it also, the fever-haunted primeval forest commences to melt through gradations of acacias and groves of precious gums into a drier and more healthy land of yellow plume-grass and isolated woods, which rolls away league beyond league until these in turn are lost in the barrens of the Sahara—and much of this is still a region of romance and mystery. The colour of its inhabitants fades from jet black through various shades of colour; and here the older civilisation of the East and the faith of Islam, proclaimed with fire and sword, have done what the milder teaching of the Cross has hitherto failed to do. The people are staunch Moslem, dwelling in strong, walled towns with their mosques and markets, practising many arts, and combined in powerful military organisations. Emir, sultan, wazzeir, and sheik rule, and, it would seem, rule wisely too, though with an iron hand, in places amid a mingling of barbaric and Eastern splendour which recalls the tales of the 'Arabian Nights' and the days of Saladin. Some of these potentates are said to maintain household cavalry dressed in beautifully wrought chain-mail and armed with silver axes. In others, they are known to be mere leaders of coffee-coloured slave-raiders; but there is always a wide gulf between them and the coast-wise negro. With all its imperfections, the doctrine brought from Arabia has set an indelible stamp upon two-thirds of Africa, casting out drunkenness and degradation, and raising the negro from the condition of a savage into a state of partial intellectual development at least. Possibly this is because the fear of death possesses considerable persuasive power, and the tribesman who might risk a future retribution finds it wise to keep the law when the sword hangs visibly above his head.

Farther yet, and beyond the latitude of Timbuktu, the Sahara stretches north, an undulating waste of sand and sun-scorched ranges, until the foothills of the Atlas roll the desert back. But the Sahara is by no means all desert; for on its western fringe at least—and the writer speaks of what he has seen—lie vast oases with groves of date-palms, leagues of barley, maize, and even wheat. In places rivers half a mile in width flow towards the Atlantic four months every year, and then disappear again, and countless flocks of sheep, besides camels and splendid horses, are reared. Its semi-nomad people of Berber and Moorish race are the freest in the world, obeying no law but their own pleasure and the will of the grey-haired sheik, if he is strong enough to enforce it. They mock at the authority of the Moorish Sultan, and insult the officers of Spain, who claim a suzerainty they are utterly unable to enforce over part of the coast; and, it may be remarked in parenthesis, nearly shot the writer, when he made a brief visit to their land south of Cape Bojador, which will be mentioned again. Yet these men—and some of them are scarcely darker than a Spaniard or Italian, lighter in colour, strange to say, than the northern Moors — carry on a commerce which extends from Sokoto to the Atlas, and much of the products of the Upper Niger passes northwards through their dominions towards the Mediterranean, instead of south down-stream to the Bight of Biafra. One caravan alone of 10,000 camels, with loads averaging £50 apiece in value, enters the district of which Timbuktu is centre yearly from Morocco. There are others from Tripoli and Algiers, and ostrich-feathers, precious gums and spices, ivory, and dust of gold are largely brought back. Attempts have been made to intercept this trade on the western seaboard of the Sahara, but the result was generally disastrous to the white adventurers. With this rough classification, which may nevertheless serve its purpose, we will turn to the Niger proper.

It would seem to have been known to Egyptian, Carthaginian, and Roman that a great river flowed through the wilds of north-west Africa, though its source and mouth were never located. At first it was supposed to run eastwards towards the Nile, afterwards westwards towards the Atlantic, and there is no doubt that men of Eastern origin travelled south across the Sahara in search of it nearly a thousand years ago. Then, as in all ages down to this nineteenth century, death was generally the reward of the adventurer who set forth to unravel the mystery which enwrapped the Niger region, men and camels perishing of thirst in that furnace of scorching sand, "the belly of the desert."

Afterwards they died of fever or by the edge of the sword, ascending from Senegal. To-day the malaria lays its burning grasp upon them as they go up from Biafra Bight, and through long generations the road to the Niger has been watered by human blood. Yet, two widely different races, who between them have opened a way into the heart of Africa from Table Mountain to Tripoli, the swarthy Arab and fair-skinned Anglo-Saxon, have ever been subject to the spell of the unknown, which calls the adventurous forth into the wilderness, to die there if need be, but at least to leave their bones for a guide to those who come behind.

It was about the year 900 A.D. that the followers of Mahommed first carried a certain light of civilisation southwards towards the Niger, and the negro embraced the new faith, or had it forced upon him, on an extensive scale. Later the great Moslem empire of Songay was founded, and its dominion extended westwards, it is said, all the way from Sokoto to Bojador, a dominion which on the whole seems to have been for good, until the Moors broke it up in the sixteenth century. About the same time another sultanate, that of Bornu, ran eastwards towards the Nile, and so the faith of Islam spread far and wide, while by intermarriage and contact with his conquerors the negro rapidly changed, and became a higher stamp of man. Thus the Arab came first, through the gates of the north, bringing with him a measure of civilisation, and then the European entered the field from the west and south.

In 1481 the Gold Coast was reached by the Portuguese, who extended their discoveries east until they reached the swamps of the Niger delta. There they traded, unaware that this was the mouth of the legendary river whose fabled wealth, like that of the golden Manoa across the western sea, fired the imagination of the adventurous and discontented. It is strange that Europeans should have visited the delta periodically for centuries, gathering strange stories along the coast about the rich country surrounding the higher waters of the Niger, and yet the real locality of its mouth should so long remain a mystery. These Portuguese left unmistakable testimony of their presence in the Niger delta, and in the last few years expeditions marching into swamps hitherto sacred to fetiche cruelty have discovered weapons and other mementoes of their visits in tabooed towns wherein it was supposed no white man had ever set his foot.

Early in the seventeenth century (1618) Thompson sailed from England for the Gambia, then supposed to be the Niger. Others followed him, and a few years later the French decided that the Senegal must be the lower waters of that river. Then came Hawkins, hero, buccaneer, slaver, and fervent Christian, and it was undoubtedly the iniquitous commerce in human flesh inaugurated by him which gave a great impetus to the commercial exploitation of the coast by Europeans. Early in the eighteenth century a Captain Stibbs ascertained that the Gambia was not the Niger, and towards the end of that century the British made determined efforts to find the river, following at first the example of the Arabs, and marching south across the Sahara.

They paid the usual penalty, for the secret of the Niger was not to be lightly won. Leyland died, Horneman entered the wastes of the Sudan and disappeared therein. Lucas came back broken down by suffering, and then Houghton, attempting the western route from Senegal, perished with hunger in 1791. Mungo Park sailed in 1795, and reaching the true Niger at last near Sego, brought back wonderful stories of the power of the Moslem races about the head-waters of the river, which seemed to change legend into fact, and awoke a fierce desire for further knowledge. Again he sailed, marched inland through Senegal, and started on his last voyage from Sansandig to reach its mouth down-stream. When he left

Goree in 1805 he had with him thirty-six white followers. When he launched out into the unknown from Sansandig in a rickety craft made from two canoes joined together there were left but one white officer, two sick soldiers, and a raving madman—all the rest were dead. So, like Henry Hudson, and in an equally forlorn-hope, the great explorer sailed, and vanished from European eyes. Yet, as Isaaco, sent out by the Government in 1810, discovered, he reached the Haussaland, one thousand miles down river; and he who had served as guide told how the little party with four surviving natives fought their way against starvation and foe, until at last, shooting the Yauri rapids near Bussa under fire, the composite craft struck a reef, and all the white men perished. Park's family, however, still hoped on, refusing to believe him dead; and his son Thomas, starting from Accra on the Gold Coast in 1827, with neither provisions nor retainers, also disappeared and was lost in the silence of Africa. About the same time Clapperton reached Bussa, and found that the tale Isaaco brought back was true.

Between 1816 and 1827 the course of the river was pieced together little by little, and the roll of the dead was lengthened. Peddie, Oudney, Laing, and Clapperton laid down their lives, the two last reaching the great kingdom of Sokoto from Fezzan, and Clapperton it was who eventually of all explorers struck the right road. He started the second time from Lagos just outside the delta in 1825, and reached the Niger at Bussa, proving finally that the Benin swamps were the delta of the river. He, too, died in the Haussaland; but his mantle fell upon his servant Lander, who went back and sailed down from Bussa to the sea in 1830, dying four years afterwards from a wound at Fernando Po. Thus Park's work was finished and the chain complete. So far it may be repeated that every British adventurer whose eyes had seen the Niger perished in Africa. Peddie, Oudney, and Clapperton were slain by fever, Houghton starved, Park was drowned fighting a grim running fight, Laing was murdered, and Lander shot. There were others also whose work will live long after their names are forgotten.

Then, in 1852, Laird, making a second attempt, established trading-posts among the Niger creeks, and the story of the delta was the usual one of native raids, pestilence, suffering, and death; but in spite of all these evils trade and knowledge steadily increased. Time after time the Jakkery savages threatened to come down and drive the white men into the sea. The Government at home listened coldly to traders' appeals, but they held on grimly with the persistence of the race until the different factories were amalgamated into the National African Company. This corporation in 1886 received a charter and became the Royal Niger Company, and in 1891 an improved administration of the Niger Coast Protectorate, first proclaimed in 1885, was inaugurated, to maintain peace and order in a savage land, and incidentally to protect the trade. But these two powers and the work they do will be discussed in another place.

And so the history of the Niger reaches our own time, and British trade and influence are supreme in the delta and upon the lower waters of the river. As will be seen, this is not a wholly desirable region. The pestilence is always there, and when forest and swamp are rolled in clammy fever-mist at the change of the seasons white men die one after another, or suffer in burning torment. The inhabitants are cannibals, devil-worshippers, and offerers of human sacrifice, and after contact with Europeans for many generations live to-day as they did when the Portuguese first entered the mangrove-shrouded creeks. The Martini carbine represents the olive branch, and the voice of peace is most attentively listened to when it speaks by the mouth of the machine-gun. It is a land where murdered slaves drift down the muddy creeks, and order can only be maintained by an iron hand—an unsatisfactory state of affairs from a humanitarian point of view; but where moral persuasion utterly fails there is no other remedy than the stern rule of physical force. It is still better that one man should die than many, and that sharp retribution should overtake the malefactor, rather than that the land should lapse into a chaotic state of bloodshed.

As a nation our record in Western Africa is not a clean one, and we would do well to ponder before we cast the first stone at the Arab. For more than two centuries after Hawkins first sailed in search of slaves we stole the negro and shipped him westwards in endless thousands, to face the horrors of the middle passage, and end his days in slavery. Afterwards, we sold him rum and gin, introducing drunkenness and further degradation on an extensive scale, while our traders grew rich by traffic in improved means of murder with the flintlock gun. Thus through long ages we dyed our hands in blood, but now a better state of things exists. Patient missionary, and highly trained Government official, suffer many evils, and too often lay down their lives for their work. In the face of hardship and peril order is being brought forth out of chaos, plague-stricken towns are relieved by white help and medicine, and the word has gone forth that there shall be no more pouring out of human blood in honour of the Ju-Ju gods. Thus the weak are protected from the strong, so far as it may be done, and the Gospel is steadfastly preached. In our colonies of Sierra Leone, portions of the Gold Coast, and Lagos, Christianity has at least taken hold, and if the state of things in the Niger delta is not very satisfactory, it was ten times worse a little while ago. We make grievous mistakes at times, but our faces are set in the right direction, and there is hope yet for the redemption of the coastwise negro. The West African legion of honour is long, and the roll of faithful men shot from ambush and slain by fever or poison as they did their dangerous work valiantly and well, is one of which we have little cause to be ashamed. The trader is improving, too. He is no longer the dissolute ruffian he undoubtedly was, but generally, we cannot yet say always, a self-respecting European, whom the native knows may be trusted, and whose word alone is taken as guarantee for the delivery of much palm-oil.

So we wait, hoping that the dawn of better things will grow into a brightness before which the shadow of old wrongs, bloodshed, and cruelty will melt away.

And some day a great colony will run northwards from the Niger swamps into a rich and healthy region where we shall rule over intelligent Moslem races already waiting for our goods. Then, it may be, the Cross will replace the Crescent above the myriad mosques, and, if not, the follower of the Prophet has shown in other lands that he can become a law-abiding citizen under British rule.

Thus, with an industrious people, already skilled in arts and strong in arms, improved by Western knowledge, it is hard to say what the future of this land may be, or where its progress shall cease. France at least is awake to the importance of the Western Sudan, for she has been busy extending her influence throughout the hinterland, and her officers work with one eye on Dahomey and the other on Algiers. Meanwhile they who suffer and die in the delta are preparing the way, sowing for what may be a great harvest, though who shall gather it, and just what that harvest will be, lies beyond the knowledge of living man.

CHAPTER II.

ON THE WAY TO THE NIGER—TENERIFFE AND SIERRA LEONE.

ONE hot afternoon in May, together with two British companions whose faces bore the unmistakable stamp the fever-land sets upon most Europeans, I lounged upon a time-worn stone bench which stands in a certain avenue of oleanders close by the bullring at Santa Cruz, Teneriffe. Behind us the volcanic cordillera, a titan wall of fused red earth and jetty lava, seamed and rent by subterranean fire, lifted its splintered crest against the crystalline azure. Heavy-scented crimson blossoms hung above our heads, and below, seen through openings in the white sheen of orange flowers, lay a sloping reach of pale-green bananas, rustling maize, a few tall palms, and then the clustering red roofs and white walls of the old-world Spanish city rising out of glossy leaves. Farther yet, the sapphire Atlantic seethed in a long line of foam upon black lava beach and scoriæ crag, and there the low, yellow-funnelled steamer which was to carry us to the Niger lay rolling from rail to rail on the sunlit swell. The rush of the trade breeze shook down the oleander petals upon our heads, and the saltness of the sea was tempered by the fragrance of many flowers. It was a fair prospect, and there was life and health in every breath of the glorious "trades"—a contrast to the pestilential steam of the swamps and the sweltering heat of the equatorial forest which was soon to be our lot.

Western Africa had long interested me. For a time I dwelt among the glacier-ribbed peaks of the Canadian North-West with a man who had served one of our African colonies, and the tales he told had turned my thoughts towards the feverland. The wish to see it grew; and later contact for many months with invalided officers and traders recruiting in the Canaries strengthened the desire; until now, after a passing glimpse, I was going back to learn a little more of what it had to teach.

Presently one of my companions rose to his feet and suggested that, while that place was quite good enough for him, and he could do very well without setting eyes on the dismal swamps and native squalor of Bonny Town again, it would be awkward to be left behind. The rest agreed, and we reluctantly turned our faces towards Santa Cruz. Soon we were among the stony streets, where white-, cream-, and pink-walled houses flung back a dazzling glare, and as a matter of course visited the market-place, where Nelson's bluejackets and marines were hemmed in hopelessly during the great admiral's unsuccessful raid upon the town. Everywhere there was life and colour — swarthy, linen-clad hill peasants hauling in supplies with lumbering ox teams; tall camels, too, swinging along beneath loads of fruit and vegetables; red-capped fishermen, mules with jangling bells, and grave-faced, sombrely clad dons. Quaint balconies, and Moorish lattice-work, four hundred years old, relieved the monotony of the glaring walls, and through iron grills we caught glimpses of the flower-filled patios inside. These were the better type houses. Then we passed through narrow and shadowy streets redolent of piccadura tobacco-smoke, garlic, and olive-oil, where handsome men lounging about the wine-shops made way for us with graceful courtesy.

Afterwards we came out upon the black lava mole, and examined the fissure in a slab made when a ball from the old bronze gun El Tigre, still preserved, tore off Horatio Nelson's arm, and soon were rowing off across the sunlit swell towards where the s.s. Kinyema lay. It was sunset when she hove her anchor, and turned her bows towards the sea; and for a space I leaned over the taffrail aft, gazing shorewards at the town we left behind, where I had passed many happy months. Beyond the clustering roofs, alternate patches of vineyards, maize-fields, and slopes of dark-red scoriæ, checkered like a draught-board, ran up towards the dark pines 5000 feet above. There the black volcanic crags of Las Cañadas walled them in with a ridge of splintered pinnacles; and far above them all, cut off from the world beneath by silvery mist, the great white Peak lifted a glittering cone 12,000 feet in air. Then the boom of a distant gun rang out across the tumbling swell, a puff of smoke wreathed about the citadel, and the faint strains of the "Marcha Real" came softly to our ears, as the red light died out behind Las Cañadas and we steamed away into the darkening east. And that was the last glimpse of Teneriffe and European life. Henceforward we were to visit very different scenes, and breathe another air amid the foul dampness of the mangrove swamps.

One trip on board a mail steamer in open water is much like another, and needs little description. For four days we steamed south and east before the fresh trade breeze. The ocean was piled on end about us in white-crested ridges, flashing green on their sides, violet in the hollows. The sky was one unbroken sweep of crystalline ether, fading into neutral on the sea-rim, while a glorious rush of pure keen air awoke weird music from every tight-strung shroud, and filled each cranny of the ship with life and freshness. And this is the weather the "N.E. trades," blowing all the way from Cadiz Bay to Cape de Verde, bring with them for eight months every year.

Now and then we crossed the course of a great four-masted clipper, storming down wind for Australia round the Cape under wide breadths of straining sailcloth, with the ocean roaring apart beneath her swinging bows, and spouting high about the quarters as she tore through it at eleven knots an hour. Once too we passed a rolling troopship, crowded with men, and wallowing from rail to rail as she fought her way to windward. Then there was only sky and sea.

The passengers were, however, not those usually to be found on board an ocean liner. They were all either traders or soldiers, while the lined foreheads, sallow skin, and listless air of many clearly showed that they had been "on the coast" before, for as a rule there is no mistaking the man who has dwelt any time in Western Africa. The exceptions were a few fresh-faced English youths, going out under a three years' contract as factory assistants, for the usual sum of £60, £70, and £100 a-year, and who would probably die before the time expired. They seemed eager to reach the land of romance, and blissfully ignorant of the lives they were to lead. True, they had been medically examined, and warned that the coast was "unhealthy"; but unhealthy is a vague term, and as yet they did not understand the full meaning of the petition—"from plague, pestilence,—and from sudden death." That, however, would come in due time. Two, I remember, hailed from Manchester, and were nicknamed by an official in the Sierra Leone service, "Bones" and "Blades." These were ostentatiously cheerful, and one afternoon were holding forth about the fine things they were going to do. "A gig with four Krooboys to row you wherever you want, lots of hunting and fishing, and only a few invoices to check. A negro girl to feed you with pine-apple, and that kind of thing. Better than slaving in a gas-lit office," said Blades; and a gaunt trader answered quietly, "Is that what you think you are going to do? Now, if you will listen, I'll explain."

Then an officer whose name is well known to the Fanti tribesmen on the Gold Coast touched the trader on the arm and drew him away. "Let the lads enjoy it while they can. Poor devils! they will find out soon enough," he said. It was a simple episode, but I venture to describe it as it happened, because the affair was typical. Six months later poor Bones was buried by two half-drunk Krooboys beside the roaring beach at Ambriz, and a little rickety cross now marks the last resting-place of Blades outside Bonny Town.

On the sixth day the blue heights of the Lion Mountain rose up from out the sea, and the

Kinyema's bows were turned towards the only good harbour along 2000 miles of surf-beaten coast, Freetown, Sierra Leone. Rolling past the twin lighthouses at whose feet the mile-long rollers of the Atlantic thunder night and day, we steamed into a wide, landlocked basin, and as seen from the water there are few places fairer than Sierra Leone. On the southern hand are palm-groves and cultivated land, where white villas stand among the glossy leaves and snowy flowers of oranges and limes. Beyond are the roofs of Freetown girdling the slopes of Tower Hill, with the bold Sierra rising steeply height beyond height above them, until its forest-clad crest is sharp against the azure. Northwards, however, are low-lying swamps, swathed half the time in steam, a waste of slime and mangroves through which the Rokell pours into the sea, and the beauty of Sierra Leone resembles that of a whited sepulchre.

Presently the anchor thundered down, and we hurried ashore. Landing on a fine stone pier, we found the town full of life and noise. Sierra Leone and Lagos have long been the strongholds of the missionary, and here the negro has been civilised to a degree. The coloured inhabitants are probably better acquainted with revivalist hymns as well as the Church service than many Britons at home; but there are not wanting sceptical traders who aver they would sooner employ a pagan negro than a converted one, and point to the fact that the Government invariably secures Mahommedans where fidelity and valour are required. The trader's statements must, however, generally be taken with a grain of salt, for he is an interested party, and for various reasons little love is lost between him and the missionary. It was then Sunday morning, and a steady stream of coloured folk flowed towards the handsome church. They were worth inspection. The young trading clerks eclipsed the Europeans altogether in the gorgeousness of their dress. Faultless silk-hats, tight frock-coats, and the yellowest of gloves were much in evidence, and the ladies were striking too. Materials of brilliant hue, gold, crimson, and green, had been made up in exaggeration of the last Parisian fashion; the sunshades were dazzling to behold; and while some of the individuals were not uncomely, the whole effect was grotesque. Dressed in white cotton or dull blue after the manner of the heathen, they would have passed as stalwart men and women with a splendid carriage: as it was, they were mere parodies of a state of life which did not belong to them. Then we strolled up the steep, stone-paved main street, where, beyond the well-built offices, the houses of traders black and white rise one above the other about the feet of Tower Hill. For the most part they stood in gardens filled with many flowers, purple bougainvilleas trailing about the verandahs, and shaded by orange-trees or mangoes. All this was pleasant to the eye, and Freetown looks well upon the surface—but there is an under side. The air was heavy and full of steamy dampness, which even in that fierce heat checked the perspiration, and made breathing difficult, while one glance at the white men we met was sufficient testimony as to what manner of climate this was. Many moved listlessly and slowly, as though exertion were impossible; others limped, for the sufficient reason that rheumatic fever had distorted all their joints; and there was scarcely a bronzed face or buoyant carriage to be seen. Instead, most were haggard, hollow-cheeked, and dragged themselves rather than walked. Those who know Central America, strips of the Brazilian coast, and the Guinea shore will recognise what the writer means. Those who have not must visit the steamy tropics before they can fully understand how the malaria sets its sign upon the white man.

It was also to be observed that the houses and stores of the black merchants were at least as fine as those of their paler rivals, and the self-importance of the first considerably greater. It must, nevertheless, be remembered that such a state of things is exceptional. It is only in Sierra Leone and Lagos—we will leave Liberia out of the question at present—that European civilisation has really touched the negro, although there are some well-educated sable gentlemen, including lawyers and physicians, on the Gold Coast. Even in Freetown there is barbarism, for beyond the harbour with its coaling wharves and stores there lies a collection of rickety huts where part of the negro population dwells in dirt and squalor, and it is said uncanny things are done in the way of Ju-Ju and Obi rites. The advancement of the negro has, however, its drawbacks, and in Sierra Leone white men say the Government has carried its policy of equal justice too far. Men of colour hold high places in the courts and councils, and a European finds it hard to get fair play there at all. Once the African obtains a measure of education and is installed in any office he suffers from an inflated sense of his own importance, and in Liberia at least "man clothed with a little brief authority plays such fantastic tricks—as make the angels weep." The result is that he is often aggravatingly rude to the white trader, who retaliates with personal violence and is straightway haled before the court, and, even if he has been the injured party, is generally heavily fined. The writer remembers a certain scene on a mail-boat, when a sickly merchant who had been systematically harassed by some of his black rivals deliberately and methodically kicked one of them down every step of the accommodation-ladder ere his steamer sailed. The applause that went up as he did it spoke for itself. There are, however, other disadvantages in partial civilisation. The pagan negro may be degraded and bloodthirsty, but he is not infrequently a fearless man, and, contrary to general belief, honest according to his light, while half-training seems to take the steel out of his nature, and teach him more of the European's vices than his virtues. To the writer's mind the finest West African types are the sturdy pagan Krooboy and the soldierly Moslem Haussa; but it must be remembered that it is not wise to look for great results all at once, and our work upon the negro has only begun. In any case you will find in Freetown black men who keep the law—they are rather too fond of it, live as Europeans do, carry on an extensive trade, acquire wealth, and attend public worship—and what more can any one desire? We had many people to see that afternoon, and early on the following morning were ashore again.

There was of course the market to be visited, and a striking scene it is. There, amid a babel of voices, we saw the humbler orders of the populace in their workaday attire, which became them best —loose garments of duck made after the European fashion, or folds of white and blue cotton swathed from shoulder to ankles, with turbans, gaudy shawls, or coloured handkerchiefs upon their woolly heads. Merchandise of all kinds was displayed —the flesh of the tiny cattle of the hinterland, smaller than the smallest Alderney, sheep which dress scarcely 12 lb. in weight, yams, cassava, and endless fish and fruit. There were huge pineapples, price one penny each, ripe oranges invariably green, crimson bananas ten inches long, and yellow mangoes. The latter is a trap for the new-comer who bites it, and finds the fibre network within draws out a foot in length and smears his face with the luscious pulp, so that the stereotyped advice to a stranger is, "If you want to eat a mango you must get into a bath." A walk along the famous "Kissy Road," past houses pleasantly situated among shady trees, brought us to the canoe-landing on the banks of the Rokell, the highway to all the wild land that lies beyond. A flotilla had just come in, and men of many races were busy among varied merchandise. There were little Mahommedan Mandingoes, jet black muscular Jallufs, and big brown-skinned Moslem from the far kingdom of Samadu. The babel of voices was deafening, and the simile of the old-world tower holds good, for they spoke with many tongues; and at least one hundred languages, or more, so some aver, are daily used in Freetown streets. They had beautiful leather-work to sell, finely tempered swords, the work of artificers in an unknown land, carved powder-horns, and other articles, often highly artistic as well as domestic and useful, coming from anywhere between the Rokell and Timbuktu. These were the productions of skilled craftsmen in the hinterland, for no coastwise native could make such things. Afterwards, and at the risk of catching fever for our pains, because it is very unwise to do too much in Western Africa, we wearily climbed Tower Hill, where the great brick barracks of the West India regiment stand. There is always a full battalion of these black troops in Freetown, and a splendid force they look, for the West India privates pride themselves upon being as smart as any white infantry. Their dress is blue serge with crimson Fez, and the men are Mahommedans of a kind—that is to say, they have mingled Obi superstition learned in Jamaica with the purer faith.

Hawkins shipped his first large cargoes of slaves from Sierra Leone in 1562, and Europeans traded spasmodically with the Rokell mouth until, in 1787, a strip of land was purchased for the philanthropic purpose of settling freed negroes thereon, and the little colony steadily developed, so that now Freetown is undoubtedly second city in Western Africa, Lagos being first. Yet but a little way behind it the bold ranges and swampy valleys are peopled by fierce savages, one of whose murderous customs alone may be mentioned, that of hunting as "leopard men." Members of this Thuggish league wearing hoods of leopard skin break into the villagers' huts at night, and carry off the inmates. These are never seen again, and it is believed portions of their anatomy are used in some horrible fetiche rites. Shortly before I once called at Sherbro, five men, if I remember rightly, were publicly hanged for this offence.

At the present day the coloured people of Freetown seem to be suffering from too much liberty, and some of the journals publish scurrilous abuse of officials, which in India at least would certainly lead to the editor's incarceration. This is, to put it mildly, ungrateful as well as foolish. We bought the land and settled their ancestors there, built up the colony at the cost of the lives of our adventurous sons, and now if we withdrew our troops for twelve months there would not be an educated negro left in Sierra Leone. The bush tribes would assuredly come down and wipe them out, for as a man at arms the Christian negro is by no means equal to the heathen one. As it is, these tribesmen periodically sweep the border; and if they failed, the great Arab raider Samadu would seize so rich a prize. He threatened to do so once, and as the story is characteristic of Western Africa, while similar collisions with the French have happened before and since in various parts of the Niger basin, it may be briefly told.

CHAPTER III.

THE BATTLE OF WEIMA.

NORTH and east of the Sierra Leone colony, and beyond the barren peaks which form the watershed of the Niger, there lies a Moslem kingdom where the son of a slave, who was once a slave himself, rules in a state which is not altogether barbaric. Amadu, or Samadu, occasionally and incorrectly rendered Samori, is the name of this swarthy emir, who is dreaded throughout endless leagues of hinterland.

In 1883 the French fought many battles with his followers of various races and languages, and in 1893 he swept their colony of Senegal with fire and sword, beating their best native levies, strengthened by picked detachments of white troops, more than once. I afterwards met some of these soldiers, and they averred that Samadu's Moslem were a very dangerous foe. Then towards the end of that year rumours reached the coast that Samadu was preparing to raid Sierra Leone, and the fierce

Sofa and Konno tribes actually marched south, devastating British territory as they came.

There was alarm and bustle in Freetown, and in December a strong battalion of West Indias under Colonel Ellis, with a detachment of the frontier constabulary, hurried northwards into the swamps to turn the invaders back. It was a memorable march. Day by day they splashed knee-deep through reeking quagmires, where germs of disease and death lurked in every breath of the tainted air, forded muddy rivers, or hewed a pathway through creeper-choked forests, until they came to a land laid waste by the sword. The villages were circles of ashes or rows of silent huts with dead men strewn about the doorways, and the weary soldiers pressed on the faster, their blood stirred by the things which they had seen. The West Indias behaved well, but a few of the frontier police, bare-legged negroes in the inevitable blue serge uniform, gave trouble. Among them were northern people, sober and orderly, but there were evidently also some hastily recruited from the coastwise tribes, and the quarter-civilised negro of the settlements is not as a rule remarkable for either virtue or courage. On the 20th December the Konno people showed fight, and for three days and nights flintlock guns crackled and squibbed from behind the buttress roots of the cotton-trees or among the tall reeds of the swamps, and there was a constant whirring of cast-iron potleg. Now, although the negro is passionately fond of firearms, he is a deplorably bad marksman; but, knowing his weakness, he adopts a surer method than long-range fire. A flintlock gun is loaded with a cupful of slow-burning trade powder and a double handful of cast-iron pot pounded small. Then the bushman (the usual term on the West Coast for any forest-dweller) crouches amid the undergrowth, with the long barrel resting on a forked twig, until he can fire the murderous charge into his enemies' back at point-blank range.

Even white troops would have grown restive under being fired at for three long days by an invisible foe, but the West Indias stood it well, and on the 23rd they cleared the native town of Seedoo with the bayonet. Later, the village of Weima was reached, and the bushmen, having heard what happened at Seedoo, did not wait for the steel. It must be borne in mind that these were forest tribesmen, Samadu's raiders being of a very different stamp. An oval breastwork of branches and banana stems was piled round Weima, and when night came the troops lay thankfully down to rest. They were worn with travel and want of sleep, for the Konnos had taken care they should have little time for rest. Their uniforms, as well as the skin beneath, were rent by stabbing thorns, and crusted with the mire of leagues of swamp, and many of them were filled with sullen fury or in a state of nervous tension, which only those who hour after hour have known that the muzzle of an unseen gun followed every move can understand. A long march in the steamy heat of Africa, where an attack of fever is the general result of over-exertion, is very trying to the strongest European, and the white officers longed equally with their men to be brought face to face with the foe at last. Their wish was gratified.

For a time bright moonlight poured down upon the palm-thatched huts, clustering, broad-leaved bananas, and dewy undergrowth. Whisps of mist rose up from the steaming earth, fireflies flashed among the dripping brushwood, and the aromatic smoke of burning wood hung in heavy blue wreaths about the weary camp. There was no sound to break the stillness save the occasional hoarse challenge of a sentinel from the edge of the forest which walled the village in, or the eery howl of a leopard, for the men were too weary for speech. Then the moon sank behind the cotton-woods, and darkness, the black darkness of the African forest when the air is heavy with steam, closed down. The last rounds were made, the officers found each sentry at his post, as well as a strong guard at the weakest points of the stockade, and those whose turn it was retired to rest. Tired as they were, it is probable few enjoyed sound sleep that night, for it is difficult even for a man of steady nerve to slumber peacefully with the knowledge that a naked bushman may be crawling like a snake through the undergrowth, watching an opportunity to cut his throat. Neither is a sweltering, fetid hut, filled with many kinds of creeping things that bite, and mosquitoes, an attractive chamber. This, however, was just as well.

A little before the dawn, 23rd December, the ringing of a rifle awakened all the echoes of the forest, and instantly the camp stirred to life. Sturdy West Indias and bare-legged policemen came leaping from the huts, buckling belts and opening pouches as they ran, still half-dazed with sleep, and uncertain if it was only another attempt to murder an outlying sentinel. Fastening their cartridge-belts over their thin pyjamas, the white officers hurried to their posts, and found the men lining the breastwork with their rifles in their hands. Then almost before an order was given the fray began.

The surrounding forest was streaked with whirling flame. The shouts of the officers were drowned in a continuous roar of flintlock guns, and a sharper, jarring crash, which even then some of the Europeans wondered at, for the ringing of a rifle is hardly to be mistaken for the report of an overloaded flintlock gun. This led them to believe that the foe were neither Konnos nor Sofas, but Samadu's men, for the latter were known to be armed with high-class weapons, how obtained in contravention of a certain clause in the Treaty of Brussels the authorities have long puzzled themselves to discover. Orders were given and probably never heard amid the din of firing, but they were hardly needed, for in an affair of this kind men work instinctively, and West India private and sable policeman fired as fast as they could load. Thus the front of the breastwork was lighted by constant flashes, while acrid wreaths of powder smoke curled down and blinded the eyes. Between the crashing of the volleys or rattle of independent fire there was little to be heard but the clatter of Snider breech-blocks, as the men turned the weapons over to fling out the empty shells, or the "click-clack" of Martini levers. Through the smoke the officers hurried to and fro, restraining or encouraging, and in their light pyjamas they were faintly visible as the first dim light crept across the cotton-woods. Policemen and West Indias wore blue serge, and their officers usually the same; but there being no time to don uniform, they stood in their sleeping garb, which accounted for much that happened.

Occasionally wild shouts and yells came out of the forest, and were lost again in the clamour of the fight. And so the men crouched beneath the

THE BATTLE OF WEIMA.

breastwork or in the shelter of the huts, firing at the flashes, until their faces were blackened with the back-spitting from the muzzles, and the barrels almost too hot to touch, while rifle answered rifle, and each red streak was the target for a ball. Then there was less flame about the edge of the bush, a crackling of undergrowth took the place of the rifle blast, and the defenders knew that their turn had come. A sharp order was given, and followed by a clatter of locking rings, as the bayonets slipped over the foresight, and the weary men, tired of being shot down from ambush, stalked by crawling bushmen, or fired at while they slept, were ready to settle accounts in full. Out from the breastwork they went, the early light twinkling on the line of bright steel above the blackened muzzles. There was a rush of feet, a dash from bush to bush, a desultory flashing of rifles among the trees; then a sound of headlong flight through yielding undergrowth, shouts and yells—and the battle of Weima was won.

When the men came back the triangular steel was red, and the faces of the officers who led them very grave. Each man looked at his neighbour, and no one cared to speak. It was broad daylight now, and four British officers lay dead beside the breastwork, or among the scattered huts. Six black privates, who would serve the White Queen no more, rested very rigidly and still among the grasses, and wounded wretches crouched with distorted faces in such shelter as they could find, or dragged themselves about on hands and knees, calling pitifully for aid. But the officers had seen such things before, and these were not the worst. Outside the breastwork, and in the forest, many of the foe were huddled among the cotton-wood roots, gripping the still hot rifles in hands that had stiffened on the trigger-guard, while their sightless eyes stared vacantly up into the brightening heavens—and these were neither Sofa tribesmen nor Moslem raiders. Ten of them wore the Zouave uniform of the French Senegalis, and the rest were people from the north. Then the pity of it all, and the useless waste of life, commenced to fully dawn upon the British, for they realised now the awful blunder that had been made. The story of a prisoner made his listeners set their teeth together, and a few minutes after seven o'clock the crowning horror came.

Blackened with smoke, dripping with blood, and shot through and through, a young French officer was carried in, and the English stood beside him with anxious and compassionate faces. The surgeon did his best, but there were at least four fatal wounds in the fever-worn body; and feebly thanking them, the sufferer gasped out his pitiful tale. It was a simple story of useless heroism, and the life of a valiant soldier thrown away. About the same time that the West Indias left Sierra Leone, a French force hewed a passage through the forests of Senegal to intercept the march of their ancient foe Samadu. Neither party knew of the movements of the other; and deceived, it would seem, by the chieftain Koronah, who was doubtless well pleased to see his powerful neighbours destroy each other, the French officer hurried towards Weima, believing the British to be either a strong body of the Sofas or the northern horde. Lieutenant Moritz had with him some thirty picked Senegali soldiers, and about 1200 other native levies, the regulars being armed with repeating-rifles, which explained the rapidity of the fire, and the natives with flintlock guns.

The attack was splendidly planned; the auxiliaries crept silently, as only a bushman can, through the dewy brushwood, and shortly before the dawn hoped to storm the raiders' camp. The steady and rapid fire which met them in the teeth surprised their leader, and he fancied he had trained fighting men from the north to deal with, while the light-coloured pyjamas of the officers he took to be the white cotton dresses of the Moslem leaders. He admitted that, in this belief, together with his best marksmen he took up a position among the flanged roots of a cotton-tree very near the camp, for the special purpose of picking these chieftains off when he saw the place could not be taken by surprise. The work was done only too successfully, for four British officers went down. He was hit several times, and knew at last that he had not long to live; but, faint and bleeding, he held grimly on, cheering his men, determined to break the power of the raiders ere he died.

The story was listened to in pitiful silence, and more than one of the auditors turned his face away. Then the hollow voice was lost in a choking sigh, a trying stillness followed, and presently they knew that a faithful soldier of France had passed to his rest. There was neither blame nor resentment in the minds of any of those who listened, and, so the writer was told, they forgot even their own dead for a space. The officer of Senegalis had done his best for the nation he served—and that was all. So Gaul and Briton were reverently laid in one grave, to rest together side by side. They were of different faith, and spoke with another tongue; but death levels the narrow barriers of caste and race, and both had fallen bravely in a righteous cause. They had done what they could to save a wide land from devastation and the horrors of a border raid; and, if they had failed, the fault was not their own. Only the work was theirs, and that they had laid down their lives to do.

The humbler dead of both sides, French Senegali, British West India, and hastily armed bushman, were honourably buried, the wounded seen to, and for three days the troops rested at Weima. Then with fierce wrath at the bushman's treachery burning in their hearts, and a wild desire to avenge their comrades' blood, they marched out into the forests again, in a very dangerous mood, as the tribesmen found. This time they met the mocking foe face to face in overwhelming force at Bagweema, and very grim work was done. When the tribesmen fled at last, they left 200 dead behind, as well as 400 women and children, torn from their homes on British soil, whom they were carrying away into slavery. A large collection of fine arms, including many high-class Chassepot pattern rifles, fell into the expedition's hands, and, having broken the power of the Sofas, for a time at least, and taught the forest dweller that neither bushman savage nor Arab raider may ravage British soil with impunity, the West Indias marched back to Sierra Leone.

Samadu, it may be because he feared the Briton more than the Gaul, or more probably because he was too busy somewhere else, apparently did nothing for the assistance of the forest allies he had stirred up to attack us, but left them to their fate. Shortly afterwards he was heard of nearly seven hundred miles to the east, and rumours reached the Gold Coast of mysterious fighting going on beyond the Mountains of Kong. If once this redoubtable leader could induce the Moslem potentates of the great Fulah race ruling between the Gold Coast and the Lower Niger to join him in a jehad or holy war, the outlook for all the European colonies would be serious, and it is not improbable that the British Government may have to grapple resolutely with Samadu yet. Lately an expedition has been sent up to negotiate some kind of treaty with him, and may or may not be successful; but the trouble is that the rulers of the hinterland occasionally find it convenient to forget that they ever entered into an agreement of this kind. A native chief Koronah, who, it seemed probable, had with malice prepense arranged the "accident," was duly hanged for his share in the proceedings, and so the deplorable incident closed. There is an ever-present danger of a repetition of such an affair when the black troops—who often have feuds of their own to settle—of two nations are patrolling the forests of the hinterland. I heard the story of the battle of Weima from the lips of men well qualified to speak on the matter.

CHAPTER IV.

LIBERIA AND THE BEACHES OF THE KROO COUNTRY.

THE morning of the day we left Sierra Leone was typical of the fickle changes of the climate. It was fiercely hot, and not a breath of air stirred the glassy surface of the swell. The sky was blue overhead, but charged with sickly yellow above the sweep of land and sea. Freetown lay invisible, hidden in fleecy mist which rose half the height of the Lion Mountain, and all on board were in a state of prickly irritation. Tired of the glare of the scorching deck, where a swarm of woolly-haired Krooboy labourers were hurrying the last of the cargo into a lighter alongside, I occupied myself with some papers in my cabin beneath the poop, and when a few minutes later a sudden dimness caused me to look up, I saw the sun had gone. Then there was a stunning roll of thunder, and the vessel seemed to tremble through every plate with the reverberation, while ere the echoes had died away a wild uproar broke out. Half-naked deck hands were leaping and struggling about the hatch covers, vainly attempting to hold tarpaulins and even stout deal planks down by main force, and some of them were actually lifted into the air and hurled against the deck. One huge sheet whirled aloft and disappeared into mid-air, and then the screaming of the wind drowned the roar of orders. The 4000-ton steamer swayed down and down, until the snowy swell lapped her scuppers, while the sea grew feather-white, and the spray flew across her in sheets. Then she span round like a top, the strident roar of cable grinding across her stem mingling in the din, and the engines began to throb. Standing half-choked and blinded beneath the break of the poop, I saw a little schooner lying at anchor close alongside list over until the water lapped high about her sloping deck, while the terrified crew clung helplessly to the weather shrouds. Her canvas was stowed tight along the booms, and the bare surface of her masts and bulwarks was all the wind had to act upon, and yet that seemed enough to blow her bodily over. Then the heavens were opened, and there was nothing to be seen but a sheet, literally a sheet, of falling water, which hid even our bridge-deck from view, or heard but the roar of the rain. This lasted, it may have been five minutes, or even less, and then the sun broke through the cloud-banks. The scream of wind was gone, and there was only the tumbling of the swell to show that a tornado had passed that way. The whole affair only occupied some fifteen minutes in all, and now the sky was clear, and the sun shone down hot and bright. As it happened, no damage was done; but such is not always the case, and that the mercury gave no warning of the tornado's approach I can vouch, for I had just glanced at the barometer. Such storms are fairly common at times, especially towards the end of the year, and the danger lies in the fact that there is often no warning at all in either sky or sea.

It was afternoon before we were on our way again, rolling eastwards over the long and sunlit swell, which flamed with reflected light on the one hand, and on the other lay purple black in the shadow of the ship. On the second night we passed close in to the lofty Cape Mesurado, which hangs over Monrovia town, capital of the black republic of Liberia,—though, and partly as we expected, there was no streamer of brightness from the lighthouse perched 240 feet above the surf-fringe at its feet. This lighthouse is occasionally cited as an example of the way the free and enlightened Liberians manage their affairs. The building is a fine one, and heavy dues are charged, but the illuminating power is said to be two or three domestic lamps, and in the Admiralty charts "Not to be depended upon" is marked large against it. I found very few men along the coast who had seen it working satisfactorily, while the following story is currently told. A certain American skipper, who had been fined for breaking some of the multifarious customs regulations of this undesirable port, was one night discovered wandering through the streets of Monrovia striking matches and stumbling in the mud. He was not quite so sober as he might have been, and when questioned by a British mate as to what he was doing, replied, "Looking for the lighthouse. I've had to pay high for the blamed thing, and I would like to see it any way." One Gold Coast surgeon also told me that, having cured a deputy, or senator, or other kind of coloured notable on board ship, he was requested to send the grateful nation a bill. He did so, and was thereupon informed that he must wait a while, as there were but seven dollars in the treasury of that particular department at the time. He averred that this was not a joke, and gave both name and place.

All next day we steamed south and east, parallel to a line of yellow sand eternally swept by spouting surf. Above this low bluffs rose steeply, and beyond were tall palms, cotton-wood forests, and a distant ridge of flat-topped mountains. And such is the general aspect of the black republic from the sea all the way from Cape Mount for nearly 400 miles to the Pedro river. Inland there is little more than cotton-trees, palms, and clusters of mud-walled huts, for in spite of the fine coffee it ships, and the cheerful optimism of its self-conceited journals, Liberia is, as a trader, who found it impossible to collect his accounts there, informed me, "a very ordinary place." But it has one product besides coffee which is of high value, and that is the woolly-haired Krooboy. Throughout 2000 miles of surf-fringed littoral he plays the same part in the development of Western Africa that the Chinese did in the building up of the Pacific States, and therefore deserves a passing mention. With a very few exceptions no negro inhabiting the coastwise strip can by any means be induced to work, and this is perhaps only natural, considering that the fertility of the soil is such that a minimum of effort produces sufficient food. It is impossible for Europeans to perform manual labour in the heat and steam of the fever-land, and it is said that even a coolie or Chinaman would succumb. Therefore, were it not for the Kroo race, trade would either have to be abandoned, or slavery reintroduced on an extensive scale. The Kroo country, which lies beyond the roaring beaches of Liberia, is, however, a hard one, and its easy-going inhabitants are forced by famine to ship themselves away in search of sustenance. The Krooboy is broad-shouldered and muscular, with very woolly hair, and a broad blue stripe tattooed down the centre of his forehead. He is a sturdy pagan, and perhaps sometimes a cannibal, but withal a good-humoured, laughter-loving fellow, the finest boatman in the world — and the writer speaks advisedly, after sailing in many seas — and when well treated, comparatively honest and peaceable. He can, nevertheless, fight at times, as the Liberian officials know, and generally cherishes a bitter animosity against the black republicans.

This is in no wise strange. For generations the Krooboy traded along the smoking beaches with neither let nor hindrance, and now he cannot understand why he should pay the Liberians a heavy duty on everything he brings in, or two and a half dollars each time he sails away in search of work and comes back again, for the doubtful privilege of being governed. The Krooboy does not want to be governed at all, and if he did, would prefer a white ruler to a black one; while as to protection, a freshly filed matchet is quite enough for him. Therefore, instead of paying the duties, he occasionally burns a custom-house, or sends a message of defiance to the nearest detachment of republican soldiers, and thus there is frequent trouble about Grand Sesters and the mouth of the Cavally river. Once, indeed, a party swam off at night and seized a small gunboat (the Goronomah) sent to burn their town, throwing all her little guns into the sea; but, unfortunately, they were unable to handle the engines, and some were scalded in the attempt. The grinning Frypan, who, so he said, was there, and afterwards occasionally steered my surf-boat, explained the matter as follows: "Them Liberia man get two dollah and halluf, sah; Krooboy get nothing. Where we come in, sah? So we dun pay no custom—the Lord give us sense too much."

Our only object in following this reef-sprinkled coast so closely was to obtain a labour-supply for the Niger factories, and the first place we called at was, I think, Sinu, or Setta Kroo. Imagine a glaring sunlit sea, running in mile-long undulations, which pile themselves on end and smite the yellow beach with a thundering crash. Hard by the shore one or two isolated rocks lift themselves out of a white smother and whirling spray cloud, and beyond the beach a row of mud huts nestles beneath the feet of immense palms, whose raw-green fronds form a feathery lacework over them. Beyond these are cotton-wood forests, while a steamy haze of spray hangs over the whole, and this is the almost invariable appearance of the Krooboy's home. Following the boom of the whistle, naked black figures swarmed about the huts, while canoes were run down the beach by scores, and launched through a fringe of breakers which would have drowned the best white seaman. Then they came shooting towards us over the steep-sided rollers, tiny craft some fourteen feet by as many inches beam, beautifully modelled and finished. As they paddled, the occupants kicked the water out with the hollowed sole, a mode of baling unknown elsewhere,— and it may be mentioned that the soles and palms of any amphibious negro race are almost as white as those of a European.

Occasionally the canoes were swamped and upset, but that mattered little. Treading water, the Krooboys raised the light craft above their heads, turned her over, and when thus emptied, by means only known to themselves climbed in again. To drag oneself on board such a craft out of deep water without turning the knife-edge of hull round and round is considerably harder than it might appear. I know this because I have tried it. Presently they were alongside, upsetting one after another as the steamer rolled down upon them; and wild dripping objects, in the attire of Adam before the Fall, swung themselves on board, holding bundles and strings of curious objects for sale in their teeth. There were probably two hundred about our deck, howling, gesticulating, and swarming into the forecastle to traffic with the seamen, who turn their quarters into a cheap bazaar; while the mates ran here and there trying to prevent everything movable being looted from the deck. Then the skipper set his engines going, as a hint for all visitors to retire, and those who had only come to trade dived from the rail in scores, throwing their possessions before them, while as we steamed away we saw them paddling in chase of multifarious floating articles. There is no surf in the world big enough to drown a Krooboy, or shark he cannot slay with the matchet, and it is not uncommon for homeward passengers to swim ashore at least a mile, pushing their belongings before them, when the canoes do not come off.

We were left with about a hundred of these emigrants on board, and whether they had paid the "two and a halluf dollah" for an embarkation permit or not was their own concern, though British steamers have been fired upon for taking them without. Then they proceeded to roll a strip of wet cotton round their loins, and spread a bundle of damp matting to dry upon the deck, while the work of collecting fares began. Each sable heathen commenced by tendering a few shillings or an American dollar in payment of a £2 passage, solemnly averring he had nothing else in the world. The harassed mate and purser had, however, heard that tale before, and with fearful threats induced the Krooboy to find another coin somewhere in his waist-cloth. Then the latter shook the cotton strip to show this was actually the last, and, as a rule, it was only when tied to the mast that he discovered a further piece of silver in his mouth. Some, however, had not even an American cent, or, if they had, kept it inside them; and as each went through much the same performance, and there were some hundred on board, it is needless to say that the patience of the two officers was sorely tried. Vivid language was used of course, partly because the Krooboy understands that kind of English best, and the following story is told of an acquaintance of mine when he commanded a steamer casually employed in the African trade. He was a man of rather severe religious ideas, which is perhaps unusual on the "West Coast," and after listening with a frown to his experienced mate and purser at work, informed them he could not permit such proceedings on board his vessel. The officers explained that it was the only way the fares could be collected, and after some discussion the skipper engaged to prove the contrary by doing it himself. He toiled on stubbornly all one blazing afternoon, and then he called the purser. "Mr Ellison," he said, "how much did you and the mate collect before I stopped you?"

"We were at it an hour, sir, and we got fifty pounds," was the answer.

"Well," replied the skipper, "henceforward I am afraid you must do it your own way. I have been all afternoon, and I have only got four pounds now."

This reluctance to discharge his debts is one of the Krooboy's vagaries, for he has several weaknesses of his own; but taken all round he is by no means a bad specimen of the human race, and the laughing, wicked-eyed amphibian was always a favourite of mine. All the voyage these passengers slept upon the bare deck on little rolls of matting, singing unlovely songs there first, from the time darkness closed down until the night was far spent, and dancing weird dances, unless some mate or engineer who pined for slumber silenced the music with a hose.

Still bound east, we called at one or two more beaches and shipped further Krooboys, touched here and there at French settlements on the Ivory Coast, where is still much fine ivory in the shape of armlets and carved work, though the elephant has long since disappeared, and then passing the Assini river were off British soil again —the Gold Coast Colony.

Now, in considering the trade of any West African colony, and that of the Gold Coast in particular, it must be borne in mind that there are two great obstacles to the extension of commerce — the want of roads and the want of harbours. In regard to the first, rivers are sometimes available, but even in such cases the mouth is generally choked by a thundering bar. Thus a great portion of the produce is brought down on the heads of slaves, through bush trails only a few feet wide, often watched by semi-bandit chieftains, who levy a heavy blackmail on all goods passing through their dominions, and sometimes confiscate them altogether. In the Gold Coast, for instance, it costs about £10 a-ton to carry rubber, which is one of the principal exports, a distance of sixty miles to the beach; and in another place, Pram-Pram, oil-casks are, or were, rolled twenty-eight miles over swampy earth. Rubber alone is shipped from this colony and Lagos to an annual value of some £150,000 to £200,000 sterling. To convey palm-oil and kernels to Cape Coast Castle from the native markets only ten or fifteen miles away costs as much as £2 a-ton, and thus it will readily be understood that the lack of means of transport is a great drawback to trade. In fact, it has been pointed out to her Majesty's Ministers several times by the Chambers of Commerce of Liverpool, Manchester, and London, that the exports might be quadrupled in one year by the subsidising of light railways, such as the French have in Senegal and the Portuguese in Angola. The merchants cannot at present do the work themselves, for the simple reason that marauding headmen would have to be sternly convinced of the desirability of leaving the track alone before the line could be operated.

The want of harbours is still more serious, for along some fifteen hundred miles of coast, all the way from Sa Leone to the Niger (Lagos, as will be seen, can hardly be called a "port"), every pound of goods has to be shipped or landed through the fringe of breakers. The West African surf is perhaps the heaviest in the world, and although there is, as a rule, little wind on the coast, the long heave of the Atlantic, carrying a momentum gathered all the way from the far Antarctic ice, piles itself on end as it meets the shelving shoals. Thus off every beach there is a fringe of parallel, thundering rollers, white-crested and steep-sided, which from year's end to year's end smite the sand with tremendous force. Sometimes this surf is worse than others, but it is always bad. These remarks are a digression, but a recollection of them will answer many questions likely to arise in the mind of those interested in the future of Western Africa. And so we pass on to a hasty glance at the Gold Coast Colony.

CHAPTER V.

THE GOLD COAST COLONY AND DAHOMEY.

THE Gold Coast was one of the first portions of West Africa where Europeans attempted to settle, the first comers being probably the Portuguese in 1481. Then came the Dutch, and in 1872 the British took it over from the latter in return for concessions in the Java seas. Between the watershed which divides it from Ashanti and the sea are forests of acacias, palms, cotton-woods, and swamps, intersected by sluggish yellow rivers, and sprinkled with foul lagoons. Its climate is at least as unhealthy as the rest of the littoral, which is saying a good deal, and the predominant native races with whom we have to deal are the Fantis and Shantis. Both are tall and powerful negroes, the colour of some verging towards yellow, which may be due to the fact that the blood of Dutch or Portuguese, or perhaps that of some brown race from the north, is mingled in their veins. Once, so the traditions of the Fantis state, they dwelt beyond the ranges in what is now called Ashanti, and the warlike Shantis on the more sterile coast. The latter drove them out, and ruled with bloodshed and fetiche cruelty inland, until, seeing the advantages of European trade, they desired to come back to the seaboard again, and it was a claim by King Coffee for the settlement of Elmina which partly led to the first campaign against them in 1873. Both are sturdy heathen, skilled in various arts, especially wood-carving and metal-work; but, as a rule, slothful, and apparently incapable of much mental development. Gold is everywhere to be found in this colony. It lies in the mud of each river-bed, and after an unusually heavy surf or torrential deluge the natives may be seen washing it out of the beaches or even the very streets. The quantity, however, does little more than pay for the labour, though now one or two British companies are obtaining fair results from the use of proper plant. There must be a great store of the precious metal somewhere in the hinterland, but hitherto hostile tribe, quaking swamp, poison, and pestilence have barred the way to the adventurous prospector. So much for the inland portion of this colony: what the coast-line is like we shall see.

Shortly after passing the boundary-line of the French Côte d'Ivoire, we anchored off the British port of Axim, a cluster of whitewashed factories surrounded by luxuriant palms, with the primeval forest behind. A homeward-bound steamer was anchored close at hand, hauling off massy mahogany logs through the roaring surf, and as she lay wallowing from rail to rail one glance was enough to show that the task of swinging on board the 3- or 4-ton trunks was a trying one. There is splendid mahogany in the forests behind, but what with the quantity lost in the surf and the risk of shipping it the business is severely handicapped, and boats are often smashed. Some of our own amphibious deck hands were hurt landing a few bales of cotton goods in a big surf-boat, and then we were off again.

By-and-by we were abreast of Cape Three Points, a succession of towering bluffs with the eternal surf spouting about their feet, and the tallest palms in the world cresting their summits. Then for forty miles we steamed north and east, beneath a line of forest-clad hills, with many villages of mud-walled huts beneath the palms which fringed the roaring beach, and the spray hanging above them all, until the mouth of the Prah river was left behind. After another twenty miles' steaming we passed the curving bay and few factories of Elmina, oldest settlement in the colony, and an hour later Cape Coast Castle rose to view. Imagine a line of glaring, yellow beach half-hidden by leaping foam; a grim stone fort, first raised by the Portuguese four hundred years ago, and rebuilt by the Dutch, rising from a smoking reef; a steep bluff where European factories and mud huts are any way mixed together beneath the climbing palms — and you have a bird's-eye view of Cape Coast Castle. It is by no means an attractive place. Native squalor and dirt stand side by side with the curious civilisation of the West Coast European; the scorching streets are crowded with noisy negroes, and the air is filled with spray. In spite of the heat, which is like that of a furnace at times, everything reeks with damp; no metal can be kept bright, and clothes unworn go mouldy in a week. Malarial fever is always there, dysentery and cholera strike the white man down, smallpox is generally at work among the swarming natives, and a few years ago a scourge which was generally believed to be yellow fever, though the authorities said it was not, swept most of the Europeans away. We managed to land a few boat-loads of Manchester cotton, and very indifferent rum, behind the reef which affords partial shelter, and steamed on east again.

For seventy miles there were more blue heights, bays of yellow sand, and lines of breakers, very fair to look upon and deadly to live beside, and then the anchor thundered down off Accra, the seat of the Government. Accra possesses one of the worst beaches I know of anywhere between the Niger and the Yukon mouth, and a few words as to how the surf is passed may be of interest. Taking my seat in the stern, for prudential reasons, of a 28-foot Liverpool-built surf-boat, double-ended, high-sheered, and as strong as iron and pine could make her, I gave the order to thrust off from the wallowing steamer. Fourteen Krooboys balanced themselves upon the gunwale, each big toe gripping a fibre stirrup, and in time to a musical chanty the three-tongued paddles whirled together. Soon we were flying shorewards over a long and glassy swell, which grew steeper and steeper, until Old Man Trouble, the grizzled helmsman, stood erect, and seized the big sculling-oar. The sea that rolled up astern was now ridged for some 800 yards with incandescent froth, and its transparent sides flashed like green diamonds in the sunlight. Up the boat went, flung 20 feet from the trough, and as we drove wildly forward on the crest the chanty broke up into a chorus of howls and whistles. Ahead there was nothing to be seen but a chaos of spouting white, and then the sea swept on, and we sank down into a hollow of muddy green 100 yards across. The next came in like a wall, roaring and frothing above the stern, and though I had passed many a bad surf before, it was with a feeling of relief that I felt the boat hove bodily aloft. Again we shot ahead, apparently with the speed of a locomotive, a fathom's breadth of foam boiling about the gunwale, and the Krooboys yelling and hissing as they whirled the paddles for dear life, until the roller passed, and we could only see its white-streaked back as it thundered majestically shorewards. Its successor half-filled the boat, and a minute later, with the water gurgling about our knees, and half the craft's length in mid-air, we swept into a whirling smother of white, dazzled and deafened at once. Then there was a jarring crash as the keel smote the sand, naked figures came floundering through the backwash, and the writer was carried out shoulder-high, while the boat was run up by sheer muscular force ere the next sea rolled in. The surf was rather worse than usual that day, but much valuable cargo is periodically carried out to sea on the undertow, and many sable beachmen are pounded out of all likeness to humanity beneath the shattered boats.

Beyond the strip of roaring beach ran a low bare bluff, and on its summit stands Accra. There are fine trading stores, verandahed houses, sandy streets, and swish huts. Tall muscular Fantis and negroes of many varieties of physique loaf about in the sun-glare. Sickly white men pass and repass in hammocks, for exertion of any kind seems almost impossible to the European, and now and then a big Moslem Haussa of the armed constabulary stalks proudly through the crowd, glancing contemptuously at the heathen around him. These are tall men with regular and not unpleasing features from the kingdom of Sokoto, which lies beyond the fever-belt, attired in blue serge uniform and crimson fez,—splendid soldiers, who follow the white officer they trust wherever he will lead. It is by their aid alone that the fierce heathen are turned back from raiding British soil, and that order is maintained. The black soldier from the hinterland is particular about his officers, and sometimes manifests disdainful contempt for the traders, whom, sad to say, together with the missionary, he classifies as "white bushmen." He is rarely a marksman, but under an officer whose ability he has seen manifested in action is capable of great things with the bayonet, and the best guarantee of peace along the frontier is a strong force of Haussas.

I had no time to visit Christiansberg Castle, a fine stone building raised by the Dutch and seat of the Government, which stands beyond the town; and after inquiring for a few friends, and finding they were either dead or had been sent home invalided, I proceeded to interview the traders. They had many rubber-gatherers and Accra coopers to go on with us to the Niger; but we must wait until to-morrow, they said—the surf was too bad that day; so, tired of the heat and glare, I returned thankfully on board, and was nearly drowned in the passage.

A student of human nature would have been interested next morning when the sable passengers came off. There were burly Fanti coopers in loose blue cotton, men of splendid physique, and some scarcely more than yellow; unsophisticated bush rubber-gatherers, wearing nothing beside a waist-cloth, devil-worshippers, and perhaps cannibals too; twenty-five dwarfs, their woolly heads not reaching our shoulders, who came from no white man knew where in the mysterious forests beyond Ashanti; men of every shade of colour, design of tattoo, and knitting of hair, speaking with many tongues. Then we steamed away, and passing the mouth of the muddy Volta and afterwards the settlement of Popo, some hundred and thirty miles from Accra, were off the coast of French Dahomey.

Such is the general aspect of the Gold Coast Colony, where, in spite of its sea-breezes, few Europeans can hope to escape the fever. In a sickly season graves are dug beforehand to receive the fallen, and in one year eleven white officials out of thirteen in a certain department went down at their post. Another time we fell in with a tramp steamer which had been trading along the Dahomey and Gold Coast beaches, anchored for three weeks and waiting for a gunboat, unable to proceed, because, out of all her crew, she had not sufficient left to raise steam or keep the wheel relieved. The imports of the Gold Coast are chiefly Manchester cotton, rum, and gin, though there are many sundries, and its black customs clerks who attend to the receiving of them are exasperating at times. We ourselves were worried by endless documents relating to the landing of "one cast-iron pot over and above the manifest."

It ships palm-oil, kernels, and gold, but its principal export is rubber. No African rubber is as good as the Para (Brazilian); but that of Accra is the best on the coast—so good, in fact, that Lagos rubber is occasionally sent there to be re-barrelled and shipped as "fine Accra."

From the settlement of Popo, which lies near the boundary-line of French Dahomey, to Lagos Roads, is about one hundred miles, and nearly sixty of these form the coast-line of the possessions of France. The whole is a narrow strip of smoking beach covered with dwarf scrub, where an occasional tall palm rises above the glistening spray. Beyond this barrier foul lagoons, still but partially explored, wind inland, and are lost amid dismal mangrove swamps or streamy forests of palms. One great lagoon, that of Hakko, or Avon Water, which, however, lies practically outside French territory, is supposed to run inland more than a hundred miles. In early days these stagnant waterways were the haunts of the light-draught slavers, and the remains of barracoons, or slave-yards, are everywhere to be seen. There is not a muddy river mouth which is not haunted by the shadow of some dark tragedy, and the story of Whydah alone is an example of cruelty worse than that of any Ju-Ju priest. The latter at least shed blood to appease the wrath of his vengeful gods for a stricken people's sake, but the white men who traded in Dahomey committed abominations from mere lust of gold. It is said that in some British families who first amassed wealth through the iniquitous traffic, insanity and blindness descend from generation to generation, reappearing in at least one offshoot. This may be coincidence, or mere superstitious fancy, though the writer has heard similar stories from mystery-loving Cubans; but it is written that the sins of the fathers shall be visited upon the children, and there is a retributive justice to which no innocent blood cries out in vain. Ghastly and awful stories, half-legend, half-fact, are still told of the slaver's doings; and although the Spaniards and Portuguese were the worst offenders, it must not be forgotten that we showed them the way. The climate of Dahomey is worse than that of the Gold Coast or the Niger mouths, which is certainly bad enough, and the French have dearly bought their hold upon this dark kingdom. Many expeditions have marched north, and came back with the loss of one-third of their men; and once spending some weeks with an invalided French trader who accompanied the troops, I heard the story of a memorable march, details of which were quietly suppressed by the French Government.

A strong battalion of Senegalis, reinforced by white troops, marched north, to impress the fact that coastwise natives under the protection of the nation might not be promiscuously raided upon the forest tribes. Pestilence, poisonous water, and treachery, however, fought well for the Dahomeyan, and thinned the invader's ranks. Some were shot from ambush; the rest died of fever, were lost among the swamps, or perished in foul quagmires which sucked them down; and for a hundred miles their march to the sea may be traced by the graves they left behind. The battalion came back—five men in all, so the trader affirmed. I remember that when we reached Madeira our friend obtained a Parisian paper, wherein he saw that some of the Ministers had publicly cast doubts upon the truth of the reports of this disaster, and it was easy to see by his indignant fury that the tale of suffering was true. We afterwards heard that a book was to be published about the affair, but it apparently never came out, and I believe my acquaintance was eventually despatched to some good appointment in Algeria, probably to prevent any injudicious *éclaircissement.*

The French "Africander" has two failings. One is a weakness for locating himself in territory belonging to some one else, and the other the habit of prohibiting trade in any place where he is established by discriminative duties or military terrorism. Thus it is well that our protective rights should be firmly maintained, but in his favour it must be admitted that the Gaul does his work very well. The native towns in French possessions become clean and orderly, which is saying a good deal for any West African town; fine roads are driven through the forests at the cost of much money and blood; and there are many things in French Senegal, including a good railway, which might advantageously be copied by the administration of British colonies. Personally I have nothing but a pleasant recollection of the frank courtesy and kindly bonhomie of the French officials and traders I met, and this notwithstanding an original bias against them.

CHAPTER VI.

LAGOS AND THE NIGER MOUTHS.

It was a sweltering morning when we anchored in the wind-swept Lagos Roads, and in spite of the claims of its rival Sierra Leone, Lagos is by far the most important town in Western Africa. Glancing shorewards you see the inevitable line of yellow beach, but no forest behind it, and the slender shaft of a lighthouse rising above the tumbling surf. Beyond lies a wide lagoon, and upon a low island therein stands what is really a handsome town, and not the conglomeration of galvanised sheds and mud huts which forms so many West African settlements. Here are fine stores, well-built houses, banks, mission-schools, and Government buildings, all imposing in their way. In Lagos, as in Sierra Leone, there are many well-educated coloured merchants dwelling in luxurious houses after the European style, and most have been trained commercially in England. Lagos and Freetown ("Sa Leone"), as has been said, have long been under missionary influence, and in this city most of the black population are Christians, and probably better acquainted with the Scriptures than are the white traders as a rule. Still, some of these converts do curious things at times, and the relations between European and African are occasionally strained. When speaking to an educated man of colour it is always desirable to allude to his people as "Africans"—the word negro is generally an affront.

Colour-prejudice is as strong in West Africa as it is in the Southern States or India, and while the white man may purchase a dusky helpmate for some £5 unreproved, if he espouse an educated negress, as is sometimes done, he loses caste at once. Occasionally a white woman marries a sable barrister or merchant who has studied in the highest English schools, but such a one disappears for ever from European circles, and her countrywomen look askance at the mention of her name. Once I heard a Government official say, "They had better have been shot"; and there are strange stories, very curious if wholly true, told along the coast about this matter, but they can hardly be set down here. It may be taken as an axiom that you cannot thoroughly civilise any savage race in one generation. Thus a man thoroughly and completely educated, possibly too a discerning and devout Christian, will lapse now and then into the state of his fathers for a space. It seems as though the old hereditary instincts are stronger yet than the power of the freshly disciplined mind, so the latter is occasionally beaten and for a while loses its superiority, and that time alone can bring about a total change.

The trade of Lagos is extensive, and its strategical importance greater still. It commands the shortest routes to most of the Niger basin, the Yoruba country, the Haussaland, and the kingdom of Sokoto, all fertile regions peopled by Moslem races very far removed from savages, and which will some day form an immense market for our goods. The Egba people, who live nearer the coast, are Christians, and have long held resolutely to their faith in spite of murderous persecution by devil-worshipping Dahomeyan, and Moslem of the north. A railway into the hinterland would do wonderful things for this colony, as will be understood when it is mentioned that in one month £10,000 worth of rubber (only) was brought down to the coast on the heads of slaves. One African merchant testified before both Mr Chamberlain and the Marquess of Ripon that he had seen a host of 9000 men march in to the river-side with burdens of merchandise, and no one who has visited the trade-roads will forget the sight of the bearer-trains winding like endless snakes through the forest-trails. Gin in millions of cases, Manchester cotton, salt, Government officials, and young trading clerks to fill the gaps made by pestilence go in, while rubber, palm-oil, and kernels in immense quantities come out, as well as broken-down invalids. Yet there are white women in Lagos, and the European inhabitants endeavour with varying success to enjoy themselves as they did at home, holding concerts, dances, and horse-races too. But dancing is not altogether enjoyable at a temperature of 100°, when half the guests are sick; and a Lagos handicap is by no means an inspiriting sight, for the horses brought down from the hinterland suffer from malaria equally with men. Dogs also sicken, a self-respecting British terrier generally declining after a few months' attempt to live any longer in such a climate. And yet there are many worse places in Western Africa than Lagos town, and men of the kind which is curiously exempt from fever have dwelt happily there half their lives.

We went ashore in the little 400-ton branch-boat, which was buried in foam and swept by frothing green as she shot the roaring bar, among a crowd of shouting negroes we had brought down the coast. The enterprising inhabitants, after spending much money in surveys of the bar, were reluctantly forced to the conclusion that nothing could be done to improve it. Therefore, as the ships cannot get to them, they philosophically determined to send their produce to the ships, and a flotilla of light-draught vessels was built, which, steaming out through the surf, land and receive passengers, and then follow the ocean liner to the Forcados mouth of the Niger, one hundred miles away, where cargo is transhipped in smooth water.

One glance at the confusion of tumbling green walls which swept towards the bar, and the clouds of foam spouting vertically from the shoal, plainly showed why this was so, and we could readily understand how these branch-boats periodically come to grief there. Much might be said about Lagos; but we are bound for the Niger, and have only time for a passing glance at its hot streets, its wide marina, and the inevitable steamy haze that rises from the foul lagoon; the Yoruba and Haussa police, and the market, where you may see representatives of endless races from a thousand miles of hinterland—turbaned Moslem, swarthy descendant of the Arabs, half-naked bushmen, and savages of the Lekki coast. There is not the colour and artistic surroundings of the bazaar in Cairo or Bombay, but the difference of type and physique is perhaps greater still.

Leaving the tumbling roads behind, we steamed nearly south this time, towards the Niger swamps, and what each portion of the delta is like will be explained in detail. All the way from Lekki lagoon, which is connected with that of Lagos, to the mouth of the Old Calabar river, there lies a waste some four hundred miles in length of festering mud and slime, out of which the leather-leaved mangroves grow. Through this desolation of rottenness the waters of the Niger find their way by many channels to the sea, and though both the most northern and most eastern branches have separate sources, and as such are strictly speaking not deltaic arms, the whole is bound together by a network of tangled waterways. In some geographies the Niger is said to have twenty-two mouths; in reality it has several hundred, though only eight or nine have hitherto been found navigable by large vessels, and with a native guide a launch could travel through five hundred miles of swamp and forest, by probably as many different routes.

It was early morning when I leaned over the Kinyema's saloon-deck rails to catch the first glimpse of the Niger delta, a region where civilisation and savagery exist side by side, the one apparently powerless to affect the other, and the naked riverman still offers up his human sacrifice. There it lay, a few streaks of mist-wreathed forest and clumps of tall palms rising like islands from out the depths of the sea. There was a flush of crimson light behind it, and as we gazed the sun swung up out of a purple haze, his first bright rays changing the dim sea-plain into a glistening reach of green. Away ahead a serrated line of foam became solid brightness, and by the aid of the glasses I saw the "bar was bad" that day,—a simple phrase in use along the coast, though it means a good deal, as underwriters know. A long trail of dingy smoke was now streaming away astern, and as we rolled inshore across the smooth-backed undulations a pulsating jet of vapour roared away from the escape-pipe, for a token that in the sweltering depths below dripping firemen were raising the uttermost pound of steam to drive the vessel through the surf. A look-out perched high in the foremast-shrouds hailed sharply, "Buoy a little to starboard, sir"; and when we made out a patch of red half-veiled in glancing smother we knew that the mouth of the Nun river, the main entrance to the Niger, lay ahead.

Soon we could see the swell, heaped as it were on end, rolling towards the river mouth in parallel frothing lines, until, meeting the bar, it dissolved into spouts of foam and a flying cloud of spray. The Kinyema was drawing 14 feet, which left a very small margin for the sink of the sea; but that surf might run for weeks, and chance it she must. Presently as the steamer drove forward with a curling mass of white lapping about her quarters, and the steering engine clattering wildly to keep her from twisting on the top of a sea, most on board tightened their hold on what lay handiest, for they knew it was at least possible she might "touch the bar."

Touch she did, with a crash that shook her in every plate, and rolled down until one rusty wallside was bare half way to the bilge, while a big roller burst across her poop in eddying whiteness. That thrust upon the quarters aided the throbbing screw, which, whirling like a dynamo, churned up foam and sand, and, grinding and scraping, the Kinyema forged ahead. A sea rolled in, its crest curling hollow for a fathom's-breadth, picked her up like a cork in spite of the 3000 tons of general cargo still below, and with froth sweeping the length of her rail, she drove on faster. There was another vicious bump, and the crowded deck passengers fled forward as a cataract of muddy green rolled across the after-well; and then with a long "grind, grind, grind" she ploughed a way through the sucking sand, until every soul on board drew a long breath of relief as they realised we had safely "jumped the bar." Sometimes the passage is smoother than this, perhaps usually so. Sometimes it is worse; but there is always risk, and the same thing applies to every bar on the Niger coast.

Swinging round a spit of yellow sand crowned by giant cotton-woods, and beaten by everlasting surf, we steamed on into the mouth of a yellow river, which flamed about us like molten brass, and burst apart in muddy wreaths before the bows. A wall of forest hemmed it in, the bright green of feathery palms contrasting here and there with the sombre cotton-woods, while horizontal strata of mist drifted in blue-white lines across their stems. Soon a cluster of dazzling white-washed buildings rose to view, a clearing opened out, and by the aid of a boatful of howling negroes and many instructions from ashore, the Kinyema was made fast to the wharf at Akassa, general depot of the Royal Niger Company, Chartered and Limited.

There are three powers ruling over the Niger swamps, and much of the drier territory behind them. The first is the British Government, as represented by the Niger Coast Protectorate, whose consuls and vice-consuls do what they can to put down bloodshed and human sacrifice, and have promised that the trade-routes shall be kept open, that the Jakkery merchant may bring down his goods by night or day, no man daring to make him afraid. What has been done to fulfil this pledge will be seen later on. The second is the Royal Niger Company, which also rules with power of life and death over a vast region, and its rule on the whole is for good, though the jealous independent traders say high-handed things are done by its officials at times. In any case, the main object of this corporation is not philanthropy but the earning of dividends, and the keeping ahead if possible of enterprising shippers in Liverpool and Glasgow. The third is the Ju-Ju, or great fetiche, whose ministers are a very real power behind the throne in the Niger swamps, as in much of the rest of Western Africa; but being at Akassa we will deal with the great Company first, and to do so it is necessary to repeat a little of what has been set down before.

Although white men had long traded in a desultory fashion among the miry creeks, Lander, sailing down from Bussa in 1830, was the first to prove beyond all doubt that these were the Niger mouths. In 1832 he and Laird together steamed into the delta with a well-organised surveying and exploring expedition, and found that the free-lance traders' reports as to the undesirable climate were correct by losing eighteen men from fever in the first six weeks. On this journey Lander was shot, and died at Fernando Po, the last of those who, piecing the Niger together length by length, perished in the doing of it. The French seem to overlook the fact that we showed them the way to the Niger, and bought our hold upon the lower river with a heavy price.

In 1852 Macgregor Laird went up the river and established a chain of trading-posts; but troubles with the natives arose, and he was forced to withdraw. Still, in spite of pernicious fever, deadly damp, and scorching heat, the adventurous traders flocked in, now holding their factories by the rifle, and now buying the worst of the river pirates off. They died in scores of the pestilence; some were poisoned, and a few were shot; but England had plenty more, and there was never wanting an adventurous youth or broken-down world-wanderer to step into the dead man's place. So, steadily and grimly, in the face of peril and suffering, the work went on, until there were four large stations owned by large merchant firms firmly established and carrying on an extensive trade. Then in 1879 Sir George T. Goldie was instrumental in combining these four rivals into the United African Company. Shortly afterwards two gigantic French schemes were floated to exploit the Niger, and shares in the African Company were offered to the British public. One million pounds was subscribed, the French were either bought or driven out by various means, and the re-christened National African Company reigned supreme, until, in July 1886, a Royal Charter was signed, turning over a vast tract on the lower reaches of the river entirely into their hands. They were intrusted with full powers of jurisdiction, the maintenance of peace, and the making of laws; and when all is said—and they have many prejudiced opponents—have certainly done their best. It is hard to arrive at the truth in details, because the independent traders who are forcibly excluded from the Company's territory, although the Protectorate is free to all, cherish a bitter feeling against the monopolists, and may not be over-particular about the truth when they testify against them. It must also be remembered that there are two sides to every question, and the directorate at home as well as the administration at Akassa and Asaba cannot control every move of their isolated representatives scattered amid forest and swamp. The officers of the Niger Company have neither spared money nor hesitated to risk their own lives in the development of this region, and now they have achieved some measure of success, it would seem unjust to ask them to throw it open to every trading adventurer, though the time for doing so will doubtless come sooner or later. Where men have broken down their constitutions, invested their last penny, or patiently accepted years of very trying and toilsome work, it is only fair that they should, at least for a time, enjoy the fruits of their labour, and that others who have done little or nothing should not be permitted to rob them of it. Still, chartered companies cannot be more than the forerunners of regular British dominion; for with the best of intentions it must be difficult for those interested in them to frame any ordinances which, though needful for the welfare of the natives, might militate against the value of their shares. Thus it is clearly impossible for the trader to rule as justly as the Government official, and while such bodies do very good work in their way, the time will come when, for the general benefit of all, the Government must engage in its completion. It always has been so, and the development of trade which followed the substitution of Government rule for that of a company in Hindustan, and the wide land north and west of Winnipeg, where once a few H.B.C. agents peddled rum for beaver-skins, and now a splendid race of settlers have covered the prairie with yellow wheat, may be repeated in the Lower Niger region.

CHAPTER VII.

AKASSA.

IT was burning noon when we landed on the worm-eaten wharf at Akassa, and found a swarm of woolly-haired Krooboys, among whom were many of those we had brought from Liberia, hard at work. As fast as the clattering winches could heave them from the hold they trotted away with salt-bags on their backs, white crystals spangling their oily, dripping skin, laughing and singing light-heartedly at their work. A haggard surgeon whom I had met before gave us a kindly greeting, and promised to show my companions, who were new to the place, all there was to be seen at Akassa. We halted a moment to watch the eddying rush of tideway shimmering in the sun-glare that swept between us and the dark forest on the farther side, and noted the wreckage of steamers lost on the bar and snags piled upon the narrow beach binding the sand together against the fretting stream. Then our eyes were dazzled by the reflection of whitewashed buildings, and we were glad to turn them towards the sweep of cool cotton-woods, 200 feet in height, which hemmed the clearing in. Next we entered the big salt-shed, and in contrast with the brightness outside it was a moment or two before we could make out anything at all. When we did so we saw a burly white man in pyjamas and sun-hat, sitting astride a salt-bag, and hurling mingled abuse and encouragement in the tongue of the West Coast, which is more emphatic than polite, at the trotting Krooboys; while a youth wasted by malarial fever kept "tally" of the bags.

"Not dead yet, you see," was his characteristic greeting; and there followed these words of encouragement to a panting Krooboy, "Oh, you low bush 'tief, you crawl along faster there, or them flies live for eat you, sure"; at which the oily African showed his splendid teeth as he grinned from ear to ear. There were endless bags of Cheshire salt, perhaps several thousand in that shed, and we had many more on board; for the quantity of evaporated salt that goes up the Niger is enormous, to say nothing of the rock-salt which comes south by camel-train from the Sahara *viâ* Timbuktu. Up leagues of yellow river it is carried in light-draught steamers, then in canoes. Afterwards it is packed in fibre cylinders, and goes north on the heads of slave-gangs, each negro ruler cutting off an inch from the roll for the privilege of passing through his dominions, until what reaches the eventual consumer in the wilds of the Sudan is worth its weight in silver, and has cost many lives.

The ways of Africa are not those of the Western world, and neither time nor distance is an object with the Arab merchant in a land where the slave-trade provides sufficient labour. By examples brought down from the hinterland, and occasionally found when the stockade of some rebellious headman of the coastwise heathen is stormed, it would seem that articles of Indian and Persian art are not unknown. Beautifully engraved gun-barrels and richly chased hilts of the straight-bladed Arab swords have been found; and though many of the inland Moslem evidently understand the smelting and working of iron, these would seem to bear the stamp of Damascus and the farther East. How they came there across endless leagues of desert, or passed from hand to hand through many different nations, no white man knows; but if the methods of the Arab are primitive, his commerce extends from the Nile to Senegal, and from Fezzan to the Zambesi. France at least is thoroughly alive to the importance of this trade, for while we British have to a great extent been calmly content with the unhealthy coast, she has been tirelessly exploring the hinterland. A repetition of this statement may be pardoned, for the fact is of supreme importance to the welfare of our colonies, and may be forced upon the attention of those at home sooner or later. The following difference between the policy of the two nations should always be clearly remembered. When we British open up a country we are content to hold the trade, if we can, by means of low prices and the quality of our merchandise, while any nation finds a free market there. Indeed, there are several prosperous German factories in our Niger Protectorate. It is not so with France. Once she establishes a protectorate, the traders of every other country are at once driven out by duties, which is one reason why associations of British merchants have periodically urged the development of the hinterland and the laying down of light railways upon the attention of her Majesty's Ministers. Now, however, a fairly satisfactory arrangement has been come to with France, and the difficulty, so far as that nation is concerned, is over, for a time.

The galvanised sheeting of that shed was far too hot to touch, the radiation, noise, and bustle almost insupportable, and we were glad to hurry out into the sun-glare again, where at least there was a little breeze. Close by stood the big gin-store, filled to the roof with thousands of cases of Hamburg potato-spirit, which is one of the staple imports of the Niger delta, and what is said of this region applies almost equally to the whole littoral. It is worth about 2½d. per quart wholesale, and there is a great difference of opinion about its quality. Some authorities endeavour to prove it is really beneficial, others that at least it is harmless. I would not care to enter the arena and try to prove anything at all, but merely say that I never found a white trader who cared to imbibe it, and I have seen European seamen who had purchased it surreptitiously ashore brought back to their vessels, not drunk, but raving mad. One scene, at least, when four strong men were needed to carry a frantic quartermaster on board, and the struggle that ensued before he was prevented from taking his own life in the wheelhouse, was a thing not to be lightly forgotten. This style of comment may resemble the method of Marc Antony in his famous oration, but it is accurate nevertheless. As to the effect of the gin on the native it is hard to judge, for the coastwise negroes can eat or drink almost anything without ill results. I have seen them absorb a whole bottle of black draught for a dose, and come back for more croton-oil, saying, "That be fine medicine too much, sah"; and one Krooboy at least used to mix the blue and white packets of Seidlitz powders in different vessels, and drink them — separately, so as to enjoy the ebullition when they combined inside him. He said this also was "fine too much." It must, however, be stated that with the exception of the big headmen drunkenness is not ostentatiously apparent in Western Africa, except in the periodical carnivals.

Near the oil-shed there stood a tree—a paw-paw, I think—whose trunk we proceeded to inspect. The bark was splintered with many slashes, some 5 feet from the ground, and even then, although it was probably fancy, it seemed that the odour of blood still hung about the hot sand below. Near at hand stood the quarters of the black clerks, a low, single-storeyed building raised on piles above the river-bank, its front pierced with shot-holes. Entering, we were shown a dark stain on the floor of a gloomy apartment, which treble salary would induce no African to occupy at night. How it came there will be explained in the following chapter. Next, we crossed the blazing compound, where a detachment of Yoruba troops were swinging through their drill, the rifle barrels glinting amid a cloud of stirred-up dust. These were tall and somewhat handsome men, black enough in colour, but with faces of a higher type than those of the coastwise tribes. They were Moslem from the Lagos hinterland, though of an easy-going kind, for it has generally been found impossible to make soldiers out of the forest heathen. At times the latter will fight hard enough, but at others they will run away; and once, where such a thing was attempted, the officers were in greater danger from their own men than from the enemy.

Across the compound stood the European residence, a long, single-storeyed wooden building raised some 30 feet on piles, with a broad verandah shaded by the overhanging roof running round it. The reason for the elevation is that, while few Europeans can hope to escape free from painful and frequent sicknesses, the white man who sleeps upon ground-level almost invariably dies. Machine-guns commanded each approach; and in the shade below a group of naked Nimbi men, with irons on wrists and ankles, squatted in the hot dust, chatting and laughing with negro philosophy, though they were then waiting sentence for some serious crime. Climbing the broad stairway leading to the verandah, we noted the way the balustrade was riddled with ball, and, when we stood above, saw that here and there the house had been rent through and through by fair-sized projectiles, and the damage not yet made good.

We were cordially received by three or four white men of the rank and file, the higher officials being away at Lokoja or Asaba up-river, and my friends were shown over the building. A central dining- or sitting-room, with bare floor, plain table, and a few Madeira-chairs, occupied one section, while beyond it the little sleeping apartments opened on to the verandah. They were of the usual West African type. A trestle cot, washstand, table and chair, a few photographs upon the wall, and a repeating-rifle or revolver-belt in a corner, was about all that each contained, but it was enough. White men do not live luxuriously on the Niger. After a somewhat Spartan lunch of tinned stuff and very indifferent bread, we lounged upon the verandah, sipping the inevitable cocktail or lukewarm claret, and listening, while our hosts discoursed about the various troubles in the swamps. The men were characteristic of the place, all listless and yellow-faced, while their duck garments or yellow *karki* tunics hung loosely upon their wasted frames. Later, the surgeon, whose own limbs were twisted by rheumatic fever, showed us the hospital, and the sight was one to remember. There was a white clerk, a mere lad, raving mad with fever delirium; and Yoruba soldiers crippled by the horrible Guinea-worm, which grows to a length of 2 feet amid the muscles of the human leg. In course of time its head breaks through the skin, and is caught if possible in a cleft stick, say a split lead-pencil, or something of the kind. Then each day an inch or so is wound round the appliance, until, in perhaps ten days, its extraction is complete. Should the creature break, however, it grows another head, and the trouble begins again. Its ova are most frequently absorbed into the system by drinking unfiltered water. Then there were Krooboy labourers bitten by poisonous spiders or centipedes, suffering from the loathsome "craw-craw," which peels off the skin, or with feet eaten to the ankles by the boring jigger insect. The latter lies in wait in the sand, and if it once penetrates the toe, increases and multiplies in the flesh, its progeny feeding thereon, until there is nothing left. There were other horrors too, but these are enough. Neither are they pleasant things to mention, still less to look upon; but it would be hard to give an adequate picture of life in the feverland if all the shadows were left out. White men also suffer from these evils, though not so much as the negro, partly because the latter goes barefoot, and the white man does not. For myself, I never even stepped from a cot without drawing on a slipper before setting foot to the floor. Ceaseless vigilance is the price of safety in a land like this. Afterwards there was the little cemetery to be visited, too well filled with sandy mounds, and brightened by a sheen of the tall African lilies, whose heavy-scented blossoms only unfold at night, though the flower remains open by day. Like most others on the coast, it consisted of a little plot of sandy soil on the fringe of the forest, railed round by roughly split laths, unkept and uncared for, and beautified only by nature with the lilies that speak of resurrection. The roughest of crosses, consisting sometimes of two barrel staves nailed together, rise above the harsh, rank grass, bearing for a few months, until the rain and sun obliterate it, the name of him who lies below. There are so many dead in Western Africa, and the living have so much to do, that but little thought is taken for the fallen. After all, as the trader says, is it not a happy release?—and you never know your luck. The latter sentiment seems to console him for most troubles, especially those which fall to his neighbours' lot.

And such is Akassa, a narrow clearing between shimmering river and steamy forest, a dusty compound, and a collection of whitewashed buildings stewing in fervent heat or swept by torrential deluge. The Royal Niger Company, its fortunate possessor, is, as has been said, a much-abused corporation, and some of its disputes with the freelance traders arise from the uncertainty of territorial rights. In the lower delta it is occasionally a puzzling matter for a trader to decide whether a certain creek lies in the Company's domains or under the rule of the Niger Coast Protectorate. In the former no outsider is permitted at any price to erect a factory or visit a native market, while the latter or Government region is open to men of every nation alike, which privilege the ubiquitous Deutscher has as usual availed himself of. The trouble is that no definite demarcation limits seem to have been settled in certain districts, and it has happened more than once that traders have built a factory, organised an extensive commerce with the natives, and finally the Company, apparently only able to make up its mind on the question after much consideration, has ordered them off. This is exasperating, to say the least, for the freelances have built up the business in that creek, and the monopolists carry it on. Still, the Company can hardly be blamed for that; the trader should have made very sure before he set the venture on foot; and it is of course possible the latter "make mistakes" in this direction because they think it worth while to run the risk. East of Akassa the coast-line and land close behind it is all Protectorate. About Akassa it is Chartered Company's domain, though the mouth and one bank of the Forcados river are claimed by the Protectorate. Then just behind the Royal Niger Company's territory here lie Warri and Sapelli, Protectorate settlements; more Company's land; and New Benin, Protectorate again; while both sides of the great river beyond the delta are the Company's for endless leagues inland. There may, however, be an explanation for the curious way the possessions of the respective parties are dovetailed into each other.

If, according to the traders' stories, the representatives of the Chartered Company execute rough-

and-ready justice at times, it must be remembered that to have a new factory burned, or one's trusted servants butchered, to please the naked savage, is exasperating to the most patient, and that unless stern retribution follow the offence the river pirate grows bolder day by day. The depredators also are not the mass of the population, but a part only, who plunder their own countrymen equally with Europeans, and thus the suppression of them is a common boon. Here, as in other new fields, men of little education and obscure origin have made a reputation for themselves by mere force of will or dogged valour, and several such, whose names are well known in the delta, if overlooked at home, have done great things, as yet unchronicled, in the opening up of the Niger region. Occasionally they made mistakes, always their hands were heavy, but they did their work in the only way they could, and the result has generally been good. The story of one or two of these would make a romance which would hardly be believed; but chartered companies do not, as a rule, encourage their confidential officials to discourse upon their doings, and indeed most Englishmen in Western Africa mention memorable events in a very casual way. They have seen so many curious things that they appear to have lost the sense of wonder. One characteristic episode among those which periodically disturb the peace of the Niger delta may be set forth, and the writer would say that, having heard the story from men of various colours on the spot where it happened, he has endeavoured to blend the whole into a faithful representation of what took place.

CHAPTER VIII.

THE RAIDING OF AKASSA.

DURING the latter portion of 1894 there was trouble between the Nimbi tribe, whose stronghold lay among the swamps of the Brass river, and the officials of the Chartered Company. The Nimbi men were devil-worshippers and cannibals; but for all that they traded largely with the European factories, and sold much merchandise to their inland neighbours. The exact cause of the quarrel was never very apparent to outsiders. Perhaps it was one of the periodical outbreaks of dislike to the regulations of the white men, though as the Nimbi people, or Brass-men, dwelt under the rule of the Protectorate, it was more likely a tariff question. The Protectorate duty on gin being less than that which the Royal Niger Company as a governing body charged itself as a trading corporation, spirits bought in the Protectorate could be sold at a profit under the price charged by the Company's factories. Now the

Brass men were gin smugglers, and as such they had occasional differences of opinion with the officials sent to put down this traffic. It is also said that the arguments of both sides were sometimes enforced by the matchet-blade or repeating-rifle. However that may be, the result was that at last the headmen of Nimbi sent the Company warning that, unless some settlement was arrived at, they would come down and burn Akassa. The Chartered officials, with a contempt of the savage tribesmen which has more than once cost the Briton dear, disregarded the message, and did not even consider it worth while to retain a detachment of troops at Akassa. They had heard such threats before, and probably considered it a poor attempt to force their hand, but they suffered for their mistake.

One sweltering night in the hottest part of the dry season an oppressive stillness hung over Akassa. There was not an air of wind astir. Wreaths of white mist heavy with germs of fever rose from the quaking slime beneath the mangroves, streaked the muddy river, and crept in horizontal strata across the fringe of shadowy forest. There was a moon above, and endless fireflies flashed among the dewy undergrowth, but air and water alike were wrapped in silence. It was too still. No tapping of monkey-skin drums, or croon of monotonous chanty kept time to the Krooboy dance, as usual when the sable labourer's work is done. Instead the woolly haired wharf-hands crouched beside the dying fires, filing their matchets keen and whispering anxiously. Some of them had fought the Liberian troops or the tribesmen of the Ivory Coast, and now it seemed they must fight again, against long odds this time. The black clerks, after strengthening their dwelling, clustered round the doorway, examining miscellaneous weapons, varying from antiquated capped revolvers to the nickelled article turned out in Belgium at 30s. the dozen. They were by no means easy in their minds, for contact with Europeans had taken the savage delight in a *mêlée* out of their nature, and had not replaced it with the methodical courage of the white man.

High up on the factory verandah three Europeans, one of whom was a French officer visiting there, lounged in Madeira-chairs, looking anxiously out into the night, and a litter of cartridge-packets lay beside the Lee-Metford rifles at hand. They had not much to say, and when any one spoke his voice was strained and dry; for each knew there was in all probability trying work before him, and none of the three could tell whether he would be alive at dawn. The Brass men, it seemed, had kept their word. All that day mysterious canoes had been seen sliding down the river, to disappear among the mangroves. The forest had been filled with a crackling and rustling, and all the troops were away. So the three officials grimly waited the attack they felt would surely come, while beneath the broad verandah two Moslem soldiers watched behind a salt-bag redoubt which had been hastily thrown up around the one Nordenfeldt gun then available. It is said that the only man, black or white, who seemed in good spirits that night was the Company's coloured printer. He had been converted and taught his trade by the good missionaries in Lagos, but that had not prevented him visiting the fetiche town of Nimbi, and, by marrying one, or several, wives of the daughters of the people, becoming a *persona grata* there. He even volunteered to take his comrades under his protection when the raiders came. Alas, poor printer!

Suddenly the "chunk-chunk" of many paddles came through the stillness, the undergrowth crackled and crashed amid the forest, and the white men leaned out over the verandah as the sentries came running in. They were just in time. Amid a confusion of howls, whistles, and hisses a mob of wild figures, many naked, poured into the compound, the curved blades of matchets and the long barrels of flintlock guns glinting in their hands. Yelling and clamorous, they swept towards the residence, and as they did so there came a jarring crash, a cloud of blue smoke curled up across the front of the building, and a heavy steel projectile ripped a passage through them. Had the gun been a Gatling or Maxim, instead of a single-shot weapon, the story of the raid might have had a different ending; but the Nimbi men came of a fighting race, and with the red flashes of the flint-lock guns lighting up the compound, and the potleg whirring angrily about the residence, they closed in and rushed towards the salt-bag redoubt. Then the little gun spoke again. Its whirling 10-foot flash burned the assailants' faces, while the second projectile smashed through sable flesh and bone; but even as the big Moslem artilleryman thrust upon the lever there was a harsh clank, and the breach jammed fast. From what the survivors saw neither of the Yorubas attempted to seek safety in flight. One would seem to have struggled with the refractory mechanism, while the other thrust and pointed with the flickering red bayonet, until the black wave rolled on, over and across the salt-bags, and the two faithful soldiers, stabbed and hacked into shapeless heaps of crimsoned uniform and quivering flesh, lay dead beside their gun. Could any white troops have done more than this?

Next a mass of the raiders, who came down about 800 strong, it afterwards transpired, ran howling and leaping to the foot of the verandah stairway with the matchets gleaming in their hands, while their comrades fired any way over their heads. Three haggard white men stood grimly at the top, their fingers tightening nervously on the Lee-Metford stocks. As it happened, all were used to the rifle, and they meant to hold straight that night; for this was grimmer work than stopping the flighting curlew with the full-choked twelve as he swept at long range down the darkening river when the sun had gone. With a howl of fury the Nimbi men poured on, up three steps or four — and then they came no farther. Bright flashes whirled out above them, the ringing "rap-rap-rap" of the repeaters deafened their ears, a pitiless shower of lead drilled through and through the mass, and when those behind gave back there was no living negro left standing on those steps — only a writhing heap of naked black limbs, and screaming objects rolling in the sand beneath. Meanwhile the rest had surrounded the oil-sheds and the Krooboys' dwelling-house, and here a fierce struggle went on. Flintlock guns squibbed and boomed, ragged, screaming potleg ripped through galvanised sheeting and weather-board; and while some of the Krooboys broke wildly for the bush, the most part stood and fought. It was a hopeless struggle, for they were outnumbered five to one: the assailants had flintlock guns, and even for a bad marksman it is hard to miss a crowd with a scattering charge of a quarter of a pound. In spite of aspersions on his character, the Krooboy is not a coward, and if some bolted, there are white men who would have done the same. It could not have been pleasant to stand still with only a short matchet or shovel in one's hand, and be shot at by a howling mob of cannibals bent on murder, but some at least of the Krooboys did it. Exactly what happened it is hard to determine, for out of all those who remained but one or two escaped alive, and they never seemed to clearly remember the order of events. There was, however, a clashing of matchet-blades on gun-barrels, yells, screams and curses, and the black clerks, gazing terror-stricken from their quarters, saw the labourers forced back against the shed. There, hemmed in, with broken matchets or naked hands, bleeding and exhausted, the Nimbi men had them at their mercy — and the tender mercy of a West African cannibal is not a desirable thing. One after another they were cut down, or seized and dragged towards the tree we had seen, and here two big river-men relieved each other in relays at their deadly task. As each victim was flung against the trunk the red matchets came down, bit through skull and spine, and a Krooboy who would see the Liberian beaches no more sank limply to the steaming sand. Meantime detachments of the raiders busied themselves hunting fresh victims from their hiding-places, and so amid yells of fiendish delight wholesale murder was done. I was informed that while it was difficult to estimate exactly, probably 120 Krooboys in all were slaughtered that night.

Then the butchers hurried to the black clerks' dwelling in search of further prey, and one coloured invoice-checker afterwards said they were smeared red, apparently purposely, from their knitted hair to ankles, while the glare of a burning shed flung an unearthly crimson light around them. A weird scene for British dominions in the nineteenth century, at a port where mail-steamers call weekly! In any case the sight was too much for the black clerks. The cheap revolvers crackled and flashed; but if the negro cannot hold a 4-foot barrel straight, he can hardly be expected to be sure of aim with a 4-inch one, and next moment the foe were at the door. Most of the occupants bolted by the farther entrance or end windows, preferring the risk of being murdered outside to certain annihilation within, and then the door went down. The ringing of one revolver alone made answer to the raiders' shouts, and a sharp spitting of red fire came out of a shadowy doorway. One clerk at least stood fast, and a comrade, who frankly owned to being ensconced beneath a trestle-bed behind the thin partition, said he heard him fling his revolver down when the last shot was fired. Next morning this nameless hero was found literally cut to pieces on the spot where he had made his last grim stand, and we had seen the dark stain upon the boards he reddened with his blood.

Now there were only the three white men left of all the defenders of Akassa. The rest were dead or hiding in the bush, and meantime various rushes upon that verandah had been made. Each time the foe charged on until the stairway was blocked with struggling forms. Then three rifles, whose holders were sheltered by the coping above, flamed out; and when it is remembered that a Lee-Metford bullet will penetrate more than a foot of oak, the result upon the packed crowd below can be understood.

At last the Brass men appear to have realised that this method of getting at the defenders was somewhat dangerous, and they set their wits to work. The result was, that while various sable marksmen were sent to keep a sharp fire upon the verandah, others sheltering beneath the house attempted to destroy the piles, or fired up through the floor from underneath. They had also with them several good-sized brass guns, probably of the kind which fires a 6-lb. ball; and projectiles which, judging from the rents they made, must have been odd chunks of cast-iron or stone,

were sent crashing through the house. And all
the time the three Europeans, soaked in perspiration, and choking with acrid smoke, waited in
breathless suspense, or crammed fresh cartridges
into the magazines, determined that if die they
must, the foe should at least find their destruction a desperate task. There is a curious feeling
of contraction in the throat and roughness of the
palate which those who have stood face to face
with death in a revolting shape for many minutes
together know too well. So they waited for the
end, until in the greyness of the dawn the R.M.S.
Bathurst swung round a point at the entrance to
the river, and the boom of a big brass gun announced that the mail was in. Now some of the
Nimbi men had seen her Majesty's gunboats at
work, and the rest had heard the tale; so in
all probability mistaking the cargo-steamer for a
war-vessel, they decided to take themselves away.
Except for this providential mistake, they might
readily have boarded and sacked the steamer too.
Soon they were in full flight, and the Bathurst's
crew saw with surprise a flotilla of dugout canoes
shooting up the muddy river as fast as the whirling paddles could drive them through the water.
No one shouted directions as to mooring at the
wharf, and those who hurried ashore to investigate will never forget what they saw. As one
man afterwards said in my hearing, "You don't

like to remember that kind of thing—and it took half a bottle of whisky to put it out of my mind before I could sleep that night."

The Nimbi men, however, took a few prisoners with them, including the unfearing printer, but he did not travel as an honoured guest. Among other writhing wretches he lay nailed through arms and feet to the bottom of a big canoe for several days and nights, tormented by scorching sun, and drenched in midnight damp, as the flotilla threaded its way through the reeking swamps. There is no doubt the prisoners suffered this, for black traders afterwards averred they passed the canoes on the way, and there was other testimony. What happened at Nimbi is chiefly known from the tale of some young children, fourteen in number, I believe, taken prisoners and afterwards returned by the tribesmen from Nimbi with a message which I was informed was translated at Akassa as follows: "Their flesh is not sweet so young." This is perhaps the only redeeming incident about the whole affair, and it seems curious that the raiders should have taken the trouble to send them back, instead of either murdering them or retaining them as slaves. These children, sent by the Chartered Company, went back with me to their homes in Liberia some little time afterwards, and they unhesitatingly declared that all the other prisoners were cooked and eaten in Nimbi town in the carnival that followed. They also said the printer was the first to suffer, and that some of his comrades were forced to eat portions of his flesh before being slain in turn. This reminds me of an account of the doings of a certain cannibal bush tribe I once listened to, and it was accepted unquestioned by men who knew the district. It seems that before any great fetiche orgy it was considered desirable to eat human flesh, and a victim being obtained, was put up for sale in portions. But and because "provisions" of any kind are hard to keep in the tropics, he was not slain beforehand. All day he stood exposed in the market, and participators in the rites bid for portions of his anatomy, which were sold by auction, and then marked off in white paint. When at last each and every part of the poor wretch had been so claimed he was slaughtered. A custom of this kind is hard to credit, but there was at least no dissentient voice when the story was told, and some very curious things happen in the Niger delta. Strange to say, white seems to be the fatal colour and livery of the doomed all along the West African coast.

And so was Akassa raided. As a sequel, on the 20th of February 1895 H.M.S. Thrush and Widgeon, as well as the Royal Niger Company's steamers Nupe and Yakoha, with 150 bluejackets and marines and 150 of the Company's black soldiers, under the command of Admiral Bedford, were sent up to teach the Nimbi tribe that such things might not be done with impunity. As the greatest lover of peace will admit, it is no use remonstrating with men like these and pointing out to them the error of their ways. Any delay in the execution of justice merely encourages the bushman to continue in his lawlessness, for he fancies the Government is either too weak or has gone to sleep, and stern measures are perforce necessary. The tribesmen at first showed fight, and there was a hard struggle with a thousand well-armed warriors before a landing was effected at Sacrifice Point. On the 23rd an advance was made upon Nimbi, and as usual a heavy masked battery—the old cast-iron guns carefully hidden among the mangroves—opened fire on the flotilla of boats, killing one lieutenant and wounding seven men. But the avengers were not to be driven back, and, shortly afterwards, Nimbi town went up in smoke and flame, the British losing in all three killed, while seven were badly wounded.

CHAPTER IX.

A BURNT VILLAGE.

WE lay at Akassa nearly a week discharging salt, partly because many of the Krooboys we had brought from Liberia were unused to the work and took much longer than they should have done. One sweltering Sunday I remember we went inland through the bush, to visit the site of a native village burned by some one connected with the Company, because its inhabitants were believed to have either slain fugitives from the sack of the factory or taken a part therein. I was careful to lace thick leggings over my light duck garments, because there are many creeping things whose bite may mean amputation lurking among the undergrowth of the African bush, not the least of which is a venomous spider. The river was blinding bright to look upon, the fierce rays burned down through the double crown of a sun-hat, turning one sick with heat, and we were thankful to enter the steamy shade of the forest. At first the tall harsh grass grew waist-high, and here a few feathery oil-palms and smaller cocoanut-trees spread their curving fronds above our heads. Then the grass gave place to a confusion of vines and thorns springing up out of earth that was spongy, hot, and steaming, and the palms to giant cotton-trees, 200 feet and more from the buttresses which support the mighty trunks to topmost spray. Festoons of creepers trailed from above, white lilies grew up among the flanged roots, while the atmosphere was that of a giant hothouse, soured with the rankness of rotting leaves. After a march of half an hour or so we reached our destination, and the scene was typical of the Niger delta. A narrow clearing lay between the wall of forest and a muddy creek, and about it were the fragrant and snowy blossoms of oranges and limes, the pale-green leaves of bananas, and the vine-like trailers of the sweet potato. In the centre lay a strip of hard-trodden earth strewn with the wreckage of huts, and ringed by blackened ashes, and a wrathful growl rose up at our approach. A score or two of big men, of the Brass race, with chests and arms splendidly developed by labour at the paddle, were busy re-erecting the huts. Their hair was knitted up into many corkscrew plaits, their oily skin—and the majority wore little else upon it—was covered with devices in blue tattoo standing out in high relief, and both matchets and flintlock guns lay close at hand. Women in the fashions of Eden were hurrying here and there with bundles of palm leaves and reeds in their hands, and the work of rebuilding seemed to be going on apace. It is little punishment to destroy a West African village, for the river-man can replace it in less than a week. Signs were not wanting that the workmen regarded us with a disfavour that might prove dangerous; but a promise of several bottles of gin induced the coloured guide to explain our general harmlessness, and after the headman had been assured that none were servants of the Company we were permitted to inspect their work.

The huts were very simple, walls of wattled branches, roofs of thatch, a palm-fibre mat upon the floor, while four or five calabashes for cooking completed the furniture. There were children everywhere—tiny babies carried in a fibre sling about the small of their mother's back, others rolling contentedly in the hot dust, and little round balls of blackness with splendid teeth and eyes tumbling and laughing through the bush. It is perhaps worthy of mention that I never heard an African baby cry, the negro's usual state of apathetic content being apparently born in him. The headman spoke a little English of a kind, and shaking his fist in the direction of Akassa, he said, "Company man, one dam low white bushman, sah. No fit burn him town again, sah,—one time one fool, two time one dam fool." He had evidently learned this proverb—which seems to imply that if a man falls into the same trap twice he is not to be pitied—from the Krooboys. It is a favourite saying of theirs.

We had seen enough of that village, and as it was swelteringly hot I beguiled a certain surgeon, who will doubtless remember the experience, into taking a trip down the creek to the Nun river, instead of marching back. I had sailed in most kinds of small craft, from Canadian birch-bark to the tight-drawn skins in which Kaloshian and Siwash hunt the most costly fur of all, the ocean-otter's skin, in the far-off Behring Sea, and bribed the owner into giving me the bow paddle. He crouched in the stern himself, and the doctor amidships, very sorry he had come. The thing—you could hardly call it a boat, for while the Kroo canoes are beautifully modelled and finished, the Niger men have the most elementary ideas of marine architecture—was some 16 feet long and about as many inches wide. Therefore it became evident the art of balance was very necessary here, and that the first rash move might result in a capsize. A race of brackish water poured down from some lagoon or swamp inland, and we slid swiftly away between overhanging walls of forest, while crawling mangroves lined the malodorous banks. Festering mire lay among the high-arched roots which rose above it like the tentacles of a great octopus, and hideous bloated crabs squatted upon the slimy bark, blowing froth about their hairy shells. So many were they that the sound of their bubbling could be plainly heard above the gurgle of the water, while innumerable wallowing things, half-fish, half-lizard, flopped along the surface of every steaming pool. The sour odours were sickening, for, wherever the mangrove grows, there is malaria, and we felt that we had done foolishly. This was the more evident farther on, for in the late troubles great trees had been felled, so that they lay right athwart the stream, the negro's favourite means of closing his creeks to intruders. The first of these was covered with a foot of frothing foam where the current roared across it, and I looked anxiously at the helmsman. To paddle back against that rush of water was impossible, a blunder meant capsize, and, while two of the party at least could swim, to attempt a landing amid the mangrove slime could only result in our being miserably smothered there. Nothing but a monkey or alligator can safely pass a mangrove swamp. The helmsman shouted something I did not understand, but doing the thing that seemed best, I whirled the carved paddle with might and main, and drove the canoe towards the centre of the log. The negro evidently intended this, for he grunted approval; and next moment, with a bang and a rasp, the keel smote the tree. A muddy rush of water broke over her stern, and then the light craft drove on down-stream again.

A passage about 2 feet wide had been chopped through the remaining trees, though why by applying the same labour at either end the river-men did not clear them away altogether they knew best themselves; and, shooting the narrow sluice-ways more by good luck than anything else, we safely reached the main river. Throughout the whole of that trip the poor surgeon's eyes were almost literally starting from his head, and when we reached the ship he expressed his opinion on the matter in terms that were more forcible than polite. We had nearly drowned him twice before, he said, and he was getting tired of that kind of foolishness.

That afternoon, as I lounged in the quarters of the chief engineer, the usual gravely-spoken, sober-minded Scot, a thirsty comrade from the Company's little foundry higher up stream dropped in, to sample some particular blend of whisky, and to inquire for fellow-apprentices of Fairfield or Dunlops, then roaming across the face of the seas. It is the writer's impression that all engineers trained on the Clyde know each other, for in every port all the way from Singapore to Vancouver the grim "chief's" room resembles a gathering of the clans. It is not so with deck officers,—they are inclined to assert their dignity, and a stranger must win their approval before being honoured with their friendship; but one man of furnace-flue and throttle-wheel is immediately on the best of terms with another. If he is not a cousin or a brother-in-law, he "wrought in the same shop"; and failing that, he can, as a rule, discuss knotty problems in calorics or theology, and assimilate whisky with equal facility. In any case, the comrade was there that afternoon, and as the West African is most at home when discoursing about Western Africa, the visitor presently commenced to tell us how he burnt the village at the imminent peril of his life.

"It was no' the kind o' work to tackle wi' a light heart," he said, "but ye could not sleep at nights for fear they deevils would come down and break the new lathe. Tamson would not come, and wi' a revolver and ten Krooboys wi' matchets I went up and drove them oot—a hunner o' them wi' loaded flintlock guns. Then fower gallon o' kerosene did the work, an' I came back happy. Thank ye, nae mair water."

After absorbing half a bottle of the chief's best, and expressing his strong disapproval of the Company's policy up-river, our guest took himself away, and the engineer said, "A weary wastrel, and noo he'll strike the second for some more. Ye'll hear them singing in a wee."

On the following day another gentleman claimed to have distinguished himself by the destruction of that village, but this individual took only two

Krooboys and a walking-stick, and did it with trade-powder, while his thirst was also prodigious. Still the story was worth the liquor, and I signed the wine-cards cheerfully. It also happened that the morning before we sailed, the last arrival at Akassa, an ingenuous youth, who seemed already to have great ideas about the extension of British commerce on the Niger, lounged in and patronised the passengers. He appropriated as many of a friend's good cigars as he could readily lay his hands upon, and after a time favoured us with this narrative as nearly as my memory serves.

"You were up at the village, I heard," he said. "It's not the safest place for new-comers yet, but nothing to what it was. I and Charlton went up just after the raid with only one or two Krooboys, and the crowd turned upon us with matchets waving, and you know how they whistle and hiss when there is mischief on hand. It seemed a shame, of course, but you see we had to burn them out, or you could never be sure they wouldn't cut some of the Krooboys' throats at night. So I made a speech to them, and I think they understood the tone, or else it was the revolver. Anyway, they bolted, and I made a great bonfire of the place. That lesson will keep them quiet for a while."

When this youth had gone, his auditors looked at one another and smiled; and I recollect that the chief, who had been listening with a twinkle in his keen eyes, said briefly, "The Lord forgie them for leein'," as he went away to take a worn shackle out of the wheel-chains.

Now, as a rule, the European in West Africa is not given to romance, and it is even somewhat difficult to draw him out on the subject of personal exploits. Various tales of heroic endurance and suffering beyond the imagination of those who live sheltered lives at home have been told me in a casual disjointed way, by which their significance would have been lost to those who did not know what the incidental allusions meant. Thus the episode was the more surprising, but I can only say that it occurred as described, save that I may have forgotten the exact form of each story; and it would seem to show that if the bushman adopts none of the ways of the white man, the white man occasionally adopts some of the ways of the bushman. Who did burn that village we never learned. Neither did all the European inhabitants of Akassa figure as heroes during the raid. One rowed off to a hulk moored in the stream, and it is said could hardly be induced to leave her after the danger had passed.

I can remember the last night we spent at Akassa well. The air was still and filled with clammy heat, while the inevitable fever-mist hung in woolly folds above the dew-damped compound. The monotonous "tap-tap-tapping" of a monkey-skin drum kept time to one of the weird but by no means unmusical chanties of the amphibious Kroo nation, while naked figures danced and sang in the red glow of a fire. However hot it may be, a fire of some kind seems to be indispensable to any African amusement. This is the Krooboy's inevitable evening recreation, and with a few handfuls of rice, a little salt beef, the higher the better, and leave to enjoy himself as he pleases when darkness settles down, he will do the most laborious work cheerfully. That is, if he sees his employer is a man whom it would be unwise to try shirking with.

Meantime, upon the iron fore-deck, the Sierra Leone and Lagos carpenters, and artificers engaged for work upon the Government Consulates, were singing English hymns, for it was Sunday night, and the refrain of a wild pagan war-chant mingled quaintly with the old familiar words. The negro is generally favoured with a splendid voice, and the elision of the harsher consonants and the emphasis of soft vowel-sounds are pleasant to the ear. Whatever may be the faults of the converted African, he is at least regular in religious exercises, and there was scarcely a Sunday when little groups did not detach themselves from the surrounding heathen or contemptuous Moslem and sing their hymns together. Still colour caste is rigidly maintained, and I remember one evening a certain second engineer, who was of a revivalist

H

turn of mind, and had been discoursing eloquently, if not very grammatically, upon the freeness of the Gospel to an audience which was not wholly appreciative, wheeling out a tiny harmonium into the alleyway and starting some hymns. A few of the rest took up the air, more for diversion than anything else, until the swing of the music seized hold upon them, and soon some of the plaintive refrains echoed and died away far out in the mist which veiled the muddy river. Then a splendid voice, ringing and clear, rose above the rest, and we saw a converted Sherbro man, who performed a very menial office on board, standing in the entrance of the alleyway. The brotherhood of man was apparently one thing in theory but quite another in practice; for next moment a savage kick drove the sable singer, who had dared to approach too near his fellow-Christians, howling across the deck.

Then the last voice died away, the Krooboy drums grew still, and there was only the croaking of frogs, the gurgle of the tideway, and, alas! the trumpeting of mosquitoes to break the silence which brooded above the river. The twinkling lights of the Residence went out one by one, the red glow of the embers faded into darkness, and I went back to my sweltering quarters, where the skin-plates gave out the heat they had soaked in by day, to seek such sleep as the mosquitoes, rats, and cockroaches might allow.

CHAPTER X.

THE INLAND REACHES OF THE NIGER.

BEING now on what may be termed the main river —for the Nun entrance is the most direct route to the hinterland of all the myriad water-ways—a space may be devoted to tracing the Niger back to its source. Here the writer would state that he is indebted to the records of the adventurous explorers who have visited its upper waters, for there are still reaches of the great river which few white men have ever seen. Above Akassa the yellow stream rolls down through a waste of festering mangrove-swamps, and alternating strips of firmer earth crowned by mighty cotton-woods or clustering palms, the country gradually becoming drier as one travels north, and the condition of its inhabitants changing little by little from that of the naked savage. Near the Company's station of Abo, and some hundred miles from its mouth, the delta appears to end. About forty miles farther the strong post of Asaba, R.N.C., is passed on the one hand, and the large native town of Onitsha on the other, and about here the change from savage heathenism to some degree of order and a trace of Moslem influence becomes apparent. Beyond Asaba a rich undulating country rolls away on either hand, diversified by patches of primeval forest, and the banks are golden sand until the river pours through a narrow gorge strewn with fallen crags and boulders, where great flat-topped mountains tower above the frothing rush. This passed, the wide expanse where the Benue, flowing from the east, mingles its waters with the Niger is reached. Here, and some 250 miles from the sea, the R.N. Co.'s station of Lukoja, now a great fortified camp, stands beside a lake-like reach, and in all frontier troubles Lukoja will figure prominently.

Near Egga town, 70 miles from Lukoja, the river turns sharply west, round the peaks of a jagged range, and flows seaward through a wide valley walled in by rugged cliffs, until near the R.N. Co.'s station of Badjebo, where a second range of hills rises steeply above it, its channel turns north again.

At Yauri, farther north, Mungo Park perished shooting a rapid under fire, and from here to Say the width of the river is about 1000 yards, and there are generally rocks on either hand. Say lies 600 miles north-east of Akassa, and probably 1000 miles from the bar following the sweeping curves, on the borders of the great Moslem kingdom of Sokoto, and forms the boundary of British possessions on the one hand, and territory under the influence of France. Doubtless the French hope, sooner or later, to extend their dominion southwards from Algiers, and consolidate the whole. Thus with caravan-routes north across the desert towards the Mediterranean, eastwards towards the Upper Nile, and free right of navigation on the Niger, they would control a vast region. The possibilities of this portion of the Dark Continent are immense; for, as we have seen, its people are of an intelligent type, and apparently capable of much progress in many kinds of art and industry. Thus far the Niger is comparatively well known, but beyond this point it traverses a region seldom visited by white men.

Still the river comes down from the north and west through endless leagues of fertile land, where are populous towns and great plantations, cotton and indigo being extensively cultivated. Indeed, along much of the coast the native cloth made by the Moslems of Sokoto is already largely purchased, and some of the indigo-dyed fabric which I have seen is of splendid quality and texture. How it is woven, or in what manner of loom, does not appear, but it is only well-trained craftsmen who could produce merchandise like this. Then there are marshes, networks of tangled waterways intersecting reedy swamps, until the country resembles the delta again; farther yet the swamps give place to dry land carefully and skilfully cultivated, where maize, barley, tobacco, and wheat are raised, until at Timbuktu the fertile region fades into the barrens of the Sahara.

For centuries this town served as a beacon to the adventurous of many nations. By some it was supposed to be full of gold and ivory, the home of Prester John, or at least of some great sultan who reigned in gilded state; and the early Portuguese gathered many legends along the coast respecting it. In due time the disillusion came, and Timbuktu was found to be merely a large walled city, filled with rammed mud houses, and mosques with flat-topped pyramids, the desert rolling north behind it, and an unknown land stretching towards the Gold Coast on the south. Yet even to-day Timbuktu is a place of importance, and the writer, being once interested in the Morocco trade, heard startling accounts of the size and wealth of the caravans which travel from the latter sultanate towards it. Some of the camels are laden with European goods imported through Morocco, and others proceed light to a mysterious location in the great desert where are said to be quarries of rock-salt. The European goods are blue selampores, American cloth, long-cloth, sugar, tea, glass and amber beads, and silk. On the return journey ostrich-feathers, gum, incense, native blankets, ivory, rubber, and gold are carried north; and, as has been said, various attempts have been made to intercept these caravans and trade with them on the Sahara coast. Such ventures, however, were never successful, and more than once occasioned the death of several members of the expedition.

The Moors and Berbers inhabiting the region traversed by these caravans are perhaps the finest specimens of the human race the writer has ever seen, and he has rambled over most of the world. Once on venturing to land an expedition to march inland south of Bojador, our little Spanish steamer was boarded by them. The captain made them lay their splendid damascene-barrelled guns and inlaid-hilted knives in the store, and two seamen armed with revolvers stood on guard over the weapons. There were thirty-nine Europeans on board carrying repeating-rifles and revolvers, and yet the fearless sons of the desert, standing with naked hands, openly mocked and threatened us. They were mostly 6 feet high, and they carried themselves like Grecian statues. Even in the case of the darkest the features had nothing of the negro coarseness; and one tall sheik told us, in the Arabic we partly understood, that they would have no white men there, bidding us promise to retire or they would cut all our throats. We did eventually go back,—in somewhat of a hurry, too; but a stronger party returned again, and a little later a grim fight was fought on a certain beach not very far from the head of Bojador, the white men emptying the rifle-magazines as they backed down towards the boats. Two at least will carry the marks of that affray with them all their lives. If the sheiks had not placed this veto upon trade, the profits would have been enormous; for sheep were purchased at an average price of about 9d., and sold for 8s. in the Canaries, and wool was acquired at a value equal to less than 3d. per lb. There was, however, trouble at both ends; for Spain claims a nominal authority over part of this region, and apparently objects to unofficial investigation. If the writer had £4000, and a bodyguard of, say, 100 British Columbian bush-ranchers or South-African stock-raisers, he believes it could be quadrupled in one year—that is, if the Spanish or some other Government did not interfere. But all this has little to do with the Niger.

Above Timbuktu the river flows north-east through a fertile region abounding in rice and other grains. Moslem emirs, dwelling in great walled towns, whose inhabitants seem to be of considerable mental development and proficient in high-class agriculture, rule over it. Some of the stories told about them resemble fairy tales, picturing a state which was that of Bagdad and Damascus in the days of Haroun Al-Raschid; but although there are undoubtedly powerful races, disillusion might also follow further knowledge here. At the town of

Segu, filled with mosques, and peopled by 30,000 to 40,000 of what Mungo Park a century ago called "highly civilised inhabitants," the famous explorer first saw the Niger in 1795. Still following south, we traverse the kingdom of the great raider Samadu; and 400 miles from Segu, and little more than 200 from Freetown, Sierra Leone, the Niger rises among the barren peaks of the mysterious Kong, 2500 odd miles from its source to Akassa bar.

There appear to have been two great epochs in the history of the Niger basin, both of them marked by the rise of Mahommedan power. Up to somewhere about 900 A.D. the inhabitants of this part of the Sudan were probably negroes pure and simple, leading the usual slothful lives, and content with cassava and yams to eat, and a strip of skin to wind round their waist, each village making war upon the next, and the stronger plundering the weak, whenever the latter possessed anything worth plundering. This is the general status of the negro untouched by any civilisation. Then the Arabs came, worn with travel and half-dead from thirst, to find a fertile paradise awaiting them beyond the burning sand. They brought the faith of Islam with them, and the negro, with a faculty which is imitative rather than comprehensive, accepted the teaching of his conquerors, and so the tide of yellow and brown men flowed steadily south for nearly a century. But they brought other things beside El Koran, including a restless energy, ideas as to the cultivation of land on an extensive scale, and a knowledge of mechanical arts which has been made manifest all the way from Delhi to Granada, and dominates the architecture of Spain to this day. Alike in the lace-like traceries of fretted stone in the Alhambra and the pillared patios in far-off Mexico the hand of the Moor may be seen, the stamp of the immemorial East plainly set upon the farthest West.

Little by little, dwelling side by side and intermarrying with their converts, the men of the north raised the negro to a higher level, and a nation rose out of a chaos of hostile tribes. Strong cities took the place of reed-work huts, great mosques rose from the sites of the blood-stained fetiche-house, and the naked savage became not only a tiller of the soil and industrious citizen, but a redoubtable man-at-arms. Then stories of the power and wealth of this region travelling across the desert excited the cupidity of the Sultan of Morocco, and in the sixteenth century he marched south and broke up the empire of Songhay. Afterwards there seems to have been a relapse, and the land sank rapidly towards a savage state again. A second time the light which dawned in Arabia broke in upon the heathen darkness, but it must be borne in mind that in the case of Songhay it was not only the religion but also the wisdom of the East, even diluted by superstition as it was, which wrought so great a change.

Some time after the fall of Songhay a mysterious race of mixed origin wandered south and east from oasis to oasis, fighting feebly at intervals, or flying from the stronger powers. Whether they came from the southern slopes of the Atlas, Algiers, or from the land where Morocco merges into the wastes of the Sahara, does not appear. It is probable that the blood of the early Latin conquerors still flowed in their veins; and even now, at the end of the nineteenth century, their descendants, the Fulahs, bear a certain stamp which marks them unmistakably as a race far apart from any purely African. Their features are well chiselled, their hair wiry, and their skin a curious darkened golden bronze. Those who have seen the Somali Arab coal-trimmers will know what the writer means. The nearest approach to it elsewhere is to be seen in a few Indian tribes tinged with Castilian blood in Lower California and Northern Mexico. For a time they became subject to the broken rulers of all that was left of Songhay, though they taught them many things, and then about the end of the eighteenth century another Mahommedan revival took place. Who first promoted it appears to be unknown, but the Fulah, who probably already held some knowledge of that faith, apparently became early converts, and gaining influence and power, suddenly asserted their authority over the original holders of the land. Thus the Fulah Othman, Sheik or Emir of Gober, in what is now the Haussaland, inaugurated a revolution which placed him upon a despotic throne; and before he died, early in the present century, founded the great empire of Sokoto. He would seem to have ruled sternly but wisely, framing just laws, quelling the bandit chieftains by the fear of death, until peace and order came forth from the confusion of raid and foray. The story of Othman would seem to resemble that of the legendary Arthur or Alfred, and he would also seem to have been inspired by religious ideals as well as endued with wisdom and valour.

There are few obstacles which do not melt before the power of a strong faith, and in spite of blind prejudice and frequent cruelty, even the religious fanatic has been an important factor in the history of the world: for downwards through many ages the man of intense conviction and single purpose, though his hands were not always clean, has swayed the fate of nations. The early and humble followers of the Prophet, the Spaniards who marched with Cortez into Mexico, the seamen of Elizabeth who wrested the mastery of the seas from the grandchildren of these, Cromwell's Ironsides — and how many more widely different in race and character—

bear witness to the fact. So it has been, and so it will probably be to the end.

Sokoto seems, however, to have again fallen from its former prosperity; for though it is a power in the land to-day, and the Haussa men who dwell upon its borders have made themselves a name for valour in the British service of two colonies, recent visitors, though they find much to marvel at, come across little in keeping with its ancient state. But much has already been written about this empire, and we may briefly state that part of it is well cultivated, its walled towns are large and strong, and its trade to the north and west and east is still extensive.

And now we have done with bygone ages and the early history of the Niger. Henceforward we will consider that portion of the region about its waters which is most in touch with European trade, and consider it as it is to-day.

CHAPTER XI.

IN FORCADOS RIVER.

It was a steamy afternoon when the Kinyema rolled in across the spouting bar which blocks the mouth of the Forcados river, probably the first in importance of the Niger arms from a commercial point of view. It is the entrance to the waterways of Warri, Sapelli, and New Benin, and here too all the exports and imports of the great region behind Lagos are transhipped into ocean steamers, for reasons already made clear. There was the inevitable spit of yellow sand with its cottonwoods and palms about the entrance, and then we slid on into what seemed to be a land rolled in eddying steam. The westering sun was veiled in yellow haze, looming through it coppery red; while on either hand the vapours hung in curious horizontal strata half-way up the massy cotton trunks, or gathered themselves together into many fantastic wreaths. Occasionally a little sultry zephyr stirred them aside, and we saw the river, shimmering with metallic lustre, run straight between the forest walls — then there was nothing but fog again. This kind of day is very trying to the European, even when well. A healthy man can withstand the fiercest dry heat — so long as he moves about; and I have travelled comfortably enough on camel or horseback hour after hour, across hot rocks and blazing sand, where one could not have stood still ten minutes on end. But clammy dampness makes breathing difficult, exertion almost impossible; and one pants beneath a suffocating weight which sometimes crushes an unacclimatised new-comer out of existence altogether, especially if he be of the florid, full-blooded kind. For the fever-stricken it is even worse. On such days they lie gasping and choking, or die suddenly; and when the anchor thundered down off Gosshawk Point, the mere roar of grinding cable troubled one's nerves. The haze cleared a little, and we saw we were not alone. A big Belgian mail-boat, homeward bound from the Congo, and a low, black-funnelled steamer from Angola, lay close at hand. A branch-boat pounded noisily towards us to receive 400 tons of Manchester cotton, gin, and sundries for Lagos; and two sister craft lay alongside a big Hamburg gin-tank, heaving on board endless cases of potato spirit, also for Lagos town. Farther yet, and half-veiled in mist, a little paddle-wheel gunboat with the tricolour over her stern lay straining at her cables in the muddy tideway, and presuming her to be a French survey vessel, one of whose officers I had met before, I chartered a native canoe alongside and proceeded towards her.

As I descended the accommodation-ladder a big Jakkery, standing considerably more than 6 feet upon his whitened soles, pushed past me. He wore a crownless silk hat, painted yellow in imitation of the funnels of the African steamship line, a pair of brass-rimmed spectacles, and a red handkerchief about his waist. This gentleman rejoiced in the name of King George, and was reputed to be growing rich by piloting confiding skippers, unaware of the likelihood of his running them hard and fast aground, into the winding creeks. Being neither captain nor Protectorate official, and thus unworthy of notice, he jostled me somewhat rudely, and was rewarded by a greasy mop thrust squarely into his face by a grinning Krooboy above; but an altercation with the fluent savage is not altogether desirable, and I was content to leave King George to his fate. He had lately distinguished himself by ramming a steamer half her length into a mangrove-swamp, and I knew that our skipper's temper, impaired by a certain internal cramp which is one of the effects of the climate, was none of the best that day.

As the knife-edged canoe, propelled by two splendid Jakkeries, slid away on the strong flood-tide, I saw King George being kicked violently off the bridge, only to fall into worse hands below. There was a confused scuffle about the deck, a knot of Krooboy seamen surged towards the rail, and then a wild howl of delight went up as the discomfited monarch, funnel hat and all, went flying through 20 feet of air, and head over heels, into the river. As I afterwards learned, on a previous voyage he had received a selection of curiously assorted merchandise from the Krooboys, who are traders born, on the condition that he brought them parrots or carved paddles to peddle along the coast. King George took the goods, but forgot to send off anything in return, and the Krooboy's idea of justice is primitive. However, he could swim like a fish, and the wash probably proved beneficial.

As we paddled away into the mist a constant clanging of winches and roar of exhaust steam rose on every hand, until one seemed to be in a reach of the busy Thames instead of an African river; and yet not far away there stood a native village where the Ju-Ju reigns supreme, and, it is rumoured, horrible rites of fetiche cruelty are performed. Few white men care to visit it, and a brave deed was done there once when two officials landed for a conference with the sable headman. They brought him a peremptory warning that he must discontinue his evil ways; and as no African ruler appreciates being dictated to in his own stronghold, one of the white men was struck bleeding to the earth. The least sign of fear or irresolution would have been fatal to them both, but his uninjured comrade was equal to the occasion. Felling the dusky monarch with his fist, he held the villagers off with menacing revolver until their Krooboys helped the other to his feet, and, facing the furious Jakkeries, who knew his skill with the weapon, retired towards the boat. It was an old story—the quiet determination of one man against the uncertain purpose of a mob. The Jakkeries would gladly have made an end of both, but they knew that the first who struck a blow would die—and no one cared to be that first. Nevertheless, all white men are not capable of work like this.

I was soon on board the steamer, a little antiquated vessel, and shall never forget what I saw and heard there. Sickness I had seen before, and had listened to tales of pestilence and suffering in various parts of the world, but the story of this vessel was worse than any I had heard. A dozen or so of Moslem Senegalis, resembling skeletons clad in tattered blue serge rather than men, were scattered about her greasy deck, leaning feebly over the rail, or stretched upon the hatches, as though unable to stand upon their feet. There is an indefinite something which characterises a plague-stricken ship. Perhaps it is the silence and neglect, where order and activity should be; perhaps it is some mysterious psychical influence; but however that may be, there is no need to explain to the initiated that death has been busy on board. I knew almost what I should hear before I turned aft in search of the officer in charge, and his story confirmed the instinctive impression. The little cabin was stiflingly hot. The angle-beams above sweated drops of moisture upon the littered deck, and processions of big brown cockroaches crawled here and there about the mildewed bulkhead. A young French officer wrapped in dirty blankets lay upon a blue-moulded settee, his hollow face seamed with lines of pain and his eyes glittering with fever. We had met before at a certain Spanish *fiesta*, when the marble-paved *plaza* of Santa Cruz, Teneriffe, was gay with coloured lanterns blinking in the glorious freshness of the north-east trades, and now I found him wasted by fever and fighting hard for breath in the steamy heat of Africa. My French was more than tinged with Spanish; and though he spoke some English, his head was light that day, so it was with difficulty I gathered the thread of his story.

Of late the French have taken what the British traders consider to be a very suspicious interest in the Lower Niger, and the little vessel had made one or two surveying trips. Then she went aground hard and fast upon a bank of festering mire hemmed in by steamy swamps, and remained there three months, so I understood, when the river fell. Sickness broke out as a matter of course. Moslem, Senegali, and white Christian perished side by side as they laboured to heave her off in the burning heat, until at last, recognising the hopelessness of the task, they lay still waiting the end. What burial in the foul depths of an African river where scaly alligators swarm, or among the loathsome forms of life in the putrefaction beneath the mangroves, means, only those who have laid a comrade there can understand. At last, when she floated off with the rising stream, the navigating officers, or the remnant of them, had to run the engines as best they could themselves, for there were no mechanics left; and before they reached Forcados the former were worn out with toiling night and day, because they were too few to change the watch. If I understood correctly, only three or four Europeans remained of all her company, and the lieutenant, recovering a little, had sent these home to give them a chance for life. Now, with the fever returning again, he waited a fresh crew from Senegal or the Gaboon to take her out to open sea, though he doubted whether he would ever return to France again.

He gave me a message to the Kinyema's captain, begging for supplies and drugs, which were readily supplied him; and being, as I have always found the Gallic official, of a kindly nature, added that he wished especially to purchase a hundredweight of lump-sugar. This, he explained, was intended as a treat for the faithful Senegalis, who are passionately fond of it. Indeed, I knew that the Moslem Senegali often squanders his last centime not on drink but sugar; and it is curious that other races abstaining from alcohol are characterised by this weakness for saccharine.

Darkness had closed down when we thrust the canoe off from the gangway, but for a time the glare of electric lights round the noisy hatches of the steamers came blinking through the vapours, and the rattle of winch-chain served as a guide, although I noticed we seemed to make very little way against the strong flood-stream. Then the mist rolled in denser than before, and soon we were alone in a narrow circle of white. Next it became apparent that the inland rush of tide-water was stronger than human muscle, the exertions of the panting Jakkeries relaxed, and we slid away northwards, I do not think even the negroes knew where. The prospect of spending a night among the alligators on a mudbank, or soaked in deadly damp beneath the mangrove leaves, was not a cheerful one, but there was nothing to be done but resign oneself to the inevitable. Therefore, shaking the dew from my clammy duck jacket, I lay down in the stern, wondering in what part of the mile-wide river we would eventually come to grief. Providence, however, was kind, and after a weary space of watching a stream of light glimmered through the mist, and, yelling excitedly, the Jakkeries drove the canoe in towards the shadowy loom of forest. Soon she grounded on the miry bank, and recognising where we were, I stepped thankfully ashore in front of her Majesty's central post-office for the Forcados district of the Niger. It was not an imposing edifice,—only a little square hut, built either of cotton-wood logs or frame-boarding, I forget which; and approaching the doorway, I stumbled over the prostrate forms of a few Krooboys, apparently slumbering contentedly upon the sloppy earth. A faint voice bade me enter, and I found the interior reeking with damp, and dimly lighted by a highly odoriferous paraffin-lamp. The room contained little besides one or two vermilion-painted barrels, whose use became apparent later, and various kinds of creeping things; but there was moisture everywhere, standing in beads upon the match-board, trickling down the walls, and filling the shadowy apartment with steamy discomfort.

A Krooboy crouched beside a trestle-cot at the farther end, and here a young white man stricken by the fever lay in a state of listless suffering. He soon explained matters. So far the post-office was used to some extent as a resting-place for Europeans wishing to catch the first steamer calling at Forcados, and he was homeward bound upon the morrow. The black postmaster was away on business, or more probably sick, and he had occupied the dwelling for three days. They must have been trying days to any one lying there destitute of every comfort, in burning pain, with only a half-naked alien to minister to his wants. For perhaps two hours we chatted, the sick man faintly voluble, discoursing out of a full heart upon the wonderful relief of breathing the pure ocean air again, and leaving the loathsome swamps behind. Still he was by no means sure he would receive the kindly welcome waiting him at home; for although the breath of the ocean is the best antidote to the malaria poison, it often happens that the change is too much for those weakened by fever, and thus the first week at sea is dangerous. Once that is passed, invalids generally begin to recover, but on the other hand they sometimes die before their enfeebled constitution can adapt itself to the change. The writer remembers leaving the Niger swamps in a steamer whose crew consisted of forty-one men, only two of whom were sick; and remarking that this was strange, a veteran mate observed, "Wait till we get outside, and then you'll see them go." Go they did, for in less than a week we had twenty-nine poor fellows sick at once, and five or six were buried in the sea.

At last my eyes grew heavy, and stretching myself out to sleep, I found but little rest. The mosquitoes, ants, and other insects took care that I should not slumber soundly, and when these failed a moan of pain from my suffering companion generally roused me open-eyed again. But the longest night has an ending, and at last the longed-for dawn arrived. Then, even as I bade my host farewell, two white-painted canoes manned by naked paddlers grounded against the bank, and the negroes solemnly unloaded two big barrels painted vermilion, with yellow cabalistics, which presumably represented the letters V.R., straggling across the end. A padlocked lid, probably closed water-tight, was placed in the other end, and a little flag fixed in a socket, while the sable postman carried a staff in token of authority. This carved staff, often a work of art, is the inevitable credential of a West African messenger, and serves the same purpose that a monarch's signet ring did in the olden days. You may treat any matter with the bearer thereof with as much or as little confidence as you might deem wise to accord its owner.

The barrels contained her Majesty's mail, and were either to be handed to the purser of a homeward-bound steamer or transferred to some consulate launch, and the reason for carrying letters so is that the 18-inch-wide canoes come to grief by capsize or otherwise at times. Then the floating cask with its flag ensures the safety of its contents, though, so rumour goes, the unsophisticated Jakkery has more than once appropriated a mail-cask to reverence as a new kind of fetiche. The vagaries of the ingenuous savage frequently harass the postal authorities in various West African colonies. One Gold Coast official informed me that when the telegraph was most wanted in outlying districts, it was generally found inoperative, owing to some sable heathen having cut out a length of the talking-wire to make hammered slugs for his flintlock gun or a necklet for some dusky beauty. It is also whispered that those in charge sometimes bow down before Baal by propitiating the fetiche gods through their representatives, so as to get a "Ju-Ju" or taboo placed upon their property, when no negro dare lay hands upon it. The African converts objects of European manufacture to very curious uses at times. It may be only a canard set on foot by the traders, but there are places where, so it is said, missionary hymn-books are greatly in demand. This is not for the purpose of worship, but because two or three of the leaves torn out and folded make a very suitable wad for a flintlock gun, and the book is such a handy size.

CHAPTER XII.

ON THE WAY TO WARRI.

SOON the Kinyema's windlass was panting and clanking, and, as the cable came grinding home, the odours of the mire it spattered about the foredeck were something to shudder at. The bed and banks of almost every creek in the Niger delta seem to be composed of a mass of fermenting putrefaction, and when river and swamp lie sweltering in fervent heat, the poisonous rankness of the atmosphere which hangs above them cannot be described. Then the clang of the engine-room telegraph rose up through the open skylights, the propeller began to throb, and, with muddy foam seething about it, and a yellow wake streaming behind her, the Kinyema churned her way inland. We are now winding through the waste of mangrove swamps which extend for some 500 miles from Lekki towards the Cameroons, and compose at least two-thirds of the Niger delta. On either hand they stretched away as far as eye could discern, a sea of dingy, olive-green leaves, streaked with clammy mist, and looking, though this of course was an illusion, as if a strong breeze had powdered the forest with dust. Beneath the interlacing branches a maze of pale-tinted stems, many pure white, and about the thickness of one's arm, ran down 12 feet or so to the network of crawling roots, some of which were crusted with oysters, while all dripped slime.

The tide was low then, and the tentacles stood up like arches 6 feet at least from the mire below, while each overhanging branch sent down shoots to take fresh hold in the foulness. Yet even now there was not always mire beneath them, but often perhaps a fathom's depth of yeasty fluid, and at high tide I should think it possible for 13 feet of water to extend several miles into the deeper portions of a mangrove swamp. All round the world, throughout a circle drawn parallel to the equator, and not far from it on either side, the mangrove thrives where there is swampy coast or muddy river mouth; and it is this fast-growing, fast-rotting tree which forms promontories and islands by gathering the mud, and in process of time binding it into land. Everything in this universe would seem to have its appointed task, and there are no truer verses written than the "Benedicite omnia opera"; but it cannot be said that, humanly speaking, the mangrove performs its work in a pleasant manner. Every half-mile or so tunnel-like openings wound into the dim green shade, and a native who knew the way could travel from Lagos to Calabar, through leagues of intersecting channels, without ever venturing out into the broad light of day. This, it is evident, seriously increases the difficulty of hunting out gin-smugglers and plunderers of trade-canoes. Many a grim tragedy takes place among these forest-shrouded waterways, for the covetous Jakkery or Idzo is frequently tempted by the news of a rich flotilla coming down. It is so easy to hide among the brushwood of a drier strip, and fire a murderous volley of broken cast-iron into the unsuspecting canoe-men. The matchet does the rest, and the few who may escape are generally afraid to carry the news to a consulate lest worse things should come upon them.

I forget whether it was here or on the way to New Benin that an accident, not uncommon in this region, befell us, which will serve to show more plainly what a mangrove swamp is like. We were swinging slowly round a bend when, and unfortunately, a yellow rush of tide-water was going that way in a hurry too. The helm was jammed hard over, but a revolving swirl caught the bows, canted them against the rudder, and the telegraph clanged sharply. The vessel trembled as her engines pounded hard astern, but it was too late. The way of a 4000-ton steamer cannot be checked in a moment, and a warning hail, "Aft with you, every man," came down from the lofty bridge. There was a rush of feet along the deck as negro and white man fled aft for their lives, and they were just in time. The wall of dingy mangroves seemed to be flying towards the big white-painted forecastle-head, and next moment, with a crash of splintering timber, the iron bows plunged right into the forest. The mangroves went down before them, groaning and creaking in a heap of sap-filled fragments; crawling roots rose up and rasped the rusty sides; while, resistlessly forging ahead, the steamer buried perhaps 30 feet of her length in the quagmire, for she was built light-draughted and with a cut-away forefoot. Then the whirl of the reversed propeller made itself felt, and as she came slowly to a standstill the exhalations of the mud, when the wash seethed among it, made one gasp for breath. Nor was this the worst. Red mangrove-flies, whose bite leaves a wound which often remains unhealed for days, venomous spiders, and legions of ants, shaken from the branches ripped off by shroud and stay which strewed the deck, commenced to stir themselves in search of prey, and the seamen fought them with squeejee and mop until the spouting hose swept them through the scuppers. Fortunately the tide was rising, and soon the Kinyema backed off again, and, with the loss of much paint and sundry awnings ripped to pieces, resumed her journey. At several sharp bends among the Niger waterways you may see great gaps in the dingy foliage where steamers have thus rammed the forest.

Before the sun lifted himself above the purple haze the river woke to life. Flocks of screaming parrots circled about the masts, gorgeous butterflies hovered along the edge of the mangroves, and we passed many dugout canoes. Some were diminutive craft paddled by women, and others unwieldy vessels, perhaps 30 feet by 7, and manned by many slaves. Beneath a palm awning aft the owner thereof squatted in state, a fire burning beside him, while several of his favourite wives were, as a rule, engaged in the preparation of some of the sticky, starchy messes made from pounded cassava or maize, which they call *kanki* or *kuse-kuse*. Strange to say, the word *kuse-kuse* in various forms is applied to many different articles of food all over Northern Africa by races as widely divergent as Beduin and Jakkery savage. It was probably not mere affection which prompted the black trader to bring them with him, for in the Niger region wives are assets worth about £5 apiece, and the river-man knows that his portable property is safest within range of his flintlock gun. Besides —and in this he resembles some of his European brethren—he likes to be waited on, and his wives can do it best. A few big retainers occupied the stern, and the inevitable flintlock guns and matchets lay beside them, for these canoes contained valuable merchandise, and the headman realises that the possessor of such things always travels safest when he travels well armed. Occasionally canoes insufficiently protected enter a region of doubtful reputation, and never come forth again.

Presently the swamps gave place to dry land, where tufted palms, great mahoganies, acacias, and cotton-trees crowned the banks, and the beauty of the tropic forest unrolled itself before us. White lilies and the crimson spikes of the wild pine-apple carpeted the ground, while creepers of every hue trailed from the boughs above, and a subtle exotic fragrance drifted out of the shadowy aisles. Then the mangroves closed in again, and the boom of the big brass gun awoke the echoes as the red roofs of Warri rose to view.

Warri stands about forty miles from the sea, and it is curious that while the river there is only some 400 feet across, the early traders in the delta described a great lagoon which stretched inland from this point. This is certainly one of the finest Government and trading stations on the Niger—by no means the largest; but everything there is clean, new, and orderly, and in this it differs widely from some of the others — Bonny, for instance, where squalor and filth abound, and many of the white traders live under very trying conditions.

On one side of the stream are endless mangrove swamps, mud, and oozy slime; on the other a strip some half-mile long has been hewn out of the cotton-woods which tower behind it like a sombre wall, and here the trading factories stand. They are four or five in number, I forget which, while another occupies a site lower down on the opposite bank, all raised on piles, roofed with red-painted iron, and whitewashed dazzlingly, with a shady verandah running round them. Beneath stand the long oil-sheds, also glaringly bright; and between them and the river lies a strip of earth trodden hard in places by naked feet, and in others covered with a little harsh grass or scattered flowers. In the centre there stretches a dusty compound, where the union-jack floats over the stately Protectorate Consulate, a handsome wooden building, white roofed, white walled—at least it was so then—with cool verandahs, and the space underneath between its supporting piles turned into a spacious court-room and offices. One's first impression on looking at it is a feeling of partial blindness. In that fierce sunlight the whitewash seems incandescent, and there is a certain oiliness about the surface of every African river which flings back the light like a polished mirror. The dust is glaringly white or painfully yellow, the palm fronds harsh raw-green, and the only restful colour is the dimness of cotton-trees and mangroves.

ON THE WAY TO WARRI.

I was soon ashore, and together with a companion also having business with Major Coupland Crawford, D.S.O., who then ruled that district for the Niger Coast Protectorate, turned towards the Consulate. A few negroes with handcuffs on their wrists passed us on their way to the white launch lying with steam up close by, and these, in punishment for various misdemeanours, were probably being sent away to perform useful labour — road-making or wharf-building — at some other station. A big Yoruba sentry stood on guard beneath the verandah, and when he informed us, "This be justice-palaver day, sah: Consul live inside," we entered the court-room.

The great square hall was partly darkened by green lattices, and every foot of space was occupied by a perspiring oily crowd. They were all big river-men, splendid specimens of animal physique, jet black in colour, with crisp hair knitted into innumerable plaits; and some were loosely swathed in white cotton, though others preferred a much simpler attire. All were either accusers, or prisoners taken red-handed by the Yoruba patrol, or sent down by the bush headmen to be tried according to the justice of the white men. Behind a big desk at one end of the room a stalwart soldierly Englishman of middle age, whose face was wrinkled with lines of thought and anxiety, and probably suffering too, leaned wearily back in a chair, two big Yoruba

K

soldiers with rifles in their hands standing like ebony statues beside him. This was Major Crawford, whom I had met before, and explaining our business, we were requested to wait until the court was cleared. My companion being curious to see how justice is administered on the Niger, asked permission to remain, and, though with some slight trace of unwillingness, the request was courteously granted. So we settled ourselves to listen, and I found the surroundings and stories almost identical with those of other courts throughout the delta. The place was stiflingly hot, and little puffs of scorching dust swept in through the lattice-work. The odours rising from that mass of raw humanity cannot be adequately conveyed in words, and a condensation of foulness stood in globules upon and trickled down the wainscoted walls.

A big negro, charged with stealing his neighbour's wives and afterwards shooting the injured man in the back with a flintlock gun, or something very similar, stood sullenly erect, scowling at his judge, while a black interpreter translated the testimony of a native witness into fantastic English. The Major listened patiently to it all, though the perspiration beaded his lined forehead, and oozed through his *karki* uniform, for he had already worked hours on end in that awful atmosphere. The witness was evidently lying boldly but unsystematically, for he contradicted his own assertions every other sentence. When he had sufficiently perjured himself, a second heathen, who had apparently learned a little English from the Krooboys, informed the court that "This man lie, sah—all one low bush tief," ere he proceeded to locate the occurrence in quite another place. Then the harassed official whose duty it was to try to sift the one grain of truth from such a tissue of falsehood, had them both arrested and adjourned the case. There were other charges of slave-stealing, attempts to murder, firing on trade-canoes, adulteration of palm-kernels with shells, and the like, to be investigated; and quietly and methodically the Consul went into them all, until at last the command was given to clear the court. And so order is maintained and justice done, while it can readily be seen that only a man of keen discernment, long patience, self-command, and firmness is fit for work like this. In all the stations of the Protectorate the law is administered in much the same way, and there are generally many cases to be investigated. It is complimentary to the character of the officials that the bushmen send in their offenders to be tried, or frequently bring their trade disputes to be settled, according to the judgment of the white soldiers, proving that, in spite of their instinctive dislike to the European, they recognise his wisdom and fairness.

We dined at the Consulate that night, in a long wainscoted room hung with trophies of the chase, for the Protectorate officials there were keen sportsmen. A big alligator's head looked down upon us, fine skins and heads of a curious kind of small leopard which inhabits the bush were artistically arranged here and there, and among them hung richly carved paddles and savage arms, including devilishly-contrived corkscrew spears, whose blades driven into the flesh with a twist can only be extracted by the knife. Two Government surgeons were present, one of whom afterwards perished in the massacre at Benin; and a haggard Hibernian, whose inborn love of mirth many fevers had failed to quite crush out, formed a brilliant foil to our grave but kindly host. While such men as was Major Crawford represent the Government in Western Africa, we can rest assured that even justice will be done between black and white, and that our rule will prosper. Speaking quietly and very unostentatiously as he did, one felt that this man might be trusted implicitly in perilous times, and yet there was an indefinite something in all he said and did which inspired both confidence and liking. Perhaps, knowing his own power, he could adopt a certain frankness and simplicity which does not characterise all the younger officials. He told us part of his history, smiling a little gravely at the interpolated witticisms of the Hibernian. He had served long in India, where in an unhealthy station a white man may learn much of life and death, before he entered upon a work which was to be more trying still. It seemed almost prophetic that he should make the following comparison, which I remember almost word for word. What happened afterwards impressed it upon my memory.

"The difference between India and Africa is this," he said. "In India with care a strong man can live even in a very unhealthy jungle if he has a good constitution, but here no one can expect to live long. Life is terribly uncertain."

Afterwards we sat chatting on the wide verandah, looking out across the moonlit river, and watching the mist rise up from the quaking swamps, discoursing upon many things, knowing not that two at least of the party had even then but a little while to live. Among other matters Major Crawford narrated incidents occurring in the destruction of river-pirate Nana's stockade, which story will be related in its place, and the hours slipped by until at last we rose regretfully to retrace our steps to our mosquito-haunted quarters. We had heard many startling things, tales horribly weird or intensely dramatic, of European life and death, and savage mythology, told, nevertheless, as matters of everyday occurrence in a quiet unmoved voice.

CHAPTER XIII.

WARRI.

Soon after dawn on the following morning we were about again; but early as it was, there rose a jingle of arms from the wide compound, where the dew bound the white dust together, and we saw our host watching his Yoruba troops swing through their morning drill. Four by four, and section by section, they passed us as we gazed, tall and upright men in dingy yellow uniform, looking what they were, splendid forest soldiers. Then, attracted by the ringing of hammers, we visited the long oil-shed, where some of the brawny Fanti coopers we had brought from Accra were at work hardening down the hoops of the big hogsheads and caulking the seams with rushes. On the way I passed a group of panting Krooboys rolling down barrels towards the wharf, each cask being carefully whitewashed to close the pores of the wood, and entering the shed, came upon a busy scene. The big Fantis, clad in blue cotton, were hammering with might and main, turning out work which seemed to compare favourably with that of any white cooper; while a young and sickly trading clerk superintended the filling of the casks with semi-fluid yellow oil, fragrant, and not unlike half-melted butter. This material is the staple export of much of Western Africa, and is indispensable in several manufactures at home, notably that of tin-plates and various kinds of soap. The nuts grow in clusters beneath the fronds of the oil-palm, which, in that part of Africa lying between the Cameroons and Senegal, at least, only grows within a certain distance from the coast. Once the land becomes drier the oil-palm disappears. In the Niger region it is rarely met with more than 150 miles from the sea, while in Lagos the boundary is considerably less than half that distance.

The whole fruit is in appearance something between a pine-apple and a gigantic fir-cone with the interstices filled in; and this outer cover contains many "nuts," though the term is not very appropriate, for each resembles a yellow plum more than anything else. The skin of the latter is soft and silky, tinted gamboge and vermilion, and beneath it there lies a mass of fibre and yellow grease. The bushman either scrapes this away or stamps the whole affair up in a foot-mortar, and the pulp is boiled, when the grease rises to the top, is skimmed off, and becomes the best palm-oil, worth from £16 to £22 a-ton, and each cargo costs it is hard to say how many lives. Then there is still left an inner shell something like a walnut, which is cracked, and the two or three little black kernels it contains are flung into another calabash. These kernels are shipped to Great Britain and the Continent—the latter principally—in millions of tons, and in Hamburg and Antwerp are pressed for an oil inferior to the outer layer. It is said to figure largely in the composition of Dutch margarine. Lately, however, Liverpool, after transhipping the kernels in endless quantities to the Hollanders and Germans, is commencing the extraction of the oil on a large scale. The whole process is very simple, and yet it is not accomplished without loss of life, for slaves are stolen to gather it, and the native markets where it is sold are periodically fought over. Marauders armed with flintlock guns waylay the canoe-trains bearing it to the coast, or the weary trade-caravans, and the Europeans who ship it home suffer many things and perish of fever. If it were not for palm-oil and rubber there would probably be few white traders in Western Africa.

We passed most of that day wandering from factory to factory, and generally found agents and assistants endeavouring to make up leeway in their accounts or lying in canvas lounges, growling at the heat and slackness, for there were no trade-canoes coming down just then, though we were to see plenty of them later. For the most part they were gaunt and sickly men, some of them wearing the stamp of alcohol, and the faces of the rest the impress of many fevers. Though for once they had little work on hand, there was no amusement possible, and little of interest that they could do. It was far too hot to wander through the bush in search of a chance shot at a leopard cat; besides, any exertion would probably be followed by fever. Trade rivalry prevented the staff of the respective factories dwelling on the best of terms with each other, and thus they lounged the weary hours away, listlessly turning over some magazine or journal of the lighter sort, and generally answering each other's remarks with gruff brevity, for the querulousness of the season was upon them. This life is not a pleasant one, and few agents or assistants intend to spend more time than they can help in Africa. They work with what may best be described as feverish energy, with the one aim of making all the money they can, so as to get out of it at the earliest possible moment and begin again in some more favoured region. One trader, from a forsaken place called Degama, explained their position frankly as follows: "We make every cent we can, and I would sooner be worked to death than idle here. All you have to look forward to is the arrival of the quarterly liquor supply. (Firms at home often send out an assortment of spirituous comforts every three months.) Then we have a carnival for a week and forget it all; afterwards it is worse than before, and we hold on until the next arrives."

That afternoon an incident took place in the Consulate which shows the desirability of an intelligent agent. Article 7 of the Treaty of Brussels binds all European Powers, the Congo Free State, Zanzibar, Persia, and the U.S.A., to prohibit the importation of modern firearms and munitions of war into "all territories comprised between the 20th parallel of north latitude and the 22nd parallel of south latitude, extending westwards to the Atlantic and eastwards to the Indian Ocean and its dependencies, comprising the islands adjacent to the coast, as far as 100 miles from the shore." This clause has been variously interpreted, and largely set at nought, for every rebellious headman seems able to arm some at least of his followers with high-class weapons, while in the Congo State it is said that a large quantity of rifle-cartridges, "made in Germany," are annually sold. In any case, the muzzle-loading flintlock guns so largely used along the coast were always considered as exempt from the prohibition until, to the alarm of many traders, instructions reached the officials of the Protectorate that the article was to be rigidly enforced and all trade in arms put down. This notice, posted outside the consulates, caused every agent to ship his consignments of flintlock guns home again, and that voyage we collected many hundred cases. Even then they stood piled high on the wharf waiting to be put on board. One agent, however, called upon Major Crawford with a copy of the treaty provisions, proved that flintlock guns were neither specified nor described in the prohibition, and placed a written notice that he would sue for heavy damages if any Government official laid a finger on his goods before the officer. Major Crawford, I afterwards heard, was considerably puzzled. His instructions seemed clear enough, and yet on reading the clause in question, as well as the official proclamation, he could see there was much reason in what the agent said. Besides, he knew the Government have occasionally had to pay somewhat dearly for the indiscreet acts of over-zealous officials, and in the end he promised to allow the flintlock guns to be taken back under protest. Then binding them over to secrecy, the agent interviewed the Kinyema's captain and purser, and persuaded them to deliver him all the flintlock guns and trade powder they had on board for several of that firm's factories throughout the creeks. As he explained, now that all the other traders had shipped back their supplies, he would be the sole holder of a stock, and could get treble price for an article in constant demand; while even if the authorities at Calabar were able to maintain the opinion that Clause 7 prohibited flintlock guns, the last weapon would be sold long before their reply arrived. He landed the goods after darkness closed down, and, I believe, made a handsome profit. Since then a wider view of the meaning of the edict was doubtless taken, for large quantities of these arms were again sent out.

Following the suggestion of one of the traders, we purchased a fowl from a bushman, tied its wings loosely, and, as directed, flung it into a forbidding oily eddy of a muddy creek which flowed past the nearest factory. The unfortunate bird fluttered once or twice, then the slimy pool heaved mysteriously, there was a sudden swirl, and a scaly head rose up out of the turbid water. I saw the oily stream slide off a plated back, and heard a clash of yellow teeth, and the fowl was gone, while the pool seethed muddily. This was sufficient explanation of the fact that negro children are often lost along the river-banks.

Then we tramped through an experimental plantation of coffee, and, following a narrow bush-trail, reached a native village a mile or so away. Here the houses of sun-dried mud or wattle-work stood at irregular intervals among the trees, overhung or half-hidden by the massy branches; for there had been no clearing of anything but undergrowth, and the usual swarm of loafing and scantily attired inhabitants followed our movements with mild curiosity. They evidently toiled not, neither did they spin, and yet the forest supplied them with a sufficiency of food and all the shelter they needed. Now and then one wonders whether, after all, there is not some reason in the savage view of life, and that a less advanced state of civilisation, with less of the ceaseless struggle after fame or wealth, might not be better for many who wear themselves out before half their days are spent in the fierce race for gold. Certain it is that some spell lies in the silence of the primeval forest, under whose influence men learn to live more simple lives, and become well content to forego many things which, although hitherto considered indispensable, they are better without. When you have once moved among his kind there is no mistaking the man who has dwelt far apart in the lonely bush. As it is beneath the great red-woods of the far North-West, so it is in the steamy tropics and under the feathery palms. There is something in this man's gaze which differs from the rest of his fellows, his hearing grows keener, and he generally seems to be listening for something as though every sound were significant. Often he has learned to think aloud, perhaps for the mere sake of hearing a human voice, and at various times and places you may hear him talking half-audibly to himself. But perhaps the most curious effect of such a life is the way he lies awake the greater portion of every night. One man I dwelt with in the midst of a great cedar-forest in British Columbia used to ramble through the bush until it was nearly dawn. The same thing characterises many primitive peoples, as it does most of the wilder beasts and birds, and in our own islands you may hear curlew, snipe, and dotterel crying all night long. I do not believe the Krooboy is ever really sound asleep in the darkness, though he can slumber well enough when he should be at work by day; and I have seen the same thing among races as far away as the Siwash of British Columbia and the Kaloshians of Alaska. Possibly there is something in their nature akin to that of the fiercer beasts, or it is the smell of the earth and trees which leads even a white man back to the ways of ancestors who died in times far off at the beginning of things.

Following the trail still farther, we came upon a little basket-work hut supported upon piles above the river-bank—a very simple affair to look at, and yet representing a great deal, for it was erected in honour of the Ju-Ju. West African mythology is, however, too complex a subject to be explained in a few sentences, and we therefore reserve the Ju-Ju system for another chapter. Meantime we noticed the offerings of dried fish, and strings of curious charms, laid upon the little platform before it, and the bunch of reddened rags — which farther from a consulate would probably have been dipped in blood not obtained from fowls—that surmounted the whole.

Then we returned hot and weary to the steamer, and next morning the Kinyema hauled out from Warri wharf. As the ropes were being cast off I went ashore to bid farewell to Major Crawford, and found him busy writing letters for us to carry to another Government station. "Don't keep the steamer," he said, in reply to my offer to wait until he had comfortably finished. "The letters will be done before they have swung her round, and I will bring them off."

He did so, in a foot-wide canoe, just as the vessel was starting on her way, and, disregarding an offer to stop her and lower the accommodation-ladder, came aboard by a trailing-line, and handed in the packets. Then, with a kindly farewell, he went down over the side, and we never saw him again. The action was characteristic. Any trading agent who shipped a few barrels of palm-oil would have made the vessel wait, and refused to have come on board unless he had a smart gig and the ladder was manned. Yet the ruler of the district, and holder of the D.S.O., could lay aside his dignity, and put himself to inconvenience for the sake of saving trouble to a few casual acquaintances.

Not very long afterwards he went down in the red massacre at Benin. Facing the ambushed foe, with only a light cane in hand, and calling his comrades to escape, he was shattered by a volley of jagged potleg fired by the skulking bushmen, and, with almost his last breath, begged his brother officers, who strove to carry their friend away, to leave him there and seek safety while they could. But that story has already been told. So, having served his country faithfully and well, he found rest at last; and what soldier could have desired a more worthy end? The words a writer puts into the mouth of our bluejackets and marines are applicable to other ranks of the British service as well:—

> "But once in a while we can finish in style,
> For the ends of the earth to view."

This reference at length to one individual may be explained by the fact that Major Coupland Crawford was the representative of a stamp of officers who have well maintained our reputation in Western Africa; and there is room for satisfaction in the thought that we have such men to do our dangerous work, and do it thoroughly. Even the best of them does not claim to be perfect, and as a nation we have made grievous mistakes in Western Africa, and elsewhere too. Still at the present time, at least, it may be said that we do the best we can, and do not hesitate at the cost.

One of the characteristics of the Anglo-Saxon is

the way in which he can rise to the occasion; and it is curious to see a young official arrive in one of our remoter colonies, often thoughtless, possibly used to luxury, and, as a rule, hitherto new to any kind of care, and change into a quiet and somewhat grim personage, who does his trying and anxious task efficiently, and endures privations and discomfort undreamt of at home, not only with philosophical resignation but frequently with absolute indifference. The secret seems to be that the man sets his work before and above everything else, and is content to become one factor in a great organisation. All this applies to the right kind of man. The other kind is quietly "invalided" back, or promptly throws up his position.

Perhaps the most prominent fault—if it can be called a fault—of our representatives in West Africa is a too rigid adherence to the letter as well as the spirit of the law. Occasionally a widespread irritation exists among the native tribes which a liberal interpretation of various clauses in existing statutes would allay. But there are few officials who apparently care to venture beyond the narrowest red-taped meaning, and the answer given over and over again to petitioning headmen has been this: "I did not make the law, nor can I change it; therefore appeal to me is useless. For your own sakes I counsel you to keep it, for I am bound to carry

L

out the instructions laid down." We are still a trifle too fond of meaningless and often unnecessary forms, and, as a rule, it takes some time to move our administration in Western Africa and elsewhere to try experiments. On the other hand, however, once the benefit of a change is conclusively proved, no expense is spared to bring it about.

CHAPTER XIV.

THE SLAVE-TRADE AND THE JU-JU SYSTEM.

HERE it would seem desirable to devote a brief space to the consideration of two customs which have played a leading part in the past history of Western Africa, and whose influence is felt to-day throughout the whole littoral in general, and the Niger delta in particular—the worship of the Ju-Ju and the traffic in human flesh.

As it has been ably demonstrated by several great writers of modern times, the natural features of a country have always to some extent determined the character of the religion or mythology of its inhabitants. This is especially true throughout that part of Africa which extends from Gambia to Congo; and it is in nowise strange that the negro dwelling in the shadow of the primeval forest, a region of eternal silence, or swamp-land grotesque and horrible as the creations of a nightmare and swept by pestilence, should people the steamy bush with malevolent deities. Danger continually threatens him, and he is ever face to face with death. Mysterious sicknesses decimate the stockaded towns, and legions of venomous insects lie in wait among the brushwood and sand whose bite may mean the withering of a limb or lingering agony. Poisonous snakes, centipedes, and spiders worse than either, crawl into his huts; scaly alligators lurk in the mire of the fords; and thus he creeps through life in superstitious terror, and in each mysterious rustle of the palm-fronds when the bush lies still at night, hears the voice of evil spirits breathing spells upon the forest.

Further, there is something in the primeval forest before which even the courage and reason of a white man gives way at times. Officials and traders whose lot it is to dwell far apart in the solitude of the bush come back now and then to the coastwise settlements strange in speech and manner, and unable to sleep at night. Among other instances, one man I knew of, although apparently perfectly sane by day, would wander about the verandah half the night, holding audible conversation with persons unseen to any one else in the mist below—a most trying proceeding to his comrade in the lonely factory. In any case, no one can enter the tropical forest with its intense virility of life, where on still afternoons there may be heard what seems to be a great pulse throbbing through the million growing things, without realising the wonderful force of nature and the littleness of man.

Every sense feels the presence of a power that is infinite, and the heathen groping through thick darkness embodies it in the Ju-Ju, or unknown divinity. No white man seems to understand the exact attributes of the Ju-Ju, but it would appear to be a mysterious essence of spiritual force which is made manifest in many ways. Sometimes it becomes incarnate in the person of a man — a dynastic king is always supposed to be indued with a portion of its power. At others, it takes up its abode in a swamp or mountain, notably a certain Ghost Mountain on the Gold Coast, whose ascent, I was informed by the natives, several white men had ventured to attempt and perished miserably. Again, it endows some hideous graven image with miraculous influence. But behind the veil of superstition there would seem to be a glimmer of truth, and the bushman clearly recognises a divinity too wonderful for him to define.

Then there follow the minor gods, in the worship of which the spark of verity is extinguished, and these are very many—crocodile gods, river gods, fever gods, and the like. There are also legions of wandering ghosts which require to be propitiated, not only of men but of beasts and things inanimate, —such as a canoe which carries belated wanderers away to Eblis; ghosts of spears which strike men dead and leave no trace of a wound; and, strangest of all, ghostly smears of blood upon the rude furniture of the huts. In parts of the Protectorate it is impossible to shake the natives' credence in this. They have found their cooking-pots full of blood, they say, or have had their faces streaked with it by an unseen hand.

The exponent of these mysteries is the "Ju-Ju man," or fetiche priest, who works the wires of every movement in Western Africa. Consul or commissioner may rule in the settlements, but the Ju-Ju man rules in the bush, and there his word is law. Very little is known about these fetiche priests, but they are apparently by no means altogether ignorant impostors. It is said they are set apart and trained from youth in traditions and learning handed down through many generations, and this inherited wisdom is not to be despised. They certainly understand the properties of every plant in the forest either to kill or to cure, the former perhaps most often, for there are no more skilful poisoners in the world than the West Africans. An agent who offends some big headman or treats his retainers brutally often falls sick of an ailment which no surgeon can identify or find a cause for. I have been told by Government doctors —one was especially eloquent upon this point—that poisons are used so cleverly that no trace can be discovered by analysis; and further, that when the sufferer has been sufficiently punished he is sometimes restored to health by equally mysterious antidotes. A frontier commissioner once said in my hearing that he believed a large proportion of the mortality among Europeans in a certain district was not due to fever at all, but to subtle venom of some kind.

It is in any case certain that the white man who has dwelt long in the land rarely ventures to speak disrespectfully of the Ju-Ju priest when he is in the bush, and more than probable that the latter is sometimes subsidised to protect an isolated factory. There are men who laugh at such suggestions, but these for the most part reside within sight of the barracks of the Yoruba troops. It is, however, difficult to ascertain definite instances, because if an official or trader should formulate an alliance of this kind with the powers of darkness he is naturally not inclined to publish the fact. Rumour, nevertheless, states that it is done; and in portions of the Gold Coast you may see a tuft of red rags, which may or may not have been dipped in the blood of fowls, set up beside a building, and there is no negro dare touch the most coveted article inside it.

One curious feature about the fetiche system is, that along nearly 3000 miles of coast, and among people of widely different race and language, the worship of the Ju-Ju is apparently one and the same, and, so I have heard, many of the symbols and tattoo-marks also. This is the more remarkable, because there is as much difference between many African tribes as there is between, say, a swarthy Cataluñan Spaniard and a gigantic fair-haired Scandinavian. The weak-kneed Christian of the settlements is generally a pagan in the bush; and even the sturdy followers of the Prophet, the soldier peoples of the north, wear charms prepared by heathen rites, which doubtless include the pouring out of blood. White traders do so also. In fact, many of the latter seem to become indued with more than a trace of negro superstition; and when the cards are brought out as evening settles down on the sweltering factories, you may frequently see each player lay some curious object upon the table. This may be an alligator's tooth set in gold or ivory and graven with mysterious symbols, a tuft of feathers, or a piece of quaintly carved wood, and is supposed to protect its wearer from pestilence or to bring him luck.

If a stranger asks questions, the Africander smiles and answers half-jestingly; but he does not abandon the talisman, nor feel called upon to explain that he paid many pieces of cloth for the insignificant object. Some of these Ju-Ju have a very tragic history, and the fame of one or two has travelled over several hundred miles of forest; but space forbids the telling of strange stories, which are at least currently believed. They would probably be smiled at in England, but men who have lived in the fever-swamps are not altogether incredulous, for most of them have seen more things in the forest than they can understand. There is probably a scientific explanation for many mysteries, but we still know very little, and the end of discovery has not yet come. I once travelled in a steamer where a fantastic clay image occupied a place of honour in the chart-room, and the skipper's wrath was uncontrollable when some slightly inebriated acquaintances flung it into the Niger. There could be no doubt that he regarded its destruction as a thing to be regretted. Another man had a similar Ju-Ju, and getting ashore on a certain bar, solemnly broke it to pieces upon the rail.

In the eastern portions of the Protectorate especially very ghastly things are done in honour of the fetiche. Only a few years ago, when a powerful headman died not very far from Bonny, several of his wives had their legs broken, and were buried alive beside him. In 1888 a somewhat similar proceeding led to the storming of the native town of Asaba on the Niger. The official in charge of the troops there heard that three living slaves were laid in a grave beside the corpse of some person of consequence. After his warnings had been mocked at he advanced upon the town, and the headman agreed to abandon the sacrifice. The same night, however, the slaves were murdered and an attempt was made to take the cantonments by surprise. The attack was defeated, and Asaba was stormed by the troops. Some of the Opobo tribe treasure desiccated human limbs as Ju-Ju, and this in a region well under British influence. Endless grotesque horrors could be enumerated, but the relation would serve no purpose, for it has long been known that the dark places of Africa are full of cruelty. So much for the Ju-Ju; and the writer would mention that while describing the white man's tendency to fall under the influence of superstition, he does not attempt to justify it, but contents himself with setting down that which he has seen or heard.

Now we may leave the subject and turn to one dark stain on our national honour which a long continuation of welldoing can hardly quite efface. Perhaps the earliest mention of the British slave-trade is a record of the fact that in 1557 one John Lok brought five negroes from Africa into London and endeavoured to obtain money for them. This, however, provoked an outbreak of indignation, and the shipmaster took them back next voyage and landed them on their native soil. Five years later the public conscience had grown less sensitive, and Hawkins, that man of many contradictory qualities, sailed, it is said, for what is now known as Sierra Leone, though it was more likely the Gambia, with three ships, and purchasing 300 negroes, sold them in the West Indies. So profitable was the venture that a little later Queen Elizabeth invested funds in a similar enterprise, and this time Hawkins disposed of 500 negroes. Presently Bristol merchants began to fit out ships, and the commerce extended, until between 1680-1700, 300,000 slaves were carried in British vessels, chiefly Bristol owned. Then towards the middle of the eighteenth century Liverpool came to the front, and soon after her merchants embarked in this trade eighty-seven slaving vessels sailed regularly from the Mersey on round voyages between the Guinea Coast, the West Indies, and the young Southern States.

In the annals of Liverpool many curious entries may be found relating to the traffic, which became of supreme importance to it; and in 1766 twelve negroes were publicly exhibited and sold in the Exchange Coffee-House. Similar transactions followed, and soon every citizen who had a few guineas to spare embarked them in the iniquitous traffic, so that in a space of ten years more than 300,000 slaves were carried over seas by vessels owned in Liverpool. Thus when early in the nineteenth century there was talk of abolition a huge outcry was raised, and the corporation toiled manfully with petition and bribe to defeat the proposed reform. The record of this city is not a clean one —some thirteen millions sterling earned in one decade alone by traffic in flesh and blood, a vast but unknown sum gained by privateering that was often murder and piracy—and the historical reproof cast upon it, " Every brick of your dirty town is cemented with the blood of a slave," was not unmerited.

One incident was brought to light which illustrated how the trade was carried on. A slaver was smitten by pestilence, as often happened, while she threshed to windward, leaking heavily: the negroes were perishing like rotten sheep, and one day more than a hundred were flung alive into the sea, because if they died on board the loss would fall on the owners. Insurance did not cover sickness—underwriters knew the trade too well for that; but if the wretched beings were " jettisoned," it constituted a sacrifice of cargo under average rules, and the latter would have to pay.

When the great Act was passed in 1807, Liverpool declared herself ruined for ever, but soon found that the trade in ivory, gold-dust, gums, and oil was even more valuable than that in slaves, and maintained the leading place in West African commerce that she holds to-day. But the spirit which sent out slavers and privateers died slowly, and for years many of the free-lance traders continued as they had done before, spreading ruin about them wherever they settled along the coast. Stories of their doings are still told among the mangrove-shrouded creeks, and there are crumbling ruins pulled down and almost obliterated by the all-devouring forest about which the memory of some revolting tragedy has lingered for a century. Fearing neither man nor god nor devil, they lived in riot and drunkenness with harems of native wives, seized the daughters of the chieftains where purchase might not avail, set one tribe to raid another, and fought among themselves. Thus it sometimes happened that when the sun-blistered, weather-beaten brig crossed the smoking bar at last and brought up to her anchors in the still lagoon, she found but a heap of ashes where the trading-post had been, and the fate of those who dwelt there remained a mystery.

Now, as it has been shown, we have made what amends we could, and for generations our gunboats have harried the slavers across the face of the seas, while our traders are of much finer stamp, and many live heroic lives marked by temperance and self-restraint. For all that, ancient abuse dies slowly, and the genus palm-oil ruffian is not quite extinct to-day.

So much for British connection with wholesale slavery over seas. As a nation we washed our hands of it nearly one hundred years ago, though the saying of Macbeth may hold good in a measure, but the colonies we raised have yet to reap the fruit of our misdeeds. With universal suffrage and a coloured population which increases much faster than the white inhabitants, the Southern States of the Union will soon have to grapple with the problem, Who is to rule the land—the white man or the black one? It may be mentioned in connection therewith that the negro race is perhaps the strongest and most prolific on earth, and, unlike most others, does not go out before the European. The Australian aborigines have almost gone; the splendid Maories are dying out; the Indian has practically disappeared from the plains of the West, save where he dwells on his reservations fed by Government bounty—a somewhat pitiful spectacle. Incas and Aztecs disappeared before the Spaniards; the white Guanches of the Canaries too: but there is no need to multiply instances to prove a fact well known. The negro, however, in spite of adverse circumstances, increases and multiplies, and a racial antagonism is now smouldering, or occasionally breaking out into lynchings and the burning of men alive, on both sides of the Mississippi, whose ending few care to look forward to.

Slavery is still prevalent in Western Africa, and is of two distinct kinds. The first is the wholesale raiding and burning of villages, whose inhabitants are carried away and sold beyond the desert as far as Morocco and Fezzan by the Arabs of the hinterland. This has been written of many times, and goes on to-day to a great extent unchecked. The second, termed "domestic slavery," and practised by the negroes only, is to be met with in many places along the coastwise strip; and as, with the exception of the races already mentioned, it is practically impossible to induce the free negro to labour with his hands, forced servitude of some kind is almost a matter of necessity. Thus it is that the British Government, in spite of the popular but mistaken idea that no slave can exist beneath the flag, finds it inexpedient to attempt its suppression altogether, and in several districts at least contents itself with doing what may be possible to alleviate the lot of the slave. Slaves are acquired in the Niger bush by the simple process of raiding a weaker village when the troops are somewhere else, by the purchase of servants so obtained, or by parents selling their children, a custom common enough. Under ordinary circumstances their life is not such a hard one as might be supposed, for in accordance with the law of many negro peoples a master is bound to provide for the maintenance of his slaves, and is punished if he allows them to go unfed. They, however, suffer in time of the fetiche orgies, for when human blood is required to propitiate the Ju-Ju a slave is naturally the most likely victim. Until a few years ago, before a negro could fill any post of importance at Asaba, he must have murdered at least two human beings in honour of the fetiche. It is said that a special race of slaves were reared for the purpose, and sold to the intending sacrificer.

The Chartered Company, however, changed all this. There is no doubt that in districts nominally under British rule slaves are occasionally buried alive under the foundations of a new chief's house, or slain on his decease; while outside Old Benin they were regularly crucified when the seasons were either too wet or too dry. Otherwise they do not seem to be badly treated, and probably work no harder than a well-watched Krooboy. In many places they are allowed to purchase their freedom, and are seldom looked down upon; in fact, on the Niger and in Ashanti, slaves attached to a headman of importance are occasionally chosen to fill their master's place.

The great Arab soldier Samadu was a slave, and the son of a slave, at least such is the general belief. It has been said that Nana was one also, though the fact has been denied. Probably two-thirds of the 8000 odd tons of palm-oil annually shipped from the Niger is brought down to the factories in canoes manned by slaves. It may also be news to some to learn that there are various ports along the coast where British steamers are regularly loaded and discharged by slaves, and that the latter are freely bought and sold in one or two great markets close to the stations of white authorities on the Niger. This was until recently notably the case at Onitsha. More than once when a punitive expedition has been sent up into the Niger bush the officials have either requested, or at least tacitly encouraged, negroes of known character from the settlements to take possession of the slaves found in the rebel town. This was done solely that the latter might be well treated under their own supervision when the punished tribe were known to be organisers of Ju-Ju ceremonies.

Everywhere throughout the delta a headman purchases his wives, and occasionally, it is said, hypothecates them when he undertakes a big speculation in oil or cloth. Comely girls appear to be worth about £5, grown men somewhat less, and as the average price of a slave at the West Indian ports was £40 to £50, the profits must have been large. Statistics as to how often white men are purchasers of the first would be startling, but it may be said to the credit of the negro vendor that he considers the white man who has thus acquired his daughter as certainly her husband, and if the woman prove unfaithful to him she dare not return to her people. Such a one mysteriously disappears, for the negro has strict, if somewhat distorted, ideas about morality from a European point of view. It is surprising how quickly some of these learn European ways. I can well remember a factory where a woman, evidently of Arab stock, for she was light in colour, of splendid carriage, and by no means uncomely to look upon, kept the place in a high state of neatness and order. Dressed in garments made after British fashion by her own fingers, she moved about the presiding genius of a well-ordered home, and the state of that factory was very different to the rest, while few of her fairer sisters could have been more anxious about the trader's welfare. As the man said, or something very much to the same effect, "There are reasons why I shall not go home. I could bring no English lady here, and this woman is devoted to me. I cannot see where there is any wrong."

There is a well-known French proverb which meets the case, and those who know the real lives of these men would be slow to judge him uncharitably. Even the missionaries, who have learned many things in Africa, become sparing of condemnation, and it may be said that here as elsewhere they have a problem of their own to grapple with. In many places they find polygamy prevalent, and they are placed in this dilemma. If they persuade the converts to put away their several wives and cleave to one, the rest would either starve or fall into a lower state still. But that is a matter for the missionaries to settle; and some, with the understanding that comes from patient and arduous toil, have done so already, though they do not always mention such matters in the annual reports. People at home would occasionally be somewhat surprised if they had a clear statement of all the questions their emissaries have to grapple with.

CHAPTER XV.

AT NEW BENIN.

EARLY one morning, some little time after leaving Warri, we slid out of the fleecy mist into a wide lake-like reach of river, bound for New Benin. The engines pounded noisily under a full head of steam, for the flood-tide, pouring through countless miry creeks and mangrove-shrouded entrances, was hurrying inland against us to fill the vast network of water-ways beyond. Here and there on either hand a tuft of tall palms or cluster of giant cotton-woods rose up above the vapours, or a jutting point of mangroves loomed out shapeless and shadowy, but all the rest was hidden by wisps of blue-grey haze. This ceaseless moisture is everywhere prevalent throughout the year, with the exception of the brief harmattan, and, it may be repeated, is one of the principal causes of the unhealthiness of Western Africa.

Presently the sun rose up out of the eastern haze, pitiless and red, and soon the long deck shone dazzlingly white in the burning rays, while every piece of brass-work gleamed like a host of stars. Then, as the mists cleared away, we resigned ourselves to the inevitable, and panted beneath the awnings, listening to the roar of the muddy tideway piling itself against the bows. Meantime the banks fell farther away on either hand, until the waterway was perhaps two miles in width, and steaming across to the farther shore, we noticed a broad swath in the sombre foliage where the mighty cotton-woods had been apparently mown down by a giant hand. For a time this gap in the primeval forest will remain as a warning to the tribesman that the power of Western science and the hand of the British Government is stronger than the will of sable tyrant or the magic of the Ju-Ju, and then the bush will swallow it up again. As will be mentioned in its place, four years ago British bluejackets and alien soldiers shed their blood to drive that road through the forest, and in the doing of it they let the light shine in upon an abode of darkness and cruelty. But the West African bushland is apparently averse to light, and already the eternal cotton-woods were closing in again. Trees 10 or 15 feet high cover the hewn-out track, a line of fresher verdure running straight between walls of sombre green, and soon the primeval forest will have wrapped it once more in the shadows of superstition. But that roadway served its purpose, and for a space after the downfall of Nana, black trader and white factory agent dwelt in peace, while the harassed consulate officials wondered if at last all was well. Then the land was startled by the news that a British expedition had been blotted out, and the war-whistle shrilled through the bush again. So it has always been in Western Africa, and so for a time it will be. Consul and commissioner know that for them there is no slackening of vigilance or taking of rest if they would escape a reckoning for the lives of the mass of black humanity committed to their charge; while missionary and teacher, sick at heart of violence and longing for the time when wars shall cease, recognise that the day is not yet come.

Soon a few clusters of wooden buildings began to appear at intervals, specks of whiteness set in the green of the forest, and New Benin rose to view. Like that of many other settlements between the Gambia and Congo, the first view of New Benin is not an enchanting one—and it looks best from a distance. Behind it lie what are perhaps the foulest swamps in Western Africa, which is saying a great deal; and among these the factories stand on piles, with fathomless mud behind them and the yellow tide in front. Presently the steamer was moored to the river front of the nearest, and we set foot on dry land again. There was very little of it, and what there was had been carried at a heavy cost from the spouting shoals outside. Eastward lay the usual desolation of mangroves and fetid mud; southwards two miles of sluicing tide-water walled in by forest and swamp; and away to the westward a haze of spray drawn horizontally across mangrove point and eyot, clammy and white against the brassy heavens, marked the river bar. New Benin stands about four miles from the mouth of its river, and some forty from the fetiche city of Old Benin, as it was then; and although in early days vessels sailed right in, or were lost in the attempt, of late years the bar has grown shallower, and now even the little branch-boats steam round through the Forcados entrance, a detour of nearly 130 miles.

Every foot of ground upon which it stands has been made artificially, and this is the manner of the building of a Benin as well as many another West African factory, which explains why the largest profits often yield small dividends. A site is chosen on the river bank, and endless palavers follow with the headman who owns the soil, or says he does, which is not always quite the same, for when work has commenced one or more other sable landowners also claim to be paid for it. In early days the trader frequently lent the first man a supply of flintlock guns, and left the native litigants to settle it among themselves, which they did in the usual negro fashion, more than once destroying the half-built factory in the process. Now, however, the help of consul or vice-consul is called in, and the officials are usually very sick of both trader and native before the dispute is arranged; while it also happens occasionally that the representatives of the Chartered Company step in too and say the land is theirs. Then the vice-consul, who is already overworked without being called upon to unravel a puzzle of this kind, refers the whole matter to Calabar, while the trader, who has to pay his Gold Coast artificers and Krooboys all the time, sits down and waits, anathematising Government and negro as only a West African trader can.

When the verdict has gone forth a little army of Krooboys chop down the mangroves and form a network of branches; several score of naked Jakkeries are engaged at exorbitant charges to carry sand from the river bar, and canoe-load after canoe-load is flung into the slime, which sucks it down and yawns greedily for more. As a man relating his experience of factory building said, "When I started this place it was very like trying to fill the bottomless pit, and I made solid ground half-way to the Philippines or whatever lies underneath." At last with good luck the whole may be raised 3 feet above the river—it would need a very large capital to go much farther—massy piles are driven in to prevent the restless tides taking it away, and now a fresh trouble begins. Legions of marine worms with things resembling diamond-drills in their heads, and molluscs with razor-edged shells, riddle the piles, which cave in suddenly, while colonies of boring-crabs take up their quarters in the sand. They tunnel it from end to end, eating the grit or otherwise disposing of it, until whole square yards sink away, and that day I remember wherever we set foot the ground rang hollow. The hairy loathsome creatures also scuttled away before us, or squatted in the mouth of their burrows, bubbling froth, and almost invariably holding a saw-edged mandible in the air, ready for the fray. Now and then a hungry or inquisitive band of pioneers invading temporary quarters in the darkness puts the human occupants to flight; and I vividly remember slipping through the sand-crust into a nest of them one night, and being violently ill afterwards at the mere sound of the crunching shells and the touch of the malodorous crawling things. Most people who have entered West Africa can recall incidents which, without being dangerous, possess a kind of nightmare horror of their own.

Eventually the factory is raised on piles, and

the agent, invariably an old hand well versed in the devious ways of native diplomacy, takes charge, with a trained assistant if the place is large. Gin, cotton cloth, salt, and sundries are stored, and one or two young clerks are advertised for. Most of the merchant firms at home honourably state that the trade is an unhealthy one, and insist upon medical certificates, warning the applicants of what they may expect, but this is not invariably the case. Young lads with a few years' commercial experience snatch at the opportunity to enter the mysterious continent, for now as ever the spirit of adventure is strong in our British youth—and it is well it should be so. Therefore they sign the contract, practically delivering themselves body and soul for three years into the hands of the resident agent, in return for free quarters and a graduated salary, which rarely exceeds £200 for the whole time. A large proportion die before the three years have passed of fever, and a few of the weak-hearted very possibly in despair at their inability to escape from pestilence or revolting iniquity; for there are factories—not many, but still some—of which the gentleman-adventurer's poet might have written equally with the cattle-boats, "They are more like hell than any place else I know." The rest, however, with the dogged resolution of their race, make the best of circumstances, carry out their hard bargain faithfully, and in the end either develop into unscrupulous agents suffering from chronic alcoholism, or a very fine stamp of men, who, walking in slippery places, have kept themselves undefiled, and have been taught many things by close contact with death and suffering. Uncomplaining patience, grim determination, iron self-restraint, and contempt for personal danger, are some of the qualities a man of good courage and clean hands acquires in the African forest; but, as may be supposed, these qualities are beyond the reach of all.

One story of a man who, deceived by specious representations, repented of his bargain, and, what was more, made the agent repent of it too, may be briefly told. I know the tale is true, because I heard one version from a fever-wasted agent, as well as another from the chief actor, who travelled home with me, and its narration still provokes a smile among the Niger creeks.

The following advertisement, as nearly as I can remember from a perusal of the crumpled cutting shown me, once appeared in several British papers:—

WANTED, young man, eighteen to twenty-five, as bookkeeper in West African factory. A few hours' work a-day in pleasant surroundings, unlimited shooting and fishing, and fine tropic scenery, with a boat and crew at his disposal. Free quarters, salary to commence £70, with chance of rapid promotion.

The latter clause at least was true, for from obvious reasons promotion is everywhere rapid in the fever-land, unless the subordinate also dies.

Henry Stirling we will call him, a young man of good upbringing, who had joined the —th battalion in the vain hope of rising from the ranks to a commission, applied for and obtained the post. With the strange blindness which characterises others of his kind, he set down the warnings he received on his outward journey as romantic exaggerations, and was duly landed one dismal evening in a certain creek of the Niger delta. There two naked Krooboys unloaded his baggage on to a scaffold of planks raised above a desolation of mud alive with wallowing things, and Stirling began to realise that the warnings might after all be true. So with a troubled mind he followed his guides along the slimy footway through a waste of dripping mangroves, until he reached a dilapidated factory reeking with damp and swarming with rats and cockroaches.

Here he found one broken-down white man with a vicious temper, and just outside saw a row of crosses which showed what had become of his predecessors. He did not sleep well that night, for mosquitoes drained his blood, legions of crawling creatures explored his frame for tender places, and he was unused to the stifling heat. At 5 A.M. he was roused to weigh in palm-kernels, and for three weeks he toiled in blazing sun or tropic downpour from that hour until dark, and then entered up the day's transactions in an office which resembled a furnace. But Stirling was not a very easy-going man, and he had learned the art of taking care of himself in the hard school of the recruit squad; therefore he absented himself one day and rowed off to a neighbouring consulate. The sickly official in charge listened to the story with his usual courtesy, and then said—

"Don't you think it would be better to face it for a time?" and in answer to Stirling's emphatic assurance that he had faced it long enough, continued, "In any case it is beyond my province to interfere. The contract was made in England, and perhaps you could sue them at home; but how you are going to get there is quite another matter, for I have no authority to send you back. You must either wait events, or obtain an order on a mail-boat's purser for your passage from the agent—and I should say that would be difficult."

"At any rate I'll try," was Stirling's answer as he took himself away. When he returned that night the agent's language was sulphureous; but after listening unmoved, Stirling said: "Your firm cajoled me out here under false pretences; that cancels the contract, and I demand to be sent home. You can't do it, and I have no money—

then you shall keep me here as long as you can, but not a stroke of work will you ever get out of me."

"Then you will get no food," said the agent, with a wicked grin, and Stirling answered quietly—

"That remains to be seen. I come in here at every meal, and I don't think the Krooboys would interfere with me — they are not over-fond of you. Further, if you attempt to turn me out, I'll break every bone in your carcass. Now we understand."

The ex-infantryman was brawny and muscular, the agent broken up by fever, while his Krooboys had private reasons for not loving him fervently. So for almost a month Stirling, who escaped the malaria, lounged in luxurious idleness, in the shade of a clump of cotton-woods, enjoying the tropic scenery, or angled for mud-fish in the river —as per advertisement, he said. At other times during the long hot afternoons he gathered the Krooboys about him in the cool oil-shed with both slides wide open to catch the pure sea-breeze, and made them tell him weird stories of the Ju-Ju and affrays with Liberian troops. Thus the sable heathen, who are never too fond of work, and love a European listener, became his devoted followers, while the agent gnawed his moustache in fury and said vicious things when he dared. Once he bade them drive Stirling from the dining-room, but the Krooboys, who consider any white man as good as another, only showed their splendid teeth as they smiled at the young " so-so captain."

Then the Nimbi trouble broke out, and the bush tribes rose to arms. The Vice-Consul barricaded his verandah with sand-bags and kept his handful of men constantly under arms, while at his advice the agents in the few scattered factories provided each Krooboy with matchet or smooth-bore, and, as I have reason to know, any one wandering along the beach at night ran a very fair chance of being shot. Then Stirling once more interviewed the agent the day a number of war-canoes had been seen.

"It's not from any goodwill to you," he said, "but we have both the same risk to face, and if you will give me a free hand I'll drill those fellows into some kind of shape, and engage that we won't be surprised at night any way."

The agent growlingly agreed, and Stirling organised his own and his neighbour's Krooboys into a by no means despicable force, established outposts and sentry rounds, with vedettes on every creek that wound away inland. So throughout the anxious time that followed he patrolled the misty bush at night, encouraged or threatened the Krooboys, and kept them at their posts, while by darkness or light the Nimbi canoes passed up and down the stream, and the bush was full of rumours of a great raid at hand. There were many men in the Niger creeks who had good reason to fear the Nimbi tribe, and when the news that Akassa had fallen ran across the swamps the white traders slept with rifle or revolver across them, or, fearing that if they slept too well they might never wake at all, kept watch beside the river.

At last the suspense was over when the boom of heavy guns rang out above Sacrifice Point, and a vast cloud of yellow smoke told that the naval brigade were burning Nimbi town, and the raiders' power was broken. Then after order had been restored, Stirling spoke again with the agent.

"Have you changed your mind, or shall we go on as before?" he said; and the agent at last gave way. Stirling came home with me in triumph, bringing an order on the purser for a £35 passage, in addition to the sum it had taken to bring him out. He arrived on board penniless, but he had learned other things than drill in the —th battalion, including a high-class proficiency at nap and other games of chance in which skill also plays a part. He made the purser his banker, and I know that when, after a seven weeks' voyage, he went over the side at Liverpool, he took a bag of sovereigns with him which he had won on board. This, of course, was reprehensible, but I merely relate what happened, and a visitor to one of the Niger creeks is still told with laughter and jesting comment the story of "The man who struck."

CHAPTER XVI.

NEW BENIN.

WE found the factory at New Benin very much the same as others we had seen before—the inevitable whitewashed oil-sheds, shouting Krooboys, swarming canoes, and verandahed residence. One might walk some 60 yards in two directions among the wooden buildings, and then had to stop suddenly on the brink of a bubbling quagmire, or the edge of the swirling tide. All day the steamer's gangways were crowded with big blue-tattooed Jakkeries, their chests and foreheads covered with what appeared to be rows of azure beads, though how the flesh is thus raised no European knows, and the native will not explain. They had come there to chaffer with the crew over parrots, baby alligators, and snakes in biscuit-tins—all of which are bought up at once by naturalists at home, as well as beautifully carved Benin paddles, hewn out of a hard wood which is sometimes as white and smooth-grained as ivory. There is a wealth of splendid timber on many of the drier inland tracts, which will some day bring wealth to the man who can get it out.

The dark quarters of seaman and fireman presented a curious mingling of the fancy fair and cheap menagerie. Every bunk had been converted into a stall for the display of papers of safety-pins, needle-packets, children's toy watches, bottles of pomade with brass tops, and the like, which were purchased with avidity, though what the bushman did with them it would be very hard to say. The bargains were as usual fought over, and occasionally there was a furious scuffle as some sooty fireman strove to collect due payment by force of arms, while the voices of chattering beasts and birds joined in the din, and the smell was indescribable. How sickly men could live in a place like that beneath the fierce heat of the tropics passed the comprehension of an ordinary individual, but wages are low, and the large profits tempting. Thus in spite of formal prohibition, and an occasional dismissal, there are few captains who care to attempt the suppression of this trade, and some tarry-fingered seamen carry on a commerce along 2000 miles of coast which would very much surprise the owners at home.

We were also entertained ashore with the lavish hospitality of the West African agent, whose liquor supply had just come out, and there sat down with us a Niger man attired in plain white linen whose name is a power in the delta, and whose counsel has been taken by the Government in times of anxiety. His fine white gig lay alongside the bank, flying the jack above her stern; and the writer was informed that when a newly arrived and zealous official ordered its owner to abandon the use of a flag sacred to the imperial service, he received a hint to let Chief Dore alone. The headman could speak but little English, and was, of course, a follower of the Ju-Ju; but there was a certain dignity about him, and he sat there with an easy quietness, listening to such part of the conversation as he could understand, or explaining some native problem in a few straight words at times. And yet we knew that this unlettered heathen had but to speak the word and a score of creeks would be closed to trade, or a horde of matchet-armed savages let loose to spread murder through the bush.

The whole party were not strict advocates of temperance, and when the fun became too furious Chief Dore, with a ceremonious leave-taking, turned his back on the noisy group. I followed him, and the Krooboy house-steward explained the matter thus :—

"Headman Dore savvy too much: the Lord give him sense. Suppose get drunk, then tell too much things about his bush to them so-so white man. Suppose trader man light matches on him jacket, then headman's boy dun chop that white man, and too much trouble live, sah." From this it was evident that the redoubtable chief understood, and did not appreciate, the eccentric pleasantries of the European after many cocktails had been absorbed.

Thereupon I called my Krooboys together, and, getting on board the gig, rowed towards the seaward entrance to visit the Consulate, where one white official ruled over what was then a very unruly district. The whole Atlantic seemed to be pouring into that river by the pace the tideway ran, and we crept close in along the bank beneath the mangrove leaves. Here at least there was shade; but innumerable insects and creeping things with wings also appreciated that shade, and hung over the boat in clouds, boring through my duck-jacket as though it were a net, and driving the half-clad Krooboys wild. Creeping things without wings also dropped upon us each time the branches rustled beneath a puff of breeze. Many of these went wriggling down one's neck, which they generally attacked with jaws like pincers, until the combination of petty miseries would have tried the equanimity of a saint, and saintliness is not a characteristic of those who go down to the fever-land. None too soon we reached the Consulate, a rickety wooden building, by no means to be compared with that of Warri, standing, if I remember aright, on a natural spit of sand with a palisade about it. Perhaps on account of the jealousy of the fetiche powers ruling Old Benin there were then scarcely any black troops at this station, and only small accommodation for them. It was evident and admitted that this place, lying as it did on the fringe of a kingdom of darkness, where every kind of fiendish cruelty was rife, should be a strong post; but the authorities only a little while ago had spent money and blood crushing Chief Nana, and had presumably no desire to force another conflict just then by too ostentatious display of force.

The patience of the officials is very long, and they have an arduous task to do, subduing and reclaiming a wild region little by little, and very quietly. The only other course would be the destruction of stockaded towns on an extensive scale, which would need a fleet of light-draught gunboats or an army corps, and no one feels justified in embarking in such an enterprise. When trouble starts in West Africa it is hard to say where it may end, so those at the head of affairs would seem to wisely content themselves with crushing abuses one by one as opportunity arises. The sickly official who ruled there fully confirmed this view, saying what I had heard others say before, " We shall have to break up Old Benin before very long, but the time is hardly ripe."

It is curious that just then the opinion of men

well versed in the ways of the delta was that the subjugation of Old Benin would be a very difficult matter. It was also a common belief that the city was full of ivory and other treasure, which, in accordance with a custom prevalent in various parts of Africa, each ruler had to store. This was sacred to the Ju-Ju, and might not be sold, and I heard one or two Gold Coast officials speak of having seen hoards of gold-dust and Aggry beads in stockaded towns of the hinterland on which no negro dare lay a finger for fear of the wrath of the bush gods. The value of such tabooed treasure has occasionally been estimated at an almost incredible sum, but when Benin was taken very little of value was found. It is of course possible that the natives removed their sacred store, but there was at least no sign of the palisade of ivory the bushmen told of.

I spent that afternoon with the officer in charge, who was in a state of partial collapse from overwork and fever, and he had much to say about Old Benin, which for several centuries but three or four white men had ever entered. He also showed me two splendid tusks, said to be of the "Ju-Ju ivory," which were given as a "dash" to the Protectorate officer who entered that city to open diplomatic relations with its monarch. The negotiations were, however, not concluded satisfactorily, for this was the final answer returned by the sable potentate: "I have been pleased to allow the White Queen to place a few small factories near the mouth of my river, but no white man shall come into my creeks. If your mistress is Queen of the traders, I am King of Benin, and the next white man who comes here will be killed." Later the monarch of Ubini proved as good as his word.

I subsequently learned that, according to native tradition, white adventurers — probably the early Portuguese—had once settled there, and actually established their dominion through the swamp-land, and various things discovered by the punitive expedition would seem to confirm this. The Portuguese and Spaniards of those days were a wonderful people, and made their power felt in regions where even now, with machine-guns and high-pressure launches, we dare scarcely venture, much less attempt to govern. But the virility seems to have gone out of the old Latin blood, and "Ichabod" may be written upon Iberia— "THE Peninsula"—as the Spaniard loves to call it. I also gathered further details about the rise and fall of Nana, which will be narrated in its place, and at sundown took leave of my host.

I left him leaning against the foot of the verandah stairway, shivering with fever, and felt, as one always feels when parting with an acquaintance in this littoral, that it was scarcely probable we should meet again. The foreboding was again justified, for this man also set out unarmed for the dark city of Old Benin, with the expedition that, instead of clearing a passage with the bayonet, carried nothing but a message of peace and offer of friendship if the headman would only rule with common humanity. Like too many others, he never reached it; for the authorities, having erred on the side of mercy, paid dearly for their mistake with the loss of their best servants shot down and cut to pieces by murderous savages. There is little doubt that these men knew the risk they ran; several of them indeed had often foretold the difficulty of any attempt to reach Benin. Yet the word came, and they went, with no weapon in their hands, looking the peril straight in the face, as they had done before—but this time they went to their death. As has been said, the West African legion of honour is an illustrious one; and if those who marched with the unfortunate expedition did nothing else, they showed that the old spirit is yet awake, and that Englishmen can still attempt perilous things without hope of honour or reward, simply because it is fitting they should be done.

It was dark when I passed the factory again, the gig driving slowly against the sluicing ebb; and through the open casements a blaze of light shone out upon the tideway, and the sound of sonorous, and, it must be confessed, somewhat unsteady voices, rolled across the African river in time to the tinkle of a banjo. It was a song which every wanderer of the far out knows. I had heard it amid the snows of the far North-West, in the flower-filled patios of Spanish colonies, as well as in the steam of the tropics—ringing, plaintive, and gripping the imagination of those who can read between its lines—"Mandalay." A mile farther on I disembarked at another factory, whose agent was a friend, and found the whole place silent and gloomy, while the Krooboy attendant warned me, "You no live for make too much palaver, sah."

So, moving as quietly as I could, I crossed the creaking verandah, and came upon what was almost too common a scene in that region to be noticeable.

The match-boarded room was redolent with stale tobacco-smoke, mildew, and paraffin, the walls as usual trickled with moisture, and the young agent with soaking hair, a face which resembled parchment drawn tight across projecting bones, and blackened lips, lay upon a square of trestle-stretched canvas. He was dictating a letter to a burly red-faced man who sat close by, looking the picture of health, and asked me to wait a while, adding, "You have probably written this kind of letter too, and you can understand."

There was no help for it, and I sat there as the feeble voice continued the dictation, and fully understood, for I had also acted as amanuensis in such a case. It was a message sent by one who never expected to send another, but having been very near death before, esteemed it just possible he might escape again. Thus, while he felt a longing to seize what might be a last opportunity of sending a greeting which could be remembered in days to come, he would not create unnecessary alarm. When it was done, and signed very shakily, he said: "Temperature's over 105°, and one can't live very long at that. I'm glad to see you, and you needn't tell me not to talk: a little more risk doesn't count here at all. I've had six fevers badly this year, and look at that fellow yonder—he came to me half-dead with consumption or something, and he has been getting stouter ever since."

At this the burly Schweitzer straightened his stalwart frame. "Ja, it is so. This is good country for me, and I die at home," he said.

I did not stay very long, but undertook to call upon various persons in England in the event of my friend's decease, and made similar arrangements which would have seemed ghastly at home, but were very matter-of-fact in the Niger delta; and when at last he sank into semi-unconsciousness, took my departure, graver than when I came. And now mark the uncertain ways of the fever. About ten days later I had reason to return to New Benin, and found the agent dragging himself about the factory again, on the way to recovery, while the Swiss clerk had breathed his last two days before, and now lay at rest on the fringe of the forest.

In connection with this subject the following is a list of the various ills to be expected on the Niger. Possibly the same person may suffer from all, and it is very unlikely he will escape without being attacked by one or two. It is extracted from a medical treatise circulated on the West Coast, and the list is somewhat startling to new-comers who peruse it for the first time. It runs thus:—

"Shivering, lassitude, headache, and backache. Cerebral excitement with raving delirium. Liver deranged—constant vomiting. Vomiting of blood. Chronic hemorrhage. Blackwater cases. Shivering and rigors. Sunstroke with staggering and unconsciousness. Acute dysentery. Asiatic cholera. Acute jaundice. Typhoid," &c., &c.—but this is surely enough. It is simply included to bear out the writer's descriptions, lest some should fancy he paints the shadows too dark—as if it were possible, for these are symptoms declared by skilful men as likely to be encountered by every European.

I remained a few days at New Benin, and found the four factories there were then doing a somewhat languishing trade, selling cloth, salt, gin, and oddments, and purchasing the inevitable oil and kernels. But the tribesmen were restless all around, and the Ju-Ju taboo had been placed upon some of the most frequented waterways, thus crippling commerce. During that time I visited Nana's creek in a launch, and made such examination as I could of the scene of a very grim piece of work which was done there four years ago, and came about as follows.

CHAPTER XVII.

THE RISE AND FALL OF NANA.

THERE are two distinct classes of rulers holding sway on the Niger. The first, and perhaps the least dangerous, is the man of a dynasty, sacred by the special protection of the Ju-Ju and by the right of long descent. Nominally he is a despot, in reality often a mere puppet, whose mind is swayed by a host of fetiche counsellors, and his every action cramped by wearisome tradition. Such a one was the King of Old Benin; and this man, in spite of the revolting practices carried on in his name, was probably less to blame than the exponents of the Ju-Ju, who, after all, were the real instigators of most of the devilish cruelty. The second is the sable trader or soldier who has grown rich by commerce or raid, and being of necessity a man of energy and ability, bound by no effete traditions, is even a more difficult person to control. Headman Nana of Brohemie was a characteristic representative of this latter type, and his rise and fall form an instructive lesson.

For a time Nana traded peacefully with the white men, and, it is more than probable, very unpeacefully in the bush, where undue competition can be suppressed by fire and sword, and desirable markets secured by a midnight raid on the towns in which they are held. He was a man of action, shrewd and resolute, though he made one great mistake and suffered for it. Thus his influence spread over a region said to be 120 miles in length by 60 broad, and Nana grew rich and powerful. But sudden success is often worse than adversity, and the aspiring trader lost his head. He set up as a fetiche ruler, and rumours of sickening atrocities carried out by his instructions reached the consulates, while tangible proofs in the shape of decomposing corpses floated down the forest-shrouded creeks. But the Government is patient, and only civil remonstrances were sent, at which Nana probably laughed, for he continued as before. Then news leaked out through the bush that the recalcitrant headman was busy building strong stockades and mounting many guns. Where he obtained these 6-pounders, and even larger brass weapons, from, is a mystery to this day, though he had nearly a hundred of them. Some white men must know, but these have probably the best of reasons for maintaining a discreet silence on that point. Later, his half-brother Serey died, and to celebrate his funeral the blood of many slaves was shed in Brohemie town, which stands amid a network of muddy creeks and almost impassable morasses about a mile and a half back from the north bank of the Benin river.

Again a warning was sent, and Nana was requested to attend before a high official and furnish explanations; but the sable tyrant, believing himself secure amid swamps which scarcely a bushman's foot might pass, while the navigable creek was commanded by a masked battery, returned this answer: "Am I a servant of the Government? If the white officers would speak with me, let them come to Brohemie." Almost simultaneously he issued an edict that no man in all the river country might trade with the British unless a heavy blackmail was paid; and when the Sobo oil-carriers, relying upon the protection of the flag, ventured to disobey, his armed retainers actually seized a canoe-load of them within sight of Warri Consulate. This was too much. The harassed officials sent word that they would surely come to Brohemie, and burn it to the ground, unless reparation were made; but the headman only mocked at the ultimatum giving him fourteen days to send back the men he had seized. Then Obobi at the mouth of the Benin river was burnt, and its inhabitants carried away as slaves; the territory of Chief Dore, who was friendly to the British, was threatened; and a little earlier, in

Efferoni town, a party of peaceful black traders were cut to bits with matchets.

On the 2nd of August 1894 a great palaver was held at Sapelli, when all the headmen of the Benin creeks gathered themselves together. They came down miles of fever-haunted waterways in canoes, through leagues of dripping forest and steamy morass in hammocks, and the sandy compound was filled with their retainers and a body of Yoruba troops. They were received in state by the Protectorate officials, and man after man, protesting his loyalty to the Government, told a tale of grievous wrongs suffered at the hands of Nana. His wives had been stolen, his villages burnt, and his canoe-men murdered; and the officials listened gravely with their eyes turned down the river, wondering if Nana would come as summoned to answer the charges brought against him. The burning day dragged by until the dusk was near, and still they talked and waited; but Nana never came, and the chiefs took themselves away, whispering that the white men were afraid after all.

Then at last the patience of the Government was exhausted, and the officials knew that the time for action had come. The talking-wires flashed messages across tangled forest and under the thundering surf to Accra, Cape Coast, and Sierra Leone, and all the gunboats on the West African station turned their bows towards the Niger. Still Nana held drunken revelry behind the Brohemie stockade, where he surveyed his rows of cannon, and gathered his naked warriors from the far corners of the bush, while again rumours spread through the forest that the white men were to be driven into the sea. And all the time the little heavily-sparred gunboats were lurching from rail to rail, across the steep-sided sapphire roll, as with streaming bows they drove eastward under top-gallants and the last ounce of steam. In the scorching Consulate compounds the Yoruba constabulary were drilling night and day, while white men wasted by fever saw to the packing of stores, and the enrolling of Krooboy carriers, or overhauled the feed-gear of the Maxims and the breeches of the Martinis.

On the 3rd of August the Alecto's cutter was lowered into the muddy waters of the Benin river, and moved cautiously towards the mouth of Brohemie creek, where Nana had built what he considered to be an impregnable stockade protected by big brass guns. It was a sweltering morning, and the bluejackets were very silent as they moved shoreward into the shadows of the forest; for some of them had done this kind of work before, and knew what they might expect. Four times they were fired upon, but the murderous charge flew wild; and with promptitude and skill the mines were laid beneath the big stockade.

Then the boat backed off, and for a while the blowing of horns and rattle of flintlock guns was silent as the bushmen, lurking among the cotton-woods, waited to see what the white intruders were about. They had not long to wait. The word was given, a sudden detonation shook the forest, and amid a cloud of yellow smoke and a giant upheaval of mould and mud and foam, the impregnable stockade leapt into the air, and came down in a chaotic mass of splinters. Before the work was finished ten mines of fifteen charges had been fired. Then a message was again sent to Nana, that as the white men had destroyed his watergate, so they would destroy Brohemie, unless he gave sureties for the payment of £500 worth of oil and better behaviour in future. But Nana still refused to be convinced that he was playing a dangerous game, and, trusting to the counsel of the Ju-Ju men, hardened his heart and maintained a contemptuous silence.

Still the authorities waited, and then, as the sureties had not arrived, on the 26th of August ten men, among whom was Major Crawford of Warri, went up the Brohemie creek in the Alecto's launch. It was a very risky business, and the Protectorate officials knew that naked artillerymen crouched somewhere among the mangroves and cotton-woods that overhung the creek, beside the breech of hidden guns, which, after a sighting-shot at a fixed mark, had been loaded to the muzzle with broken cast iron, and lashed fast at the ascertained range. But it was necessary to discover just where those guns were, even if they lost their lives in the attempt, rather than that a whole flotilla should be wiped out at once; so with eyes and ears strained to the uttermost to catch the faintest stirring of leaves, they steamed on into the forest. At last there was a stunning crash and the creek was hidden in smoke, while whirring cast-iron screamed overhead or ripped up the muddy water, and the launch trembled beneath a rain of projectiles that rang upon her iron-work and tore crunching through her side.

As the smoke cleared it became evident that the bush artilleryman had done his work too well. One bluejacket lay dead beside the feet of his officers; two others, horribly torn by jagged missiles, writhed in agony; three petty officers were bleeding from lacerated wounds; while Major Cawford, badly torn by potleg, and Captain Lalor, also seriously hurt, did what they could to extricate their men from a very evil place. The launch was sinking beneath them, the water pouring through her shattered side, the steamy bush was filled with the yells of tribesmen gathering to the attack, and a thudding of rammers told that the gun was being charged again. Then the order was given to return to the ship, if they might by any means reach her in time, and a humble hero proved again that the rank and file can bear their part in time of need as well as their officers. Leading stoker Perkins, whose foot and leg were smashed to ribbons, in spite of weakness from loss of blood and excruciating agony, forced the roaring fires, and dragging himself, gasping and bleeding, towards the engine, opened the throttle wide. There followed a very grim race with death, for all on board knew that if the launch sank, such as escaped drowning would either be shot down swimming or hacked to bits with matchets; and all the time the water rose higher above the floor-plates, and licked hissing towards the furnace front. But the grimy stoker was equal to the task, and at last, water-logged and just on the point of sinking, they reached the Alecto's side.

After this it was decided that to attempt the passage of that creek would be too dangerous, and by the aid of explosives and an army of Krooboys with matchets a road was hewn into the bush. On the 29th of August some 170 blue-jackets and marines from the gunboats Phœbe and Alecto, with 148 Moslem Yorubas of the Niger Constabulary, and their Protectorate commanders, as well as carriers, marched inland until they reached the usual desolation of oozy swamp and tangled bush echoing with the yells of the tribesmen and the crash of flintlock guns. Up to their knees in slime, floundering through miry creeks, or hewing a path with the matchet through thickets of matted trailers, they held doggedly on, dragging with toil incredible their light guns and rocket-tube behind, until a grim stockade 300 yards in length opened up before them.

Then the two 7-pounder guns and Maxims joined in the din, while the rocket-tube sent its fiery missiles screaming across the logs; and presently, amid the crash of splintering cotton-wood, the word was given to charge. The yell of the negro Moslem mingled with the British cheer, and there was a fierce rivalry between the White Queen's servants of different faith and colour to be first at the dangerous work. A creek opened up before them, but bluejacket, marine, and negro went through it with a rush, and, daubed with mire and slashed with the sword-edged blades of reeds, swept on towards the flaming guns. The stockade was reached, and the bushmen flying before the rush of bayonets, a halt was called behind the carried works. There were twenty-three fair-sized guns there, with an ample supply of ammunition in the shape of ingeniously contrived bamboo shells filled with cast iron, and had the negroes understood the working of a time-fuse the British loss must have been heavy. But, as we have explained, the bushman's favourite artillery practice is to lie perdu behind a gun carefully tested at a known distance and then made fast. The swift rush of determined men with flickering steel in their hands disconcerts him, and he has no means of traversing his piece.

So for a time the allied forces recovered their breath, and the next step was considered. Contrary to the reports of natives supposed to be friendly, the space between that outlying stockade and the main defences of Brohemie was found to consist of a quagmire intersected by waterways of unknown depth. Forty guns of calibre also opened fire behind the negroes' lines, and the anxious officers decided that to attempt its passage without canoes or any materials for bridges, in the face of a shower of broken cast-iron, could only result in the loss of half their men. Thus the order to retreat was given, and worn out, disappointed, and sullen, the men retraced their steps. It was a very trying march. The bushmen hung upon their flanks firing from cover, the heat was almost unendurable, the odours of corruption even worse, and some of them were sick, while the bites of myriads of mosquitoes had almost blinded their eyes. Part of the time detachments were up to their waists in mud, and occasionally in peril of being smothered altogether in the mire, as they scrambled among the mangroves, while every now and then a rush of shadowy figures slipped through the forest and the potleg screamed about them.

It was dark when, too weary to drag themselves

another step, and ashamed that they had left their guns behind, they reached the boats, grimly determined that the ending would be very different when they went back again. It was,—for, reinforced by men from the Philomel and Widgeon, with appliances for the work and an improved scheme of attack, they marched back into the swamps soon after daybreak on the morning of the 25th September; and this time, without any prolonged resistance, probably owing to a number of its defenders having deserted, Brohemie town was taken by nine o'clock. They found there 14 tons of powder, seven batteries of guns, heaps of neck-irons and hide whips with hardened edges for the discipline of slaves, and a very large store of miscellaneous arms. The guns were destroyed, the defences went up in smoke, and for hours together the dingy vapours rolled across the forest to tell the naked bushman that henceforward he might dwell in his hut in safety, fearing neither tyrant nor Ju-Ju devilry, while no man dare hinder him bringing down his trade.

The headman also found out, too late, that it is not wise even for a forest potentate to try the patience of the authorities too sorely, and repented in durance vile of the evil he had done. He apparently took the lesson to heart, for when there was once more trouble in the forests of Benin after the massacre of the unfortunate expedition, and the call to arms ran through the swamps again, he sent word from his place of exile that if the Protectorate officers would give him a few troops and allow him to arm his own people, he would go up "and smash Benin." The authorities, however, declined the proffered assistance. It had cost them too much to lay hands upon the redoubtable chief, and now they had him safe they were too wise to let him go.

CHAPTER XVIII.

SAPELLI.

IN due time Benin was left behind without very much regret, and after accepting the hospitality of an agent in what is probably the newest trading-station on the Niger waterways, I turned out of my trestle-cot in a factory at Sapelli as dawn was breaking across the east. I had not slept there, only passed the night, for one mosquito beneath the muslin "bar" had played a very active part in keeping me awake. When one gets used to things, and has been well bitten at the commencement, it is possible to slumber more or less peacefully among a number of mosquitoes; but a single insect is worse than a host, especially if that one be an epicure. Then the tormentor does not settle down with business-like promptitude and bite, after which, being gorged with blood, it may be killed, but hovers trumpeting around, looking for a tender spot for what seems hours, and will resist the most cunning hand laid out for it to alight upon. A mosquito-sting is a trifling thing, but the expectation of it is sufficient to keep the average individual awake in a state of suppressed fury, as many know. Still, mosquitoes are by no means so vicious in the tropics, though undoubtedly bad enough, as they are on their northern limit, and there are muskegs in British Columbia into which neither man nor beast dare venture at nightfall. Several times we were driven out of camp there by the winged legions, in spite of damp cedar-bark smoke, and I well remember one night when half the party plunged into the eddying pool of a snow-fed stream in the vain hope of easing the maddening pain. Next morning several of them could not see, so badly were faces and eyelids swollen.

Further, that mosquito had been assisted by a monotonous and exasperating croon of weird music which rose from under the verandah, where a ring of Krooboys crouched in the damp hot sand. They tapped a monkey-skin drum, and sang chanties which were probably five hundred years old, for on hot nights the African becomes endowed with an energy quite foreign to him by day.

The first thing I did was to draw on a pair of slippers, as a precautionary measure, for fear of the humble jigger, which lies in wait for the unwary foot. The slipping on of a duck jacket completed the toilet, for in this region thin pyjamas are clothing enough, and I hurried towards the river through the dewy freshness of the morning. Disregarding various warnings about evil results likely to follow, I stood for a moment on the steep-to bank, and then went down head foremost into 10 feet of sparking water. Differing from most streams in the Nigerland, which ooze like pea-soup streaked with oil out of fermenting wastes of mire, the Sapelli river is crystal clear, and comes flashing down between stately mahoganies, acacias, cotton-woods, and tall-shafted oil-palms, whose feathery fronds dripped dew. There is no luxury like a swim in the tropics where it may safely; be enjoyed, which is seldom, and after shooting through water cool and limpid among the starry cups of floating lilies, I made my way ashore a very different being. The listless lethargy of Africa had gone, and for twenty minutes at least I felt that life was a good thing after all, and the fragrance of the forest glorious to breathe. But the feeling did not last — it never does in the Niger delta; for the grip of the climate takes hold again, one's step grows heavier, the shoulders droop, and light-heartedness fades like the morning mist.

That plunge reminded me of one sweltering night when we lay rolling in Lagos Roads. A little steamer was anchored close astern, and in the clear moonlight we saw two men dive from her forecastle-head. A few minutes later a half-choked cry rang out across the shimmering swell, and one of the two was gone, doubtless drawn down by the tiger-like ground-sharks that swarm below. Both were sober men who had been engaged in some hot and dirty task in the engine-room, and their common-sense was probably somewhat dimmed by fever, or they would never have made the attempt. A little earlier another artificer lay asleep on the bridge-deck of a steamer moored inside Lagos Bar, and just how it happened no one knew, but the man rose suddenly, leaned against the rail, and, being probably only half-awake, overbalanced and fell. A long grey shadow rose swiftly through the glass-green depths, a fathom of black back broke the oily surface, and the two disappeared in the twinkling of an eye. But all this has nothing to do with Sapelli.

When I went back to the factory I found three miserable individuals leaning upon the verandah balustrade, hollow-faced, nervous, and irritable, which is perhaps the usual state of most white men at 6 A.M. in Western Africa. One of them was sucking the inevitable thermometer, for on board ship and in the factories a European is anxious about his temperature the moment he awakes. If it varies from 98° to 100° he begins work satisfied; if over 100° he wears a harassed look all day, and wonders when he will be forced to roll himself in thick blankets, and with the aid of hot lime-water endeavour to check the fever by unlimited perspiration. This is frequently effectual, and the juice of green limes is an excellent febrifuge. It is scarcely strange that the temptation to resort to stimulants is too strong for many men. They have hard and trying work to do, they awake unfit for anything, and they know that alcohol, of which there is generally an ample store, will supply at least temporary energy.

We breakfasted in the usual fashion, on palm-oil chop, yams, and tinned stuff, and there was provided for me alone a luscious pine-apple. The rest would not touch it, for this fruit is regarded with suspicion in Africa, where they say its injudicious consumption is followed by a journey in a gun-case and top-hat. This is a somewhat grim allusion, and explainable as follows. In all the swamps of the steamy delta the rough deal cases in which long-Dane guns are shipped are used as coffins, and they are sometimes a trifle too short. In seasons of unusual pestilence—so at least the story goes, and stranger things are done—there is no time to lengthen them for a man above the average stature. Then the end would be knocked in, and if the head of the occupant projected beyond it in an unseemly fashion an old silk hat was nailed across. The story may or may not be fiction, but it is at least characteristic, and the reference to a top-hat and gun-case is always understood on the Oil Rivers. I remember watching the face of a missionary recruit as he listened to it for the first time with horror and disgust, while a gaunt trader elaborated other gruesome details, some of which I knew to be true.

While breakfast was going on upon the verandah I had time to look about, and the prospect was worth inspection. There are no swamps immediately round Sapelli, but a glorious forest instead, through which the limpid river flows. On the farther bank the sea of foliage rolled away wave beyond wave of eternal verdure, with the feathery tufts of palms rising like crests above it, while below and about us there ran a stretch of clean, sharp sand. Here stood the usual whitewashed sheds, then there was more forest, and another yellow clearing with its line of Yoruba barracks, while beyond a jutting point luxuriant with palms and fringed with a lacework of reeds, where white lilies starred the clear pool beneath, the red roof of a third factory peeped out among the trees. Behind the forest rim the east blazed with purple and crimson and gold, and soon long shafts of brightness touched the sand with fire, and steam rose up beneath them as the blazing day began.

Sapelli is at least a fair place to look upon, but by no means desirable to dwell in; for the fever is almost as busy among its luxuriance of tropic beauty as in the hideous swamps, and if a newcomer doubts this he can visit its cemetery and see. In spite of its few years of existence Sapelli has already a history. Here the great palaver or durbar of native chiefs was held in the time of the Nana raid, when once again there was talk of wiping out the white men. Here, too, the unfortunate expedition started for Old Benin, when the fever-worn officials set out on their last march through the bush. It must have been a somewhat impressive scene—the long lines of half-naked carriers with burdens of presents on their heads, the few tall *karki*-clad Yoruba soldiers, and the handful of sickly white men, with one stalwart figure among them, whose hair was tinged with greyness that was the work of anxiety rather than years. Then there would be a ringing of bugles, an exchange of farewells with the foreboding traders, and the expedition swung away into the shadowy forest, very few of those who marched with it ever to come forth again.

All this, however, happened afterwards, and presently my host said that as a big flotilla of trade-canoes was expected, we would see lots of fun that day. He was not mistaken. Soon the distant thud of paddles rose out of the silent bush, and later canoe after canoe came sliding down the stream. They were of all kinds and sizes, varying from huge dug-out craft down to knife-edge hulls 14 feet by 2, paddled by naked slaves or women, and loaded down to the vanishing-point with yellow oil or kernels. On they came, the long blades ripping through the water in time to a monotonous chant, and the river gurgling beneath the bows, while the headmen traders in many kinds of fantastic attire stood upright in the stern howling wild encouragement to the swaying crew. Opposite the factory a simultaneous rush was made for the landing, and truly the fun began. The clumsy craft, for the Niger man is no marine architect, drove crashing athwart one another, as some thirty canoes strove to pack themselves into a space where there might be room for ten. Method and order are qualities unknown to the tribesmen, and each crew sought to get their vessel first alongside by the primitive process of driving her through or over the rest. Thus there was a howling and shouting, some of the smaller canoes overturned, and when the larger became hopelessly entangled their occupants belaboured each other with the paddle-hafts, or clawed at their rivals' throats, while bushels of palm-kernels and even calabashes of sticky oil began to hurtle through the air. Meanwhile the agent, who had paid for some of that cargo in advance, danced upon the river-bank, hurling frantic abuse at all; and even a bargee would have admitted that he did it with proficiency, though unfortunately the Jakkeries neither understood nor heeded. At last when the stronger had secured first place, and the weaker were laving what the Krooboy calls "blue" eyes, trading operations began, and a succession of very scantily-attired retainers carried basket after basket of greasy little kernels towards a big tub mounted on trunnions in the weighing-shed.

A youth of perhaps nineteen summers stood beside this "cooler," and amid a pandemonium of shouting examined the proffered merchandise critically. "It's kernels, no dirrt, I want, ye rascals," he said every now and then in the Clydesdale tongue, and a Krooboy made a sweep with his wooden spade at the heathen who would have cast a basket one-third filled with empty shells into the receptacle. His chief difficulty arose from the fact that the servants of different headmen, with the negro's disregard of consequences, desired to empty their loads all at once, which would naturally lead to confusion, and the Krooboy's shovel was kept busy impressing this fact upon their naked skin.

Meantime sticky yellow oil, and a few coils of plastic green rubber, whose smell is beyond all things disgusting, were being weighed and probed in another shed. This probing is essential, for the unsophisticated bushman is very apt to slip a clod or piece of wood inside the calabash

P

or coil, these things being considerably cheaper than oil or rubber, and weighing just as well. It may again be remarked that it is not so easy for the unscrupulous white man to victimise the guileless heathen as some would make it appear. Among other instances the writer has purchased parrots which died mysteriously, and proved to have been fed on powdered glass, doubtless with the intention of keeping up the demand; therefore it may be taken for granted that the simple forest-dweller knows what he is about, and those who doubt this have only to try and beat him at a bargain to realise the fact. There was one trader on the Gold Coast who, it was rumoured, occasionally sent out watered gin until he received in payment certain packets of gold dust from a headman far up in the bush. The trader tested a sample from each packet in a rough-and-ready manner, and as usual found the metal genuine. When the consignment reached home, however, it was discovered that while the upper layers were fine alluvial gold, the lower consisted of brass filings. Now brass filings are not a product of the West African hinterland, and how the headman obtained them puzzled many people; for they must have been brought from Sierra Leone or Lagos, if not across the seas. Also the bushman dwelt beyond our jurisdiction, so the trader had no redress, and it took him six months to make up the commission and salary deducted by his employers at home.

As each lot of produce was completed, the black trader or his representative received a stamped brass tally as a voucher for his goods, and straightway proceeded to the store-shed or shop to exchange it for value. Endless square green cases were being counted out by another youth, who had to keep all his wits about him to see that the native claimants got no more than their tallies called for, and he was probably not altogether successful. Meantime the agent had entered the shop, and following him later, I found the space behind the counter crammed to suffocation by a howling, gesticulating mob, who fought for first attendance, and usually claimed three times as much as they were entitled to get. Rolls of Manchester cotton, worth 2s., 6 yards long, I believe, and standard currency, were in most demand; but flintlock guns, and such odds and ends as tennis-caps, brass-framed mirrors, German oleographs, blue-and-white jerseys, battered silk hats, discarded cavalry uniforms, and the like, found ready sale. Now and then a Jakkery would steal his neighbour's tally, or slip some coveted article to a comrade in the rear, while another innocently declared that he had lost his voucher, but had brought so many baskets of kernels down. The agent, however, had heard that tale too many times already, and the ingenuous bushman was generally forcibly ejected by two grinning Krooboys, while the bargaining went on again. The trader was soaked in perspiration, kept constantly running to and fro; the clamour was nerve-trying, the effluvia even worse, and already the galvanised roof radiated fervent heat. He would probably work there until sunset, with scarcely time to snatch a mouthful of food, and, all things considered, certainly well earned his daily bread. There are men who lose their heads over this kind of work, or break down altogether after a brief experience. Others, if they escape the fever, get to like the rush and excitement; and it is a curious fact that many of those who have toiled and suffered in the tropic forest, making strenuous efforts to earn enough to escape therefrom, when they finally succeed and start afresh in healthier climates, become restless, and, against both reason and inclination, feel themselves drawn irresistlessly back again.

What the fascination is they cannot say,—they abuse their own stupidity; but the tropics have woven a spell about them, and they go back there to die. Among several others I remember one of these well. He had once been somewhat famous in Lagos colony and the delta, and had just abandoned a calling at home which brought him in a reasonable living to return to Africa with empty exchequer and no contract of employment, simply, so he said, because he could not stop away. Perhaps the entire absence of outside restraint has something to do with it, as well as unlimited influence; for in this region every man does that which is right in his own eyes, and, obeying no law but his own pleasure, is accountable to none—so long as he makes the factory pay.

It should be remembered that the negroes thus crowding in the shop were only the small-fry traders, or the confidential slaves of inland merchants. The larger dealers come down in state and do their business in a very different manner, and among these dishonesty would not seem to be common. Their transactions are often very large, and mutual confidence is necessary, as whole flotillas go up loaded with gin and cloth, for which the oil may not be sent down for many months, and *vice versâ*. The big bush-trader thoroughly understands the system of current accounts, and when his indebtedness grows too large sends down a sop to quieten the agent's mind as regards the interests of his employer's property, and often a handsome "dash" for his own particular benefit as well. This sending of "dash" is a universal custom in West Africa, and even with the smallest bargain it is usual to give some trifling present, while no important business or political contract is ever made without the exchange of costly gifts. The writer has received some curious "dash"—miraculous Ju-Ju talismans, live snakes in boxes, and once, and this was a very special favour, a few Aggri beads. These are curious ornaments made out of a substance somewhat resembling jasper, dug from the earth in the Gold Coast, and worth more than thrice their weight in gold. No one yet understands where the "Aggri" came from, and in spite of many attempts to counterfeit them, the native is never deceived. A Government official once told me that he had seen similar things in the North-West Provinces of India, also said to belong to past ages; and throughout the fever-belt of Western Africa one comes across hints of an ancient civilisation whose history has never been written, and which may have been as old as Babylon. After all, we know but little about many parts of the Dark Continent.

CHAPTER XIX.

DOWN THE SAPELLI RIVER.

THE following morning I visited the headquarters of the Protectorate authorities for the Sapelli district, the Government hulk Hindoostan. Here the dignity of the law was maintained, and well maintained, by two young officials, apparently under thirty years of age, and for a time I lounged with them beneath the poop awnings, as we had done before. It is curious that most of the hard and trying work of the Niger delta is done by young men, and yet it is very seldom one hears of any piece of official stupidity.

The Hindoostan swung idly across a limpid pool strewn with the white cups of lilies, the luxuriant and spicy forest walling it in on the one hand, while on the other there lay a space of dazzling sand whereon the barracks of the Yorubas stood. Here a third white officer dwelt ashore, together with the district surgeon appointed by the Government, who also marched to Benin. This gentleman was one of the thirteen medical officers then maintained by the Protectorate, though I believe the number has since been increased, at salaries varying from £350 to £500 a-year, and well earned his pay. I used to meet him in the early dawn hurrying along the forest-trails on foot—a hammock was too slow—or came across him, always moving with quick impatience, about the Yoruba barracks in the blazing heat of noon, while we could hear his canoe-paddles thudding across the misty river long after darkness had settled down. He had much to do, and he did it with all his might.

What had once been the orlop or "'tween-decks" of the Hindoostan had been converted into a court-room, and here at regular intervals the two officials administered justice after the manner described at Warri. The result was apparent, for, glancing at the bank of steaming mould between the reed-beds at the river's brink and the forest behind, we saw a swarm of sable figures busy with matchet and shovel, or moving to and fro with baskets of earth upon their heads. These for offences many and curious had fallen under the grip of the law, and now were employed excavating a slip-way for the Government launch, a proceeding they by no means enjoyed; but two big Yoruba privates standing on guard with rifles in their hands saw they did it thoroughly. Now and then I was told a prisoner got away, but so satisfied were the Sapelli tribesmen with their new rulers that they generally sent the fugitive back again.

It was far too hot to lounge all day about the deck of the Hindoostan doing nothing—the most trying task of all in the sweltering tropics—and when one of the party suggested that I should accompany him down-stream in a canoe to look for an alligator, and be towed back by the launch in the afternoon, I gladly agreed. We took our places gingerly in the canoe, a beautifully moulded craft about 14 feet by 3, the work of some Krooboy or Fanti artificer, for it was far beyond the skill of any Niger man. My companion had contrived a centre-board and trunk, and we hoisted a large and by no means badly cut lugsail, the work of his own fingers. In spite of the heat a breeze blew down between the walls of forest; and while we balanced ourselves to windward the tiny vessel listed over until her lee gunwale was awash, and, flinging the crystal water from her bows in hissing showers, drove away down-stream. It was not the safest kind of travelling, but my friend was skilful with the tiller, and I had handled the mainsheet of ticklish craft too often to let her ship more than was judicious. Thus with one eye on the bevelled ridge of fizzing water slanting off from her down-pressed gunwale-bead, I caught confused and kaleidoscopic glimpses of tropic scenery.

Now we swept by a cluster of feathery oil-palms,

slender-shafted, and crowned by curving fronds delicate as lacework. Again we slid into the cool shadows of mighty cotton-trees and hardwoods, or beneath the gigantic leaves of paw-paws; and here the hot air was filled with a fragrance as of frankincense, myrrh, and all manner of spices. At times the forests fell away, and we rippled on by tall beds of golden reeds, where starry lilies swam in the clear pools between; past islets which, with the crimsons and yellows fringing their base, the raw greens above, and the intense azure behind them, formed visions of vivid colour. And all the time the rush of hot wind followed us, and the clear river frothed beneath the bows, while it was only by watching the shores roll by that the pace we travelled at became strikingly apparent. The flow of an African stream is always deceptive. As a rule, it oozes down, muddy, smooth, and oily, with no ripple on its surface nor gurgling along the bank. Stagnant water, one would say at a hasty glance; but when with engines panting their hardest, and a fathom of froth beneath her roaring bows, the big oil-tank makes barely five knots against it, one begins to understand that things are not always what they seem, and the power of the river is made manifest.

So we left the miles behind us until, when tired of the heat and glare, for there was no coolness in that breeze, we ran the canoe in through a gateway among the reeds, and dropped the calico lug.

For a time we dipped the paddles, and the light craft slid on past wastes of tall blades, yellow above, lush-green below, their feathery tassels rolling in long ripples overhead, while the water at their feet grew muddier. Then these too were left behind, and we entered a dim green tunnel beneath the mangrove shade, where we floated on what seemed to be a stream of crusted oil. On either hand the tangled tentacles rose out of noisome depths of foulness, fantastic and horrible, while above them a maze of white stems stretched away and was lost in the shadows. Overhead the wiry branches interlaced, shutting out the light of day and veiling the whole in steamy shade, while drooping withes crept downwards to take fresh root again. The air was heavy with that triple essence of corruption which has been described before, and used to it as we were, at times one felt inclined to drop the paddle, and lie down overcome with nausea.

My companion, however, produced a flask of the inevitable bitter mixture of spirit and quinine, and we pushed on steadily into the home of the fever and the haunts of the scaly alligator. Presently we passed a tiny scaffolding of branches lashed together, above which was perched a little Ju-Ju house. It was the kind of structure one may see in scores throughout the Niger delta, but lying thus remote from observation, it seemed good to my companion to inspect it in an official capacity. So we lashed the canoe alongside and climbed to the platform; but though the latter was strewn with offerings, they were innocent enough, and the searcher was satisfied. He explained, nevertheless, that very gruesome things were sometimes found in such places, which testified very plainly as to what went on in the bush around, especially at one season of the year. Then a mysterious orgy is supposed to be held in some remote fastness of the swamps only known to the bushman, and in places for several weeks together the negroes about the factories become restless and unsettled. One by one they slip away when unobserved, or are absent all night and crawl back at dawn clearly worn by hurried travel, but decidedly unwilling to explain where they have been. Even Fantis from the distant Gold Coast, and Kroomen from the far Liberian beaches, who have nothing whatever in common with the Niger men, and do not even speak their tongue, are said to be mysteriously absent. This would seem to show that the fear of the Ju-Ju overrides the distinctions of race and language, though just what is done no white man has ever discovered.

Volatile, fluent, and careless as he is, the negro can be very reticent, and work to good purpose with very little noise now and then. The gulf fixed between white Christian and sable pagan is a wide one, and in times of trouble the few officials who hold the outposts feel that they have no guide or clue to anything that goes on beneath the surface. They, however, have this protection, that almost every soldier or military servant of the Government is a Moslem from the remote north, and though the latter would seem to be by no means altogether free from a lurking fear of the heathen gods, there is a fierce racial antagonism between them and the bushmen. Thus, apart from their general fidelity and soldierly qualities, the former have generally their own quarrel to settle, and the difficulty has rather been to restrain than encourage them to strike hard on the British side.

So we left the Ju-Ju house behind, and the writer at least was quite content that we had not been called upon to inspect offerings of desiccated human limbs or strings of finger-bones, which things are not unknown in the delta, notably in the neighbourhood of Bonny. By-and-by we reached a little miry basin walled in by mangroves and bubbling like a cauldron, while a haze of steam hung above it. No pen or brush could adequately depict the strange horribleness of all the eye rested upon, and we seemed to have been transported to a region of the nether world. The sunlight was obscured by deadly vapours, the whole place worked with fermentation, while the mudbanks heaved and seethed. The rotting branches and logs which cumbered the surface occasionally tilted endways and sank, or disintegrated before our eyes; the heat was awful, and every fathom of water or mire swarmed with loathsome forms of life. I had dwelt in a tent alone many days together amid the wholesome pine-forests of the North-West, and had camped in solitude amid the leagues of white grass south of the Saskatchewan, but I felt that a very little of this place, even with company, would be sufficient to unhinge the reason of most men, and there was a curious comfort in the sight of the Lee-Metford and Martini rifles in the canoe.

For a time we lay there alongside a screen of mangroves, silent and, it may be confessed, somewhat overcome by the surroundings, as well as possibly a little sick, until something that seemed to be an upheaval of sun-baked mud disturbed the margin of the swamp. Then my comrade's Lee-Metford went up, and crouching gingerly in the tender canoe, I dropped the blue Martini barrel upon the gunwale. We were bound by no superstition as to firing at the throat or waiting for a glimpse at the undersides, and when the wedge of foresight filling the rear-slide V trembled across the long-snouted head, I stiffened my left fingers upon the barrel and steadily squeezed the trigger. The sharp, quick ringing of the Lee-Metford filled my ears, and without hearing the heavier report of the Martini, I felt the heel-plate jar against my shoulder and the muzzle tilt. Then there was smoke in my eyes, while a great splashing commenced somewhere near at hand. Next I saw what appeared to be a misshapen log drive straight for the wall of forest, and with a yell my comrade seized his paddle. A moment or two later the bows grated on the mud, and we heard something floundering through the mangrove-roots ahead, muddy foam washing behind it, while the other gripped me by the shoulder as, obeying a mad impulse, I reached up towards a branch. A moment's reflection showed my comrade's wisdom, for the first step would in all probability have landed me waist-deep in mire, and the next overhead altogether in plastic corruption, from which no swimmer could hope to escape. Therefore we let the stricken alligator go, and took up the paddles again; for, as the sportsman said, "A very little of this place goes a long way."

An alligator will carry off a considerable quantity of lead—in fact, it seems almost impossible to kill the beast at times. While, however, it may have been quite true once that its scales would turn a ball, in these days of high explosives and accurate twist of rifling the idea is out of date. Possibly the hardest scales upon the ridge of the back might cause a shot at an angle to ricochet, but certainly nowhere else; and I saw a big alligator drilled clean through both sides by a Lee-Metford bullet at fully 80 yards near the Warri Consulate. I think it was Major Crawford who fired the shot.

When we reached slightly more pleasant surroundings we made the canoe fast alongside the reeds, and amused ourselves by driving off insects and venomous creeping things while we made shift to get our lunch. Then we took up the paddles again, and reaching the main river, waited the arrival of the Government launch on her way from a forest patrol. In due time the handsome, white-painted vessel, with her cream-tinted funnel, and the flag which, of late years at least, has represented justice and mercy among the swamps streaming above her stern, came panting up the stream. We gladly went on board her, and as with throbbing engines she cleft the river apart, and the forest rolled endlessly away behind, realised how far we had travelled down-stream under sail.

It was dark when I left my entertainer and went back, hot, worn out, and sleepy, to the sweltering factory. But there was little rest that night either, for once I was aroused to fight a procession of ants that seemed intent upon eating me alive. Fortunately these were not of the most vicious kind, for when the driver ants invade a dwelling its human inhabitants flee for their lives. They have good cause to do so, because the driver battalion wipes out every living thing that comes in its way: rats, centipedes, or snakes—nothing may escape the mandibles; and I have heard the natives tell of helpless sick men being picked to the bone. They say, however, that the sun kills the drivers, and that unless the latter reach the shade before dawn they shrivel up and die,—an eventuality no one regrets.

Then there was another disturbance; for a steamer having arrived that afternoon, some of her crew got ashore, and after holding a wild carnival in a cluster of reed hovels along the river-bank, apparently found some reason to attempt the chastisement of the dwellers therein. The latter evidently retaliated, for the night was made hideous with shrieks, forecastle objurgations, and the rattle of paddle-hafts on naked skin as well as the smashing of glass. Then the natives, being routed, fled wildly across the moonlit compound with a line of shouting seamen in vigorous pursuit, and took refuge upon the stairway of a German factory at hand, much to the agent's disgust. Leaning over the balustrade, I saw the exasperated Teuton standing on the verandah brandishing a gun, while a cluster of panting men flung empty gin-bottles at him from below amid shrieks of merriment, until there was a splash of oars in Sapelli creek, and with some difficulty one or two officers drove their men away. After this I gave up the attempt to secure a little much-needed repose, and, disregarding the risk of fever, lounged in a Madeira-chair upon the verandah, as I had done before, until red dawn flushed the eastern sky.

CHAPTER XX.

ON THE BRASS RIVER.

SOME little time after our visit to Akassa, on board a wheezy oil-launch, which was as full of wicked tricks as any jibbing horse, I slid out from among the mangroves into the muddy waters of the Brass river. Here, in case the reader should wonder that there is little mention of travel by land, it may be pointed out that in the region of the Lower Niger the winding creeks are practically the only roads. A journey by land necessitates an expensive gathering together of carriers and hammockmen, and is therefore seldom undertaken, while so numerous are the waterways that one can almost invariably find a route for canoe or launch.

The mouth of the Brass river lies some ten miles east of the main outlet of the Niger, and is, as usual, guarded by a jutting spit of sand and surf-swept bar. The settlement, which stands just inside, is not unlike New Benin, for some three or four factories rise at intervals above the narrow beach of yellow sand. But in place of rotting swamps there is comparatively dry land and forest behind them; also there are roads, paved with the shells of palm-kernels, which tread down hard and smooth, and any kind of made road is practically unknown elsewhere in the Niger region, with the exception of Calabar and Bonny. The presence of so many shells is partly due to the fact that once upon a time a certain enterprising agent decided that if kernels could be extracted by the primitive process of breaking the shells one by one with a hammer, and crushed for oil at home, after paying freight and comparatively high wages, there should be a handsome profit for whoever could introduce proper plant for performing the operation on the spot. So he managed to persuade his employers to invest a good round sum in the attempt, and then that agent's troubles began. The machines got out of gear, partly because the river men stole any easily detachable portions that were made of brass or polished steel; while the Krooboys instituted a series of experiments on their own account, which would have tried the endurance of the strongest plant, and, occasionally damaging their fingers in the course thereof, refused to work at all. Thus the venture was a failure, and if any one desires to commence the extraction of palm-oil in the locality where the oil-palm grows, he could no doubt purchase the whole concern for the price of scrap iron, if it has not rusted clean away.

We could not see much of Brass that day, for the rain came down as it only does in the tropics, beating the muddy river into whiteness, and, swirling across the awnings, said to be waterproof, drove through the quivering fabric upon us in powdery spray, while the air seemed filled with the roar of falling water. Along the dripping shore-line I could see the steam rise up in clouds as the hot earth sucked in the rain, and, sick of the constant Turkish-bath atmosphere, I longed for just one breath of pure ocean air again.

The oil-launch, as frequently happened, was working very badly that morning, her little propeller alternately whirling like a dynamo, or thumping and grinding at about quarter-speed, while she poisoned the air far away astern with the odours of half-burnt paraffin. My companion, the black engineer, made no attempt to set matters right, but sat as far away from the machinery as he could, and I pitied the good missionaries for the trouble that craft had given them. She came out on the same steamer that I travelled in, under charge of a young Englishman, who was to instruct the black artificer how to run her; and the Society had treated him very well, purchasing for him, although he was only to stay a very short time, every comfort that could be enjoyed in the tropics, over and above his ample wages.

The young man came on board in Liverpool in high spirits, but when he heard the traders' stories his face grew long and anxious, and ere we reached Grand Canary he had firmly made up his mind to go back. Therefore he interviewed the captain, and I can remember the expression of disgust on the bronzed commander's face as the former said, "You see I am afraid of it, so I will be sure to catch the fever; and I wouldn't like to die in a place like that. Now the fare on to the Niger is much less than it is back from Las Palmas, and you can leave word for the next ship to take me home."

The answer was hardly reassuring: "The Society paid £25 to take you out—a good deal more than you're worth—and out you go if I have any say in the matter. Scores of better men than you will ever be have died on the Niger anyway."

Afterwards there never was a more miserable man, and when we lowered him and his undesirable craft over the side together at Akassa the chief engineer had to go on board and start the thing away; for her proper guardian sat huddled in the stern, apparently unable or unwilling to do anything at all. This particular morning his black successor seemed to have become affected with the same uselessness or fear of the fizzling engines, and appeared chiefly bent on keeping a safe distance from them while the launch meandered on into the rain. Presently I desired to board a little white-painted gunboat, H.M.S. Thrush or Sparrow — I forget which, for I had afterwards occasion to visit both several times—then straining at her cables in the tideway, and explained matters to the engineer. He did not offer to help, but said: "If you stop them thing when they be hot, sah, she blow up suah. Be feathering gear to propeller, and you reverse them handle while the engine runs ahead. Then turn him half-way, and them screw turn round without them blade."

It was not very lucid, but having seen a similar, and equally exasperating, contrivance before, I did as I was bidden, and jammed the tiller down abreast of the gunboat's gangway. It, however, became very evident that something would not work, for the launch careered on at full speed, and next moment, with a bang and a crash that flung me off my feet, hurled herself into the steamer, rebounded, and came on again. While I recovered my breath, and made efforts to recover my temper too, several bluejackets swung themselves down with lines from the channels, and the foremost grinned when I said: ": Tie this thing up with a good strong rope before she knocks the whole bows out of her. Those engines were not made to stop."

Of course there was unlimited banter to be faced when I reached the quarter-deck, and afterwards I was hospitably entertained in the little cabin beneath her poop. The whole place was covered with a crust of powdered cork and white-lead; for the reason that cork being a good non-conductor, the ever-present moisture does not condense upon it in a constant trickle as it would upon anything else, and thus clothing and other articles can be kept in a state less like that of wet blotting-paper.

The vessel was a typical specimen of the fleet of little gunboats which keep watch and ward over the African coast—narrow-beamed, heavily sparred, with a wide spread of sailcloth, and engines of moderate power. She and her class have little time for rest. First they patrol the south-east seaboard, where there is also sickness, from Natal northwards past Zanzibar, watching night or day for the skulking dhows packed to the beams with slaves, or ready to lend aid to adventurous British traders in trouble with Arab or native or Portuguese,—eventualities which happen much oftener than many suppose at home. Then as the white seamen weaken beneath the climate, or fall sick of malaria, the bows are turned southwards, and plunging through the great combers off the Cape with streaming forefoot hove fathoms clear of ocean, they steam to St Helena or Ascension to gather fresh health again. Afterwards they steer for the Gambia or Niger mouth, and creep rolling and wallowing along 2000 odd miles of surf-hammered beach, where they generally find much to do, for if there is not trouble at one end of this littoral it is sure to break out at the other.

Probably nothing impresses the wanderer in the far corners of the seas like the ubiquitous nature of the British cruiser. It may be there is a native rising in some river of Western Africa, or a raiding of traders' factories in an isle of the Southern Seas. Also it occasionally happens in the mushroom republics of the tropics, where the Latins revel in a form of liberty which is by no means good for them, or possessions of Spain and Portugal, that rapacious officials become dangerous, or in time of red revolution her Majesty's subjects run considerable risk of their lives. Then if there be an end of a cable anywhere at hand a message is flashed under the sea, and the British citizen sits down and waits comparatively tranquil in mind. He knows that message will call up a guardian spirit out of the vasty deep in the shape of a little top-hampered steamer with two big guns amidships, and quick-firers fore and aft. He is rarely disappointed, for before many days have passed, as if by magic, a gunboat has answered the summons, and when the cable roars out through her hawse-pipe his troubles come to an end.

Thus there is no one in the world enjoys the same personal safety abroad as the Briton. In one Spanish possession my aid was occasionally invoked by the officials to persuade inebriated countrymen to desist from smashing up a wine-shop or similar vagaries and go quietly on board their ships. One Ayutante de Commandancia, I remember, explained the matter as follows: "I do not speak their language, but if you will talk to them I will send our launch to take them off. If they stay here making *escandalos* like this they will surely get themselves stabbed, and there is always so much trouble when an Englishman gets hurt."

I think that was the time I found a squad of Cazadores protecting a few intoxicated seamen with their bayonets against a howling mob, who would probably only have executed rough justice had they rolled the Britons into the harbour, but the *sotto teniente* in command trembled lest a scratch should come upon them.

It is easy to understand that the commanders of these police of the seas must be men of tact and discernment as well as determination, especially on the West African coast, where is much international jealousy, and yet one rarely hears of them blundering, and all I saw were young. Creeping into little-known waterways, sounding for reported reefs, sweltering in the pestilential lagoons with soiled decks and grimy paint—for so careful are they of their men that they will not wash down with the river-water the merchant seaman drinks—landing bluejackets and marines to drag the machine-guns through bubbling mire or trackless forest, blowing up stockades under fire, or rolling from rail to rail as they watch the thundering beaches, they carry on a work whose results spread far and wide.

However, that morning our conversation was interrupted by a gunner entering the poop-cabin to say that the launch was "a-fizzin' badly, sir, an' a-surgin' backwards and forrards, an' a-scrapin' off fathoms of paint." With a muttered blessing on both stupid negro and unmanageable craft I hurried on deck, and finding that the propeller was whirling as if it would shake itself off the shaft altogether, and the engine sputtering very suspiciously, I bade my hosts farewell and dropped on board. We cast off the lines, and an attempt to reverse the propeller drove us madly ahead, rasping off long streaks of the Government paint, until, grinding across the gunboat's cable, we shot away upstream, doubtless amid the derisive laughter of all on board. In the end we stopped the engines by cutting off the fuel altogether, and I breathed a sigh of relief when at last we got the anchor down off a trader's-landing at Brass. A canoe took us ashore, and shortly afterwards I saw that unlucky craft had broken loose, and was driving down on the ebb towards the spouting bar with three big canoes in wild chase astern. They caught her eventually, which was, all things considered, perhaps a pity; for sooner or later it seemed only too probable that launch would take an active part in the translation of some hard-worked missionary, who, instead of Elijah's chariot of fire, will go up amid the rocketing remnants of an exploded oil-motor.

During my stay at Brass I was present at a function only too common in Western Africa, a funeral. It was not a new experience, for more than once I had shuddered at the curious mingling of the ghastly and the grotesque that characterises a funeral upon the malaria coast, and one is very like another; but there were special reasons why that particular occasion should impress itself upon my memory. I had known the man about to be laid to rest, a hard-working patient individual, who had been warned at home during a brief recruiting visit that he had already been too long in Western Africa. But, as he afterwards explained when we sat watching beside him one sweltering night shortly before the end, he had a wife and family to think of, the tropics had weakened him so that he was unfit for other work, and there was nothing left but to go back and face the risk. It was not, perhaps, the soundest logic, but the same argument has driven many others to meet their fate. The possibility of death will not outweigh the certainty of want and hunger falling upon those who look to the man for bread.

CHAPTER XXI.

A FUNERAL IN THE DELTA.

It was raining hard when some dozen sickly men straggled away from the factory behind a flag-covered gun-case borne on the shoulders of four half-naked Krooboys. The palm-fronds above us quivered before the rush of the deluge, the miry trail was ankle-deep in running water, and the forest was rolled in steam. Presently we splashed on through a cluster of mud-walled native huts, where big river-men of the Nimbi race lounged in the doorways, jabbering as they pointed significantly to the gun-case, while the broad paw-paw leaves above the dripping thatch throbbed like drum-heads at the beating of the rain. By the time we reached the little cemetery, however, the downpour suddenly ceased, and a glare of fierce sunlight broke through, while the flash of unexpected brightness photographed, as it were, each detail indelibly upon one's memory.

The forest hemmed us in on every side, great

A FUNERAL IN THE DELTA.

drops fell splashing from the leaves, and sparkling streams trickled here and there across the space of yellow sand. A shallow trench had been scooped through this surface-crust, and a mound of slimy ooze lay heaped about it, while two Krooboys were hard at work in the water they baled out of the narrow hole. The gun-case was laid upon this mound, and commenced to settle in the ooze which sucked about it, while the party, coming to a halt, looked at each other furtively, and whispered as they glanced towards the forest. So what might have been ten minutes dragged away in silence, only broken by the "splash, splash" of water and the clank of the Krooboys' buckets as they strove to keep the trench from filling to the brim, for there is abundant moisture within a foot or two of the surface almost everywhere in the Niger delta. At last one man said, "He must be nearly dead, or he would certainly have come. You are the oldest, and you will have to do it."

The individual thus addressed bore on his bloated yet pasty-complexioned countenance the stamp set there by too many cocktails, and hesitatingly produced a dilapidated Prayer-Book from his pocket. He fumbled with it shamefacedly for a space, either because he could not find the place or for the purpose of gaining time; and though few of the party were very particular, it seemed as though the sight of an alcohol-soaked gin-trader blundering over the solemn words of the last office jarred upon even their sense of the fitness of things. The latter evidently felt it too, for he began to read nervously, and as he did so the memory of another funeral I had once witnessed in the islands off the coast persistently rose up before me.

I could see the line of rickety tartanas jolting through the scorching streets of an old-world Spanish city, the inhabitants standing still bareheaded with Castilian courtesy and wonder on their faces as the procession passed, while in the clattering vehicles a nondescript rabble of British extraction lounged in unseemly disorder with their hats over their eyes, sucking at foul pipes or chatting volubly. They had also driven far, and the day was very hot, so every now and then bottles were passed around. Thus it happened that when at last their comrade had been laid to rest in the little Protestant cemetery by a clergyman tourist, and the company would have concluded with a hymn—the attempt was a signal failure. A dusty drive in tropic heat is trying, and "vino Jerez" a tempting thing, but the ears of some of those present must have tingled long afterwards at the memory of what that clergyman said.

After reading a sentence or two the trader closed the book with a look of relief upon his face, for a sound of splashing footsteps came out of the forest. Then two Krooboy bearers swung into sight with the poles of a lurching hammock upon their woolly crowns, and later a very haggard white man was lifted out, while a trader beside me said, "I knew he would come if he was fit to stand at all."

The new arrival, a representative of a certain missionary society whose emissaries have poured out their blood very freely for the redemption of Africa, was certainly fit to do little more, but straightening himself painfully, he beckoned the trader aside, and when the latter complied with alacrity, said, "Take off your hats and listen decently."

Then standing bareheaded in the fierce sunshine, which had now succeeded the rain, he read the service in a voice which occasionally rang clear and true, and sank to an indistinct murmur as he caught hard at his breath. Once, too, the reader staggered, but recovered himself again, and at last a sign was made and the Krooboys tilted the gun-case into the trench. But the poor remains of humanity within were wasted to skeleton lightness, and the buoyant deal rising level with the surface shook off the mould shovelled upon it, and resolutely refused to sink. Then the two naked aliens stood upon it to hold it down, while the bearers shovelled in the sand and mire until the last words died slowly away.

Afterwards, with a brief salutation, the missionary was lifted into his hammock, for he could never have got there alone, and we went back silently towards the factory, leaving one who had fought manfully against long odds at rest at last beside the muddy river. He had endured much climatic suffering, quietly faced pestilence and sudden death, and now his labour was over there would be £50 for the widow and a message of condolence. But, as we had heard, this was not the end, only a release from weary toil and work done faithfully, and one realised again that while the honours are to the few, the rank and file have also done their part in the building up of our dominion in Western Africa.

Possibly some may read with disapproval, or question the writer's discretion in setting down these incidents with direct plainness. But there is more than one side to our national character, and in an attempt to set forth the real aspect of life in the tropics, it is only just to show the failings as well as the virtues of those who dwell there, and they have many of the latter. As Froude, and many others who have surveyed our possessions abroad with understanding eyes, have said, so Gordon said as plainly as he could speak in a letter written shortly before the fall of Khartum, "Our empire has been built up and extended by our adventurers, and never by our Governments"; while if the privates in this legion have their faults and weaknesses, it must be remembered they also suffer many evils and work on, while others enter into the fruits of their labours. After all, they do very heroic things at times, and at least know how to endure and be silent; and who is there, living sheltered and safe at home, should venture to condemn them?

Another incident connected with the Niger trade once came under my observation, which may serve to show some of the curious tricks the malaria plays. The —— had left the river homeward bound when her bos'n, a well-conducted, sober man, was stricken down by fever. Shaken by paroxysms of delirium, he grew rapidly weaker, and his comrades wondered how long it would be before the engines were stopped while a weighted roll of canvas was launched from the gangway. One moonlight night, when the steamer was swinging like a pendulum on the mile-long glassy swell, a wild cry startled the sleepy watch on deck, and a half-dressed figure slipped stealthily in and out among the shafts of the bowl-head ventilators upon her forecastle. A long knife glinted in its hand, and the man seemed to be following some unseen object, leaning forward every now and then as though about to strike.

One glance was sufficient for the quick-witted mate: "It's the bos'n raving mad again," he said. "One or two of you slip in behind him and knock that knife from his hand." A seaman hastened forward to obey, but on his approach the bos'n leapt from the forecastle-head on to the narrow bulwark-rail, and in spite of the vicious lurching ran along it with the long knife flickering in his hand. Next with a yell he sprang into the foremast shrouds, and climbed upwards in frantic haste, screaming incoherent nonsense all the time, while the mate and two seamen followed breathlessly behind him. Then he reached the eyes of the rigging where the spreading shrouds converge upon the mast, and the mate prepared for a desperate struggle to save the madman's life, and possibly his own. The bos'n, however, was beforehand with them, and reaching aloft, caught at the triatic stay and swung himself up upon it. Now a triatic stay is a line of wire drawn horizontally between the masts,—a thin black strand of steel, on which Blondin would scarcely have dared to set his foot in a wildly rolling ship. But, holding on to the mast with one arm, the bos'n gripped the wire with his coir-soled slipper, and crouching a little, seemed to tighten his grip upon the knife and prepare to move forward.

"Come down, Forrester, you fool, there's nothing there," said the mate; but the other answered, "I can see her pointing—the other one's there as well;" and so suggestive was the attitude of anxiety and desperate purpose, that the mate afterwards averred he almost fancied he could see a shadowy figure moving along the wire. So nearly a minute passed, and the fever-stricken man above them swung across the moonlight as the masthead reeled in a wide arc to and fro, and no one dare move for fear lest, losing his hold, their comrade should be flung headlong to the narrow wedge of iron deck that heaved so far beneath their feet. Then with a hoarse cry he actually let go the mast, and stood balancing unaided on the thin strand of wire. This time, however, the mate was equal to the occasion, and in a steady voice he said, "She's not there, Forrester. Can't you see them slipping down the shrouds to starboard?" and the poor delirious wretch fell into the trap. Doing what no sane acrobat could probably have done, he moved back a pace along the wire, seized the mast, and lowered himself into the shrouds, when at a signal from the mate the man there slipped aside to let him pass.

When the friendly pursuers reached the deck they found the bos'n huddled against the bulwarks, shaking like a leaf, and too weak to stand erect, now the temporary strength of the malaria madness had passed, and they carried him gently back to the forecastle. His story, as told by a seaman comrade, was a simple one. His wife had died two days before he reached home last voyage, and the shock of finding her body had been too much for the poor fellow's fever-weakened brain. He was sane enough when well, but each time the delirium laid hold upon him, he became possessed with the idea that the dead woman called to him for help against some one who followed her with murderous intent. He never recovered from the last outbreak, and was buried at sea three days afterwards; but few on board wondered at what had happened, for they knew that men almost on the point of death occasionally become possessed of unusual strength in the accessions of malaria madness.

There was much talk on the subject of missionary influence in the factory at Brass that night, and it is almost a pity that for sufficient reasons the conversation might not be set down in full. The missionary question is, however, a very difficult one to discuss, for in a region of darkest barbarism one would hesitate lest any chance word should depreciate the patient efforts of those who only too often perish while trying to let in the light. Endless sacrifices have been made, man after man has been stricken down by the pestilence, and yet Christianity would seem to gain ground but slowly, and it is occasionally hard to see much improvement in the negro when his conversion is said to have been effected. Still no treatise on Western Africa would be complete without a passing mention of the missionaries and their work, and the attempt must be made.

To begin with, it may be taken for granted that the majority of the missionaries, especially on the

Niger, are long-suffering earnest men, who in the face of many difficulties are sowing for a harvest which in its own due time will be reaped. But with equal frankness it must be said that the conduct of others is either marked by mistaken zeal or undue consideration for the loaves and fishes, while a few apparently only cumber the ground.

CHAPTER XXII.

MISSIONARY INFLUENCE.

Two mistakes at least would seem to be made by those who send out unsuccessful missionaries. Among one or two of the smaller denominations an unquestioning belief in the somewhat exclusive virtues of their own particular creed and an abundant flow of language are apparently considered sufficient qualifications, and the results of this error are apparent. It is true that among the apostles and the first teachers of Christianity were lowly men strong in faith and all untrained in earthly knowledge; but there is no Pentecost in these latter days, and in place of being gifted with sudden wisdom, power, and eloquence, a man may only attain thereto by continued effort and patient study. Thus it happens that the missionary of the "converted policeman" type sometimes fails, and fails lamentably, if he attempt to propagate his teaching among people of a certain stage of mental development whose religion is, after all, founded at least upon truth, such as many of the Moslem races. Why policemen should be chosen it is hard to say; but although it may have been a mere coincidence, the writer remembers coming across three at least endeavouring to spread the Gospel along the coast of Western Africa and the islands adjacent thereto.

It is needless to point out that the man does not fail because he has been a policeman, but because such a one is lacking in the stamp of intellect and refinement which, strange to say, the savage recognises. Even the half-naked swamp heathen appreciate what may be termed natural rank and dignity, either inborn or acquired by self-command and patience, while among the swarthy desert tribesmen of the north-west this perception is even more marked. Thus it happens that a young Government officer journeying almost unattended is received with a certain respect which is not always accorded to a missionary travelling, as he is apt to do, with a retinue. How the swamp-dweller acquires this power of classification it is difficult to see, but the man of plain straight-forward speech, quiet ways, and unostentatious self-respect, wins at least his attention; while another, arrogant, assertive, loud-voiced, or marked by any coarser attributes of the kind, is at once set down as a "so-so white bushman."

I remember once chatting with a Spanish padre,

a man who, being paid 11 dollars a-month, eked out this sum by tilling a strip of land himself, toiling long hours each day, and nevertheless kept a village of superstitious Canario peasants in a high state of morality and order, which is a hard thing to do. It was on board a coasting steamer near the shore of North-West Africa, and on the square of the forward hatch a somewhat blatant British missionary was holding forth in very indifferent Castilian to a crowd of emigrants for Cuba. Now, although a Protestant by conviction as well as upbringing, it jarred upon me to hear a countryman not preaching the Gospel, but hurling abuse at another creed; and, somewhat ashamed, I endeavoured to apologise to my companion. But the old *cura* was wise with a wisdom acquired in many walks of life, and I remember there was a faint smile in the far-seeing eyes as he said, "He speaks well, but he speaks too much; my people are not children. No, I do not mind; we have seen many of his kind come and go: why should we heed such idle talk? But surely your countrymen are foolish to send out men like this."

There was another of the kind I came across in the Niger region — domineering, tyrannical in little things, violent in temper, and a lover of the smooth things of life, who would have been improved by a period of probation in a four-master's forecastle or the barracks of a recruit battalion. He seemed genuine at heart and possessed a rough eloquence of his own, but one could hardly help the feeling that this was not the kind of man to set forth the merits of a religion in which humility is combined with majesty. There is often a curious affinity between apparent opposites, and the highest and the lowest are sometimes nearer each other than the divisions of the middle grade. Thus it comes about not infrequently that the man of good birth and high education can live contentedly amid more trying surroundings, suffer hardship better, and win more influence over the degraded bushman than another chosen from a humbler state of life,—and this is less of a paradox than may appear at first sight.

One society at least makes the mistake of allowing its representatives to trade,—in cotton cloth ostensibly, though the factory agents hint that gin-cases change hands as well. In any case, it is rather hard to see how any commerce with the natives could be carried on unless the Hamburg potato-spirit is occasionally dealt in. Another man I heard of did a good deal of the work about his station by the aid of slave labour. As his wife naïvely explained, "We have to hire some of our boys from the headman, for we cannot always get enough ourselves;" and a smile went round, for all present knew that the headman's boys were neither more nor less than domestic slaves.

"What do you do when they won't work—none of those people are fond of labour?" asked a listener with malice prepense; and the answer was plain enough, "My husband has a whip, or he tells the headman and he thrashes them."

One new-comer seemed astonished, and when I afterwards came across the gentleman in question I felt I would hardly care to be one of those headman's boys.

Nevertheless there are some men of scanty training who occasionally accomplish much, or make a heroic end, through the power of a single purpose coupled with dauntless resolution. We met one of these once wandering aimlessly round a certain semi-Spanish settlement not far from the borders of the wild region that runs southward from Morocco in a vain search for quarters. He could speak but a few words of Spanish, knew nothing of the Berber dialect, and only one or two phrases of indifferent Arabic, and yet he was waiting for a schooner that was to land him on the fringe of the wilderness of hot sandstone hills into which he would penetrate to convert the nomad tribes. We took the man in hand, entertained him for the night, and found him absolutely genuine and filled with a conviction of his ultimate success that was almost pitiful. I remember thinking as I listened what a desperate and yet heroic forlorn hope it was. One man about to venture alone into a region peopled by fanatic

Moslem who would have no white intruders in their domains, and made short work of even the Sultan's officers if they set foot therein without a force of cavalry behind them, filled with a childish faith in his ability to controvert the teachings of the grey-haired sheiks who held absolute temporal as well as spiritual rule! Many of the latter, we knew, were men of considerable intellectual power, in which our acquaintance was clearly lacking, and yet he was troubled by no doubts and certainly felt no fear. He gave me a copy of a Spanish Bible he had been distributing before we sailed, and I have it now, a memento of a very brave man. We heard long afterwards that a European, supposed to be the same, had been shot when crossing a dangerous wady into a forbidden region.

I also remember a certain detachment of missionaries, fourteen in all, I think, sailing for "the coast," and afterwards being told that nine out of the number died there before their first year ran out.

Another weakness of some missionaries is an over-fondness for fine quarters and comfortable surroundings, with a hankering after political influence. It is scarcely necessary for the teacher of humility to have the finest house in the district, or travel with many bearers to carry his personal comforts. In this he sometimes errs; and speaking of the out-of-the-way corners of the earth in general, as well as Africa, it is not always pleasing to find the missionary intent on making himself a power in the land, and dwelling amid comparative luxury, while his flock live and die around him like the beasts of the field.

Perhaps one of the great secrets of the success of the Jesuit missions is that the messengers of Rome almost invariably live as do their flock, often labouring with their own hands to gain a sustenance as well as preaching, and thus win a hold upon the hearts of the people, because, living as they live, they can understand their needs. In various parts of the world I have met them, patient, indefatigable men, wise in all the wisdom of ancient Greece and Rome, speaking many modern languages, and yet not infrequently proficient in manual toil. One who honoured me with his friendship in British Columbia was perhaps the most expert axeman in a region where the colonists are born to the felling of trees. He had raised a little church, not by collections made at home, but with his own axe and auger and the aid of a few Siwash converts; and he was always as ready to advise his followers about the caulking of a whale-boat or the stripping of a Winchester breech as he was about matters spiritual. I often fancied, and I know that wiser men think so too, that some of our own missionaries do not interest themselves sufficiently in the earthly wants and miseries of those they would convert, and thus knit themselves together in a bond of common humanity; for, after all, the heart of a man is very much the same, whatever be the colour of his skin.

There are, however, many Protestant missionaries now who live amid the swamps and forests with only the barest necessities at their command, building dispensary or tiny church with their own blistered or bleeding hands, and, accepting privation instead of comfort, have won strange power thereby. Some among them, too, have been sent forth by a Church which at home loves magnificence and a stately service, and these would seem voluntarily to take up a deadly post or plunge themselves into the awful isolation of the swampland with equal readiness. Imitation is easier than the obeying of precept, and the savage can more readily understand when the preacher himself sets the example of abstinence, restraint, and diligent labour; while there was reason in the Egyptian trooper's explanation of his preference for a Frankish rather than a Turkish officer. With the latter it was, "Go on, you accursed fellaheen;" with the other, "Follow me."

After all, to preach Christianity in Africa is a hard thing, and it is reassuring to find that, in these days of ever-increasing personal luxury and reluctance to endure bodily pain, there are men willing to suffer for their religion. It becomes occasionally only too apparent that among those who hold leading places in our churches and chapels at home there are some impelled by vanity and a desire for the worship of their fellows, who labour chiefly to advance their own particular glory, or at least that of the sect they ornament, rather than the good of the cause.

But when a man has voluntarily turned his back upon all the brighter side of life, and, casting aside fair prospects, accepts derision instead of respect and hunger instead of plenty, there can be little doubt that he desires to serve rather than rule his fellow-men, and does all things not for personal honour but to the glory of God. And there are such in the Niger delta,—men who have given up, humanly speaking, all that the heart could desire, while the crosses of many more moulder beneath the palms, and of these it may be said that we gave the Dark Continent of our best. Surely those who stayed on in the disease-scourged stations when they knew their strength was gone, willing to risk death rather than that their district should suffer, deserve the name of martyr as well as any saint of olden days.

In the amphitheatre or on the scaffold death came more or less swiftly, and a man of good courage might face the Numidian lion or bow his neck to the sword with triumph rather than shrinking, that he might show the wondering multitude how the faithful could meet their end.

So many died, and through long ages their memories have served as a great encouragement. But the modern martyr in the fever-belt has even more trying things to face. He is not called upon to go forth before the eyes of assembled thousands to meet a splendid death, but to walk daily and hourly beneath the shadow, alone in a barbarous land, and when the end comes, often to give up his life in the isolation of the swamps, deserted it may be even by his alien servants, and—there is little doubt it has happened—attacked by ravening insects before the last breath was drawn. In this there is neither romance nor the enthusiasm of a crisis, only a weary struggle year after year amid squalor and misery, which probably requires a higher kind of courage to maintain than to accept the risk of a violent end. And this has been done many times in the Niger delta, and elsewhere in Africa.

Probably the missionary's great weapon is medical knowledge, for the African is a fervent believer in physic. He will take gallons of it if he can obtain it gratis, and always credits the dispenser thereof with almost superhuman wisdom. Thus the medical missionary has a means of gaining widespread influence, which it would be his own fault if he did not turn to good account. Even supposing no great spiritual progress resulted, there is so much unchecked native suffering in Western Africa that the man who merely alleviated the lot of a pestilence-stricken tribe, and taught them how to live cleaner and healthier lives, would have done a great work in the cause of distressed humanity.

There was one English lady I remember meeting on her way to take up mission work. She was young, fragile, and pretty, and at first sight far more fitted to be sheltered by a husband's care at home than to venture among the barbarity of the bush. The grim old Clydesdale engineer looked after her as though she had been a child all the passage, and every now and then when out of a full heart she spoke of what she hoped to do, the Government officials smiled pityingly, and afterwards said hard things about those who had sent her out. The day the first swarm of Krooboys, howling, and many of them absolutely naked savages, came off several hundred strong from a thundering Liberian beach was a revelation. These were not the benighted forest-dwellers of her imagination, guileless heathen waiting for the Gospel, but very real devil-worshippers, and some of them cannibals, ever ready with keen matchet or gouging thumb to rip out an enemy's eye, who promptly got wildly intoxicated on the gin they procured on board, while the little English they spoke was half profanity. The poor woman stared at them gasping, then burst into tears and fled; and when the engineer, who had daughters as old at home, played the part of rough comforter, she choked out, "It is all so very different to what I expected. Surely they cannot all be in this awful state." But the man of steam and fuel could only hold his peace, for he knew the Niger tribes were considerably worse than that.

It was hours before the missionary lady appeared on deck again, and for several days she was very white-faced and silent; but she had no thought of turning back, and I believe did a good work before she too died and was buried in Africa.

Everywhere the world over the climate of the tropics bears much harder on women than men. Where it is dry and free from malaria you may see Englishmen thrive and grow bronzed, broad-shouldered, and wiry; but their wives and daughters almost invariably weaken and wither, or drag out their lives in chronic listlessness. Now, one society at least insists upon its messengers being married, and in doing so, although there may be strong reasons for it, condemns many Englishwomen to untold misery, or death, which is more merciful. And yet there are plenty ready to bear with fortitude whatever may befall them by their husband's side, and when you meet them in Africa one glance at the drawn white face, as a rule, tells the tragedy of their lives. Of these may it not be written, "They also serve"?

Once a Niger trader told us an instructive story,

which he said was true. A young and energetic missionary, in order to teach his flock the blessings of labour, procured with much trouble a Haussa from the north to instruct them how to make the beautiful Kanu cloth and embroidered leather-work. The negro is curious and imitative, if not over-fond of application, and the converts learned rapidly. At last a satisfactory assortment of passable goods was ready, and then that missionary made a grave mistake. He allowed his people to take it down river to the factories themselves for sale, giving them as encouragement in this case only a free hand to make purchases in return. The converts came back, most of them in a state of blind intoxication, with cases of Hamburg gin and murderous flintlock guns, and—so the trader expressed it—"there was unlimited Sheol about that station for two days afterwards."

In the end, while they may not all be perfect, and a few perhaps even unfitted for their task, there are many noble men among our West African missionaries. There are good and indifferent in every calling, and who would venture to discriminate? So they must grow together side by side, and by their work they shall be known, for at the end of all things that which is true must prevail.

CHAPTER XXIII.

BONNY AND OPOBO.

BONNY was inspected next, and the visit was not a particularly pleasant one. I had not looked forward with any degree of satisfaction to a call there, for several acquaintances were good enough to inform me that this was "the ghastliest place in Africa," and I had already seen a fair number of ghastly places. The settlement appeared to justify the description, for standing as it does near the mouth of one of the foulest of foul rivers with a maze of quagmires about it, Bonny town is a singularly uninviting spot. This watery desolation occupies what is strictly speaking the eastern extremity of the delta, for the Opobo river, which hems it in, thirty miles to the east, is the last of the waterways connected by interlacing creeks with the parent river. The Niger Coast Protectorate, however, stretching about a hundred miles farther east, takes in the estuary of Old Calabar, fed chiefly by the wide Cross river, which rises no white man knows where, in a mysterious land to the north.

We lay rolling wildly all night in the deep-loaded steamer somewhere outside the spouting shoals, with the rush of a south-wester howling through the rigging, and the roar of the rain drowning the thunder of the surf. When morning broke we groped our way shorewards through a thick curtain of falling water, which for the most part hid the forest from sight, and having spent an unpleasant quarter of an hour on one or two African bars, I felt considerably easier in mind when at last we made out a plunging buoy. Presently the rain thinned a little, and we could see apparently detached islands of mangroves swathed half their height in steam. Here lay a clump of dismal foliage, there a broad stretch of mist and tumbling water, then a patch of trees again—and of all kinds of navigation the entering of a West African river mouth must be about the worst. Looking at it from seaward, the ways in are apparently innumerable, and one patch of mangroves is exactly like another; while the low-lying forest behind is either hidden in mist, or, in fierce hot weather, hangs as it were suspended in air above a shimmering lagoon, which on nearer approach proves to be only the effect of a mirage-like refraction.

This is one of the difficulties which keep the

whole trade of the littoral practically in the hands of three or four steamship companies; for a native pilot is not, as a rule, to be trusted, and it would be a very risky matter for a bewildered stranger to take his steamer in. Thus when there is a cargo to be picked up anywhere between Singapore and the Nitrate Coast the prowling ocean-tramps leave West Africa severely alone, and when in times of great depression a wandering freighter with empty holds, tempted by 20s. or more a-ton, ventures along this dangerous coast, she frequently either leaves her bones there or loses half her unsalted crew from fever.

As had happened elsewhere, we struck the shoals, which lie in the shape of a V off the twin mouths of the Bonny and New Calabar rivers, and struck them badly too. There was a rush of foam across the after-deck, a cataract of muddy water spouted up and hid the poop from sight, and then with a pounding of iron on sand the steamer drove ahead. Most of those on board her felt thankful when she slid into smoother water, and presently the anchor thundered down,—for so heavy was the renewed downpour that every surrounding object became invisible, and this was no place to navigate with any kind of rashness. Then as the forests lifted themselves out of the rain again, and once more took shape and form, we slowly moved ahead, and in due time brought up off the settlement of Bonny.

The rain had ceased when we went ashore, and the wind had also fallen dead away, until there was not an air to rustle the dripping foliage, and the whole place lay still beneath an oppressive weight of steam. Beyond the narrow beaches, where the factories stand and the cemetery, lies the native town of Bonny, and it is as filthy and squalid a place, or at least was then, as could well be imagined. Splashing along a road beneath big trees, from whose branches cascades dripped upon our already half-soaked garments, we came upon a mixed-up collection of native dwellings, inferior to anything we had seen in Africa. The forest had given place to an undergrowth of mangroves crawling out of mire, and among these, perched apparently in the foulest places that could be found, were endless rickety huts. Some were walled with mud, others mere bundles of reed-mat trussed together with sticks; and, where possible, they hung above a hollow of mud — a natural ditch, most likely, for no Bonny man would waste labour on anything of the kind, doubtless for the convenient jettison of refuse. There were, I should say, nearly three hundred huts in that collection, and the place swarmed with life,—big men, women who could hardly be described as other than hideous, and naked children crawling and wallowing wherever they could find a patch of greasy slime. We had seen the Krooboys' dwellings beside the thundering Liberian beaches; and these, with their well-built walls and neat thatch, the hissing surf in front, and the stately palms behind, were picturesque and even orderly. Also in other parts of the Niger region we had wandered among well-constructed huts where a certain degree of cleanliness was observed, and the inhabitants of fine physique. But in Bonny the case was different, and it was evident that long contact with European traders had done nothing for the negro. White men have visited this river for almost three centuries, and yet the condition of the Bonny people can best be described as "sickening." There is in many parts of Africa a wise regulation which enforces the erection of sanitary arrangements upon the river-bank or beach, and requires the wearing of at least a certain amount of apparel. In this settlement, however, the former were not in evidence; and as we passed very cautiously between the huts, we saw that a proportion of the inhabitants of both sexes disdained such vanities as garments. Many of them also bore the marks of various loathsome diseases which are chiefly seen in places where Europeans congregate, and a brief inspection was sufficient to turn us back disgusted and silent, while few thoughtful men could have gone through that place open-eyed without being oppressed by the inferences to be drawn from that which they had seen. It is a difficult matter to give an accurate idea of West African life, for there are so many things which cannot be set down, and the curtain may not be wholly lifted. Further, the men best qualified to grapple with grave evils become, as it were, so used to encountering things which would once have shocked them that insensibly they come to accept them as part of the natural order.

It must, however, be borne in mind that the work of reformation is a very difficult one, and the authorities meet with serious obstacles in their efforts to make improvements. From what one can gather here and along the coast, the tribesmen between the Bonny river and the neighbouring estuary of the Opobo have long been probably the most barbarous and intractable savages in Africa. In the swamps and forests behind these two settlements the most revolting practices are carried out—cannibalism, human sacrifices, and atrocities almost worse than the burying of women alive. To increase the difficulties of the white rulers, these natives are also the reverse of cowards, and have shown they can face uneven odds with a dogged endurance worthy of a better cause. One instance may be given.

In 1889 the Opobo people were reported to be arming themselves on an extensive scale, and when the Consulate officials found that the rumours were true, and that almost every tribesman possessed a firearm, many of them weapons of precision, they feared that a general rising or great bush-raid was on hand. Therefore the headmen of Opobo were summoned to give up their guns, and, as might have been expected, contemptuously refused. Further palaver followed, but the black warriors remained obdurate, and a gunboat was sent to enforce the mandate. Still the natives held out, and as it appeared only too probable that an attempt to seize the weapons would meet with fierce resistance and result in much loss of life, a notice was again sent to the mutineers that until the guns were given up a strict blockade would be enforced, and no canoe allowed to enter or leave the place.

It was an unfortunate affair all through. While the gunboat lay there sweltering in fervent heat until her paint peeled off in blisters and the caulking spewed from her seams, the white seamen sickened one by one. Inside the blockaded town it was even worse: men ate vermin, and fought like wild beasts over the boring crabs when they came up out of the slime, or lay still and starved; but the answer to each summons was the same, "We will not give up the guns."

So, beneath the scorching glare of noonday or through the deadly vapours at night, the seamen patrolled the creeks with gig and launch, though each day the boats' crews grew fewer, and now and then the bluejackets were sickened at the sight of the floating bodies of women and children starved to death inside or drowned trying to escape under the cover of darkness. But the spirit of the heathen was still unbroken, and they yelled defiance at the oarsmen, or crawled among the mangroves for a quiet shot at any who might venture into range. Then the gunboat's commander died, and of all the sickly skeletons on board there were scarcely enough left to get the gig over the side, and the starving men of Opobo held out grimly yet.

At last the authorities in mercy ordered the war-vessel to return; and manned by broken-down, half-dead wretches, some among them raving mad, she steamed away to sea. And so the people of Opobo kept their guns, and showed that the heathen savage possesses a few heroic qualities, as well as many vices. After this Englishmen were not looked upon with loving eyes in the region which lies between Opobo and the Cross river, and a few years later several strong expeditions had to be sent up the creeks, and Itu on the latter stream was held by a picked garrison because the natives threatened to march south and burn all the white traders out.

On my way back to the river I visited two graves in the Bonny cemetery, having known the men who lay there, and the story of the last was a very common one. He had traded for many years among the oil rivers, and eventually set up a factory on the coast. For a time he prospered, and suffering but slightly from fever, returned home an old man with a sufficiency. During a little time he enjoyed a well-earned repose, and then became, as often happens, unsettled and discontented. The life was too tame, he was bound fast by so many customs, and it always rained, he said. Africa was bad, but this was worse; and, disregarding the remonstrances of all his friends, he went back to the Niger coast to take charge of a factory. He had been there but a little time when he fell sick—of fever it was generally believed, though some whispered of poison — and two weeks later was buried beside the Bonny river. This man was driven by no financial necessity, but he had lived the life of the rivers too long to settle down to the narrow ways at home.

After what we had seen in the heathen town that morning, it was a relief to visit the settlement about the Church Mission a little way downstream. Here it was evident the preachers had not laboured in vain. The huts were clean and orderly, the inhabitants decently clad, and there was a general air of comfort and prosperity about the village which formed a marked contrast to the other. It was reassuring to see there were places where Christianity had power to change and sweeten the negro's life, and teach him to live soberly and industriously. The triumph was the greater that it had been brought about by mere force of example and humane influence, without the aid of either gunboats or Yoruba bayonets; and one felt that if wise and earnest men could work such a change in the condition of a race like this, there was hope of great results elsewhere. This was one of the favourite stations of Bishop Crowther, the black man's bishop and ruler of the see of Western Africa. His story was a romantic one, and in spite of much testimony to the contrary, shows the latent possibilities of the negro race.

Whether the good bishop was originally a Moslem or a Christian does not appear, but he came of the Yoruba race dwelling in the Lagos hinterland, and few of these people or their neighbours, the Egbas, are heathen. The latter have long professed a kind of Christianity, and have suffered much persecution for it. When young he was seized and carried away as a slave, but the vessel on board which he was stowed with many other miserable wretches fell into the hands of a British cruiser, and the future evangelist was freed and sent to a mission school at Lagos. Various people took an interest in him, so that he gained an opportunity of study, and was eventually ordained in England, and then went back to preach the Gospel in his native land, where strange success rewarded his efforts. Once when entering Abbeokuta market-place with his retinue of carriers he met the mother he had not seen for many years, and had long thought was dead. It must have been a strange meeting between the old negro woman, an untaught dweller in the forest, and the civilised gentleman and ordained priest, who had learned all that the white men could teach him, and travelled with a twofold authority. The venerable bishop has done his part well—so well that even the traders, who are not as a rule over-fond of the missionary, have little but approbation to speak of him. After all, he may have been but the forerunner of a host of sable evangelists; for if native converts occasionally fall away, and sometimes reflect little credit upon their faith, it must be remembered that great changes do not come suddenly. The ground must first be prepared with tireless patience, and the purpose that can hold on in spite of apparent failure and sickening disappointment will win success at last.

CHAPTER XXIV.

THE OPPOSITE ENDS OF THE NIGER.

EQUALLY with the unhealthy delta through which its muddy waters empty themselves into the sea, the spot where, amid a wilderness of broken peaks, the Niger first springs from the earth is included in a British Protectorate. What the coast-line of Sierra Leone is, and a little of the character of its inhabitants, the writer has endeavoured to show, as well as what may be seen among the mangrove-lined mouths of the great African river. Now it may be interesting to glance at a few of the principal races dwelling between these coast-wise strips and the semi-civilised interior.

Behind the little colony of Sierra Leone there stretches northwards a British Protectorate whose area it is difficult to exactly compute, rich in palm-oil, kola-nuts, and rubber. Taken as a whole, it is a rugged region intersected by parallel ranges crested to the summit with eternal verdure, or rising bare masses of granite from the forests at their feet.

Between lie deep valleys where every product of the tropics might be grown, in addition to those which only wait the gathering; but from two reasons—the lethargic condition of its inhabitants and the lack of means of transport—little has been done. This is not surprising when it is remembered that carriage on almost any goods down to the harbour of Freetown would cost as much as 20s. a-hundredweight for a distance of one hundred miles, and that its only roads are tiny trails winding in and out like serpents through steamy forests or brakes of giant cane. Also every here and there they are crossed by swamps, the like of which is probably not to be found elsewhere in the world. In this region there are no mangroves to gather the river-mud, and in process of time bind it into land, after which the water-loving tree, having accomplished its task, gives place to palms and cotton-woods. Instead, and along the hollows of almost every waterflow, there winds for league after league a waste of shivering mire bare and loathsome, or hidden by a treacherous covering of grass and reeds. These must be crossed by the bearer-trains waist-deep, and it sometimes happens that the carrier-boys, weighted by the burdens upon their woolly heads, are sucked down by the hungry swamp. Now, however, a railway is being constructed towards the interior of the country, and when the locomotive has replaced the

T

human bearer a great change will be wrought in the destiny of the Protectorate of Sierra Leone.

Three thousand three hundred feet above sea-level, a little to the northward of Mount Daro, and 2500 miles from the Nun river bar, there lies a lonely ravine. All about it ramparts of igneous rock, whose defiles are choked with forest or fenced off by thickets of giant cane, rise in tumbled chaos; while its sides are lined by mighty trees bound and festooned by creepers, which shut out the light of day and wrap the gorge in perpetual shadow. At the upper end there stands a moss-grown boulder, and the tiny rill that trickles from the bubbling pool beneath it is the first of the Niger, or Diuliba, as it is called on its higher reaches. For year after year only the wild creatures of the forest enter that silent gorge, for the Kuranko bushman believes it to be an abode of devils, and no reward will tempt him to venture there. Indeed for many miles it is said no native will drink the waters or build his hut beside its banks.

Perhaps the most numerous race of the Sierra Leone bush are the Mendis, dwelling behind Sherboro,—men of great muscular strength, and, curious to relate, capable of arduous labour, but intensely ignorant, and degraded almost to bestial stupidity. Thus for generations this people has been forced into servitude by neighbours of somewhat higher scale; and even the naked bushman looks down with contempt on a Mendi, though the latter have done good work on one or two Government expeditions.

Farther north and along the fringe of the Niger watershed dwell the Kuranko heathen, superior to the Mendis in mental development, but, with the exception of a little desultory trade, living after the usual manner of the West African bushman in slothful indolence. Still here and there a few towns and villages have received the faith of Islam, and a change becomes manifest. Every such place is said to have a school, and its commercial standing and prosperity are in marked contrast to that of the district around. Then there are the Limba Moslem to the south, civilised to some extent, cultivating the land and selling their products both upon the thundering beaches and northwards across the Kong.

Yet for decades these races have dwelt with the sword hanging above their heads, for just beyond the great mountain barrier of the Kong lies the kingdom of Samadu and the territories of his tributary emirs. These, with their occasional allies the Sofas and Konnos, are greedy of conquest, well trained to the use of arms, and regard the blotting out of a heathen village, or even a Moslem one of doubtful orthodoxy, as a very virtuous act, the more so if there is anything worth carrying away therein. Thus the native of the Protectorate dwells in constant terror of a visit from his soldier neighbours, and more than once only the strong arm of the Government has stood between him and extermination. Not very long ago periodical collisions and much friction took place between parties of French and British black soldiery marching against small bands of Arab raiders, including the tragedy at Weima, though there were others in which loss of life occurred whose details were little known outside the colony. Now, however, the frontier limits have been more clearly defined, and the bush policeman has only the marauder's weapons to face.

In this region we see the same old story written very plainly again, and one cannot too strongly emphasise the fact that a wave of Moslem conquest is steadily rolling southwards across the whole of Western Africa. In places a way is cleared with fire and sword, and emir or sultan grinds down his new subjects with tyrannical cruelty. In others the waste places are cultivated, a state of at least partial order is maintained, and on the frontier of every British Protectorate the testimony is the same—the whole trade and prosperity is to be found in Moslem districts. Already there remains only a comparatively thin line of coastwise forest untouched by Mahommedan influence, and, if Christianity is ever to win a permanent footing in the fever-land, its teachers have little time to lose. As we have shown, the possibility of a great "jehad," or holy war, is not to be overlooked; and, judging from the struggle France had to hold her colony of Senegal against one emir alone, such a struggle would be a very terrible one, and its end impossible to foresee. Probably Samadu, if joined by one or two of his neighbours, could give more trouble in the Western Sudan than the Mahdi has done in the east, and some day a great war-cloud may break across the length of the hinterland.

The semi-Arab peoples do their work in ways which seem strange to European eyes, but for all that they bring about great results, and there are few corners of Africa north of the line where their merchants have not been. For one example, it may be stated that cutlery and weapons of European make are carried by them across the desert from Tripoli and other Barbary states, and sold within 300 miles of the Guinea coast in competition with the white traders of the factories. How this is done it is hard to understand, but the fact remains.

And now looking eastwards again towards British territory at the other end of the Niger, we also find that the negro steadily improves mentally and morally as one travels north. Following the great river inland from its mouth, at a distance of about 100 miles the Ibo country is reached, and here there is already a marked contrast with the races dwelling among the mangroves of the estuaries. The Ibo people, though they have very little love for white intruders, seem to be a brave and particularly intelligent race, the men short in stature but of splendid muscular development, and the women when young said to resemble statues in ebony. Their huts are scrupulously clean, and an Ibo village is remarkable for its orderliness and freedom from the many things which sicken the white observer who enters a coastwise town. They have good, if somewhat draconic, laws of their own, probably acquired by contact with the people farther north, for the Ibos are also shadowed by fetiche superstition. Murder is punished by death, theft by death or the selling of the culprit into slavery, and the penalty of adultery, which is especially abhorred, is the confiscation of everything the offender possesses. Indeed, on the northern fringe of this country, the guilty persons, if of any rank, are forced to drink poisonous sassa-water before the assembled people, and their death serves as a public warning. Thus the Ibos, in spite of occasional outbreaks of African cruelty, are already far in advance of the tribesmen lower down the river.

Both Roman Catholic and Protestant missionaries have laboured in the Ibo country, but, it would seem, hitherto with slight success. It is said, however, that they waste time and energy trying to controvert each other's teaching, or at least allow their black adherents to get up feuds among themselves, and all the time — one and irresistible — the influence of the Crescent is spreading south to meet them.

Next, and still farther north, above Onitsha, we find the Igaras, who have made a further advance; and again the traveller notes that just laws are made and firmly enforced. Here, too, murder and theft are punished by death, adultery by slavery, lying and malicious slander by the drinking of sassa poison, and, curious to relate, in the case of domestic slavery a kind of trial by jury exists. No master may either kill or dispose of a servant of this kind unless with the consent of the latter's equals; that is to say, the power of life and death lies in the hands of the slaves themselves.

In the native town of Onitsha, which, with a population of 17,000, lies opposite to the Royal Niger Company's station of Asaba, and just south of the Igara country, the missionaries have gained a footing, although here until very recently, and the writer is not sure whether it is entirely abolished yet, a large slave-market was held. In the time of low water a great bank of sand filled the middle of the river, and almost within sight of the white ensign with its red St George's cross and quarterings of " Ars, Jus, Pax," men and women were bought and sold at the rate of about one hundred a-month until the Niger rising with the rains swept market and slave-dealers' huts away. The usual vertical rise, from June to September, is nearly 30 feet, so the force of the river can be readily understood.

Of these two races there are many subdivisions, marked in case of the former by tribal tokens in blue tattoo or vertical cicatrices in forehead and cheeks, some of whom paint white rings about their eyes and use antimony on the lashes, though the Igara peoples disdain any decoration of the kind. But, as we have seen, none of them are utter savages: the latter dwell under our consul's eyes, close to the seaboard factories.

Then at Lokoja the edge of Moslem influence is reached, and this town is a close collection of grass huts or buildings of rammed-down earth, each standing in a tiny compound screened by partitions of matting 6 feet high; for here, as generally happens, the family life of the follower of the Prophet is screened from public gaze. In Lokoja there is a constant coming and going of trade canoes and caravans, and a gathering of all the races of the hinterland. Haussas, Nupes, Fulahs, Yorubas, merchants, slave-dealers, fanatic Mallah missionaries, teachers of the Koran, and men of all shades of colour from ebony to golden bronze, many of whom can read Arabic, throng its streets, for Lokoja holds the keys of the gateway of the north. The Church Missionary Society has a fine station here, but the preaching of peace is at a discount just now. News comes in periodically of bands of splendidly armed horsemen riding through the hinterland on some mysterious quest. Rumours are carried down the river of preparations for some hastily organised "jehad," to burn a village and make proselytes or slaves, and the Chartered Company's stern-wheelers steam panting against the current loaded with swarthy troops and piled-up ammunition-cases. Lokoja is at present a great depot camp, and it may happen before very long that its name will be in many mouths, for there would seem to be a growing restlessness among the powerful races beyond it. In any campaign against them there is one possibility of danger, or at least uncertainty, which affects both the representatives of the Government and the servants of the Chartered Company. Our West African troops, with the exception of the West India battalions at Sierra Leone and a few Gold Coast Fantis, are all Moslem of the hinterland. I have heard the stories of some of these men, and they were much alike. Often they are the sons of the less esteemed wives of some northern ruler, proud of their birth, or persons who, having fallen from places of dignity through intrigue or misfortune, disdain to work or trade. Thus they come south, being already skilled in arms, to enter the service of the British Government or the Royal Niger Constabulary, and have many times given ample proof of valour and fidelity in action against the heathen. Also in the campaign against the robber horsemen of Ilorin, and when they marched with the famous expedition which seized the slave-raiding stronghold of Bida, Haussa and Yoruba served their white masters gallantly against men of their own faith. There are also stories told in the coastwise consulates of acts of heroic devotion to their fever-stricken leaders, or the sound sense and courage of some black sergeant who, when his white officer lay unconscious in delirium, held the beleaguered outpost or carried him out through trails that were ambushed at every ford.

For all that, things have happened which show that the fanatical hatred of the infidel may break out some time when least expected, and that it is chiefly the military prowess of the Government and the ability of its officers which commands the respect of these men. Thus if it should come about that in the event of a great Moslem rising our black soldiers failed us, the Government would be helpless; for, as the French found to their cost, white soldiers are of little use in the hinterland. After all, we rule by prestige and by a strong hand, for the nomad free-lance seeks to serve the most powerful master. If we lost that prestige, which is practically intrusted to the keeping of a handful of sickly men, it is very hard to say what might not happen.

So far, however, the Protectorate troops and the Royal Niger Constabulary have done faithful service, and in return the Chartered Company takes good care of its men. At most of their stations may be seen the neat iron-roofed barracks of the unmarried troops, clean and wholesome, while beyond these lies what is called the "soldier town," where those who in return for good conduct have been allowed to marry, live in comfort with their families. With their dazzling white walls, red roofs, the stalwart men in *karki* Zouave uniform armed with Snider and sword-bayonet on guard outside, and the little battery of mountain- or machine-guns drawn up in front, these camps strike the new-comer with a degree of admiration as well as surprise. The troops are well fed, soldierly, and apparently thoroughly contented, and I have heard officials who have been there say that the Yoruba quarters compare not unfavourably with one or two cantonments of white troops in Hindustan. When last at Akassa, I heard the Royal Niger Constabulary numbered about 500 in all, though I believe it has been since increased. This is not a very large army to hold and control what is, after all, a vast empire; but, as pointed out, supremacy is a matter of reputation and moral force as well as numerical power.

CHAPTER XXV.

THE EVOLUTION OF THE BLACK TRADER AND HIS MERCHANDISE.

UNTIL very lately our trade in West Africa has been practically confined to dealings with the seaboard native, and after several passing allusions to this interesting individual it may not be out of place to consider just what kind of man he is, and how he conducts his commerce.

It is unfortunately true that the pure negro with no strain of alien blood is on the West African coast at least an indifferent specimen of humanity. Through many centuries he has been stamped as a being capable of very little more than an animal existence, and often degraded, as it were, below the level of the nobler beasts. There may be some at home who will cavil at this statement, but even a brief personal experience of the negro's ways will fully bear it out, and we have always history. As a matter of fact, every swarthy race which has set its mark upon the Dark Continent north of the

Equator was not originally African but Eastern, and to-day it is only those infused with a strain of the blood of Moor or Arab that make any pretence of civilisation.

In the earlier ages contact with Egyptian, Persian, Carthaginian, Roman, and Greek left the negro unchanged — a savage; and the work of Egyptian sculptor and artist proves that thousands of years before the coming of Christ he was exactly what he is to-day, apparently fitted to be a mere hewer of wood and drawer of water. One glance at the inhabitant of the swamps is sufficient to show why this should be. The facial angle, long arm, long thin leg, prehensile toes, flat foot with its projecting sides and heel and beast-like pad where the hollow of the instep should be, have all analogies to the lower creation and bear out the Darwinian theory. His entire absence of foresight and the power of anticipation show inferior mental capacity, and it is instructive to watch a bushman traverse a forest or inspect the trails he makes. Such a being never walks straight to his destination, but creeps sideways and in bends, as though impelled by an instinct which prompted him thus to deceive some predatory creature as to the direction in which he would go. You may see the small leopard of the coast working in an exactly similar manner, with a stealthy furtive gait, turning aside or hiding every few moments among the brushwood. This is in some measure accounted for by the obstacles in the way; for if he had to traverse the same path a hundred times, the heathen negro would never think of hewing down a projecting branch or slashing a way through a thicket instead of making the perpetual detour around. But even where no obstacle exists, a trail through tall grass never runs straight, but winds in serpentine curves; and one is forced to the conclusion that the bushman travels so because the influence of savage nature is stronger within him than reason.

Neither will he work if it can by any means be avoided, or if he must do so, labours just long enough to secure food for the day, and then squats in listless contentment until he feels the pressure of hunger again. There are one or two notable exceptions, but this is at least the general characteristic of the seaboard races.

Still the negro is covetous, being possessed of the lust of the eye, and if he is a failure as a producer, is not averse to barter, though even so he declines to improve or cultivate the natural riches of the soil, contenting himself with gathering such products as grow ready to hand in the bush. On the Lower Niger the following is the usual way the sable middleman with whom the Europeans deal is evolved from the naked swamp-dweller.

When the young bushman has, by stealing them or otherwise, become possessed of a couple of wives and raised a reedwork hut, some day when more than usually energetic he strolls off into the forest and hews down a certain fine-grain white-wood tree. This is split into boards, and when these are carried home the negro's hard work is done. His wives under the fear of the rod carve it into quaintly worked paddles, and then sliding down-stream in a canoe, if they escape molestation on the way, hang about the steamers at the factories until they can barter them with the seamen for cheap-jack odds and ends, or to the Krooboys for lumps of very high salt-beef saved from their daily rations. Then they return, and their lord goes off into the bush with this "trade," which he exchanges at the nearest native market for so many baskets of kernels or calabashes of oil, while his wives carve more paddles, or catching the little mudfish, dry them in the sun, and set out for a second venture. With good luck the stock of pomade-bottles, needle-packets, or children's toys increases, until at last when the would-be merchant becomes the owner of a puncheon of oil, say 220 gallons, and worth £5 to £6, 10s., he abandons the paddle-making and takes it down in triumph to the factories. With what he receives in return he sets up as a wholesale trader, takes to himself another wife to help with the canoe, and visits remoter markets among the waterways. Later, if opportunity affords, he steals a slave or two or more canoes, and becomes a personage who is admitted to the honour of the white trader's acquaintance, and often induces them to finance him with a considerable value of very curiously assorted goods.

But it is not all plain-sailing. When the consul or other "officer-man" who rules that district is away or sick, the bush tyrants levy a heavy toll on all travellers with merchandise, some of whom occasionally disappear. Again, when a native market has become famous as a suitable centre for the collection and distribution of merchandise, some powerful bush merchant whose business is affected may burn the place to the ground or constitute himself its master at the matchet's edge. It also happens not infrequently that the fetiche priests, being jealous of their followers' relations with the white men, put a Ju-Ju on the creeks, and when this taboo has been declared no negro dare traverse them with his trade-canoes. This is for two reasons. He is to some extent afraid of incurring the wrath of the myriad river-devils, and very much in terror of the poisoned draught or thrust from a corkscrew spear which would follow disobedience. Such a proceeding, it will readily be seen, sadly hampers European commerce in the fever-swamps, and the one offence for which a sable ruler is never forgiven by the authorities is the "closing of the creeks," while free trade is occasionally enforced on the Niger by Yoruba bayonets.

A curious custom was prevalent there a little time ago, and was known as "chopping oil." It happened now and then that a black trader who had obtained a large quantity of British goods on credit found himself unable or unwilling to pay for them, and disregarded the agent's messages urging him to send down oil or kernels in return. Thereupon that agent, especially if he was one of the dissolute ruffians who formerly disgraced their nation on the Niger, armed his Krooboys and lay in wait beside a frequented creek. When a sufficiently rich canoe-train came down he laid violent hands upon it, and informed the owner that So-and-so owed him a certain quantity of oil, and he could collect the debt with interest from the defaulter. Strange to say, the negro merchant did not always object, and if strong enough also seized the first lot of goods he could come across. So the debt was passed on from hand to hand with usury, until some European whose property was confiscated rose up in wrath against a gross injustice he had probably practised himself, or a plundered headman retaliated with the matchet. Then bloodshed began, and whole villages were burnt and sacked over disputes about a few barrels of oil. It was an iniquitous practice, which like other customs of the kind was with difficulty suppressed, and it is whispered that somewhat similar proceedings are not yet altogether unknown in the remoter districts.

Still, in spite of these troubles, the bush trader often manages to extend his business little by little, and in the end becomes the proud owner of a flotilla of canoes with a market of his own, and builds a stockaded village. Then, as in the case of Nana and many others, he sometimes does foolish things, and forgetting that in a British Protectorate justice sooner or later overtakes the offender, wipes out his rivals with the flintlock gun or collects unlawful toll upon the rivers, until some harassed consul sends for a light-draught gunboat and nips his career in the bud.

So much for the black trader, and we may now consider the principal articles he deals in. Palm-oil, kernels, and gin have already been mentioned, but there are also other products of the Niger basin which are exported to a considerable extent. Among these are precious gums of many kinds, from copal, unequalled as a body for varnish, to acacia gums and frankincense, worth almost any price from 90s. to 320s. a hundredweight. These, however, do not as a rule come out *viâ* the delta, but from the higher waters through Sierra Leone, or southwards across the Gold Coast hinterland. Some kinds are not collected from the trees, but dug up, partly fossilised, out of the soil; and I have seen many beautiful specimens, clear as amber and quite as hard, which contained embedded flies. Senegal especially ships large quantities of precious gums obtained from near the source of the Niger.

Then there are the dyes, the bright orange-red barwood, worth up to £5 a-ton, and the beautiful yellow-pink camwood costing as much as £30 a-ton, besides split pieces of ebony at about £13. All these are also sought after by turners of delicate woodwork, but the trade is crippled by the negro's distaste for labour, and timber-cutting is no child's play in the tropics. There are great mahogany forests in many places worth fabulous sums which lie idle through dearth of hands to work them, although now the Gold Coast ships this wood, notably from Axim.

Coffee will grow well anywhere, especially in clearings of the virgin forest; in fact the best in the world is produced in Liberia, but owing to the universal difficulty about labour very little is sent over-seas.

A curious tree of the screw-pine family is to be found about the higher waters of the Gambia and Niger, whose withered seed-pod bursts spontaneously into flame, and often fires the bush.

It may not be generally known that cotton grows wild throughout the greater portion of the Niger basin, and in the time of the American war a large quantity was shipped by way of the Gold Coast and Lagos. It is also sent home periodically at present; but here again the indolence of the negro prevents the development of a prosperous industry, for as he cannot be induced to undertake systematic care of the bushes, the staple is short and brittle. The Moslem of the hinterland, however, cultivate it carefully, and, weaving it in quaint but ingenious handlooms, send down a beautiful fabric dyed blue with indigo to the factories, as well as northwards across the desert. Almost as far as the Nile, and certainly in Southern Morocco, the blue haiques and burnouse of the semi-Arab and Moorish tribes are the products of craftsmen in Kano and Sokoto, and this "country cloth," as it is called, is worth much more along the coast than any turned out in Manchester. The particular cotton-bush which produces the best (the *Gossypium herbaceum*) thrives well near the lower reaches of the Niger in the Lagos colony, and a very large quantity of country cloth comes out over Lagos bar.

Indigo also grows wild in many places in the shape of a woody creeper, and is largely used by the Mahommedans as follows. The leaves are boiled in a large pot, and the juice being strained, is put aside to ferment. It is then poured from pot to pot until thoroughly aerated, when a precipitate begins to settle which is pressed into cones and discs, and if not used for local dyeing is sent down to the factories.

The wonderful properties of the kola-nut, which were well known to the Arabs seven hundred years ago, are just now beginning to be appreciated at home, and this article may be found every here and there along the Niger. It is an insignificant object, something like a crushed-down Brazil kernel, and has a bitter astringent flavour which once tasted can never be mistaken. Thus there need be no question about the genuineness of any preparation said to contain kola. If any extract of the nut is there it will bring its credentials with it. It is eaten with a small piece of ginger, and its stimulating and nourishing properties are such that half a nut will enable a man to march three days without food or drink,—at least, so I was informed by some interior traders, who also said that the Arabs invariably used it when crossing the dry wastes towards the Mediterranean. The nuts are costly, even in West Africa; and once being concerned in the bursting of a small bag which we were heaving on board a launch, the damage was assessed, if I remember rightly, at 3d. for every single nut we lost overboard. In any case, I am sure it was one of the most expensive accidents I was ever personally concerned in. These nuts are also largely shipped to Brazil, though I was informed they often go bad on the way, being perishable, and the natives generally store them in wet clay. A Protectorate doctor told me they owed their sustaining qualities to the amount of caffeine they contained.

All these products of the Niger region, with many others as well — such as ginger, groundnuts, copra, gold-dust, and feathers — are largely exported from its upper waters *viâ* Sierra Leone, the Gold Coast, and Senegal, or from the other end through the Lagos colony and the Niger Coast Protectorate. Before all these, however—and probably destined shortly to become more valuable than the present staple, palm-oil—is rubber: but rubber deserves a chapter to itself.

CHAPTER XXVI.

RUBBER-GATHERING.

Owing to the many mechanical purposes for which its elastic qualities render it almost indispensable, and partly to the rapid extension of the cycle trade, there is now an enormous demand for rubber, which occasionally outruns the supply, even at treble prices. The higher qualities are found upon the Amazon and in the virgin forests of Brazil, and the "best Para" commands considerably more a pound than any other kind. Nevertheless, now that some pains are being taken with its collection and preparation, West African rubber may be used for almost every purpose, and the trade in it has increased by leaps and bounds. A year or two ago a deputation of West African merchants pointed out to the Secretary of State that of all our colonies the West African ones were those whose commerce extended most rapidly, and rubber was given as one instance. In 1882 £1 worth of rubber was exported; in 1883, £2371; and during 1890, 1500 tons were sent home to a value of £131,000; and the quantity has again been largely added to. As one of the deputation said: " This gives an idea of the capability of the West African trade for increase; and yet we say that this trade is only in its infancy, because it has been curbed and crippled by the want of proper means of transport. For instance, rubber costs £10 a-ton for porterage a distance of fifty-five miles. We know that the French and Germans have railways in course of construction, or actually constructed, while we have not got any railway at all, even commenced."

The answer was, " There is no doubt that at the present moment there is hardly any portion of her Majesty's dominions which present greater opportunities for a rapidly increasing trade than the colonies on the Gold Coast " (Gold Coast being here, as often happens, incorrectly used to indicate the whole Guinea shore).

Rubber is to be found in almost all the forests between the Niger and the sea, and abundantly near its mouth in Lagos, though the same difficulty of transport and labour hampers its production; and it is principally shipped from Lagos, Accra, and Sierra Leone. In Africa, as in Brazil and elsewhere, rubber of somewhat similar quality can be obtained from widely different trees and vines—the former of the Ficus or Fig order, and the latter of the order Landolphiæ.

The Landolphiæ, or trailing plants, are the most common source of supply, and a Lagos rubber forest is a striking sight. The creepers, many of whose stems are almost as thick as a man's leg, crawl and plait themselves like twining serpents about the trunks of the trees, hang in festoons from their mighty limbs, and wind in knotted tendrils about the buttressed roots. Their dark-green glossy leaves closing the openings between the branches, shut out the light of day and wrap all below in dusky shade, while the rank odours and smell of steaming earth are almost overpowering. Here and there are clusters of pure white star-cupped flowers, or bunches of fibrous shelled fruit resembling an orange, whose inside pulp is sweet with an acid sweetness and tolerably palatable. There is, however, something unwholesome about the rubber-vine, and I have heard the native gatherers say that where it flourishes the black man dies; while with the exception of troops of chattering monkeys, who delight in the fruit, it is seldom that the silence of a rubber forest is broken by bird or beast. Lagos colony, which forms part of the Lower Niger region, was almost the last district to develop this industry; but its citizens lost no time when they started, and I once travelled with 300 gatherers—raw, and some absolutely naked, savages from the Gold Coast bush, who were going there to collect it. Each succeeding steamer for a long period brought almost as many, and there were probably a score of different races among them, varying from dwarfs 4 feet high to splendid Fantis of over 6 feet. Also I remember that one Government commissioner, who knew the natives well, said he had never seen several of these types before.

The juice should, and in any other place than West Africa would, be collected from a neat incision made in the outer bark, from which the vine would recover. It is, however, almost impossible to teach the negro the simple lesson that if he destroys the creeper he cannot obtain any more rubber from it, and, as a rule, the whole thing is ruthlessly hacked to bits. This stupidity has ruined what would now be acres of very valuable forest behind one or two ports, including Accra. A thick white juice at once exudes, and those who have seen the euphorbia plant bruised will best understand what rubber-sap is like when it is mentioned that the juice of both seems almost identical as regards its smell and colour.

Then the bushman gatherer, who has probably finished that tree for good, looks on and grunts approval, after which he sprinkles it with a little weak salt water, and, instead of tapping another meanwhile, settles himself upon the moist earth and discourses to his fellows. Presently the exuded sap commences to coagulate, and, pouring strong brine upon his naked arms and chest, the woolly-haired lounger touches the opening in the bark with his skin. Immediately the rubber sticks, and so firmly will it adhere to human flesh that every particle at once loses its hold of the bark, while a skilled gatherer can even draw rapidly hardening sap out in strings from the fibre of the tree. I was told no white man could learn this trick, but did not believe it. There are very few things a bush negro can do that a white man with very little practice cannot improve upon. So the gatherer winds it round and round his arm, and sometimes round breast and shoulders as well, and then slipping off the clinging folds, squeezes them up into a rough-shaped cone and flings them into a basket—that is to say, if he is paid as a labourer for some one else. If he is working at so much a pound, he not infrequently searches for a convenient piece of bark or broken end of a branch to lie snugly inside that cone, an ingenious means of helping out the weight. The bushman can be very stupid when required to do anything, but he is quite clever enough to invent exasperating tricks of the kind, as every factory agent knows.

The product thus obtained is not a nice article to handle, and the negroes engaged in the industry are frequently smitten by loathsome skin-diseases. Some I have seen could scarcely be looked at, objects which it was not good to remember even after a lapse of time; and the effluvium of raw rubber is one of the most disgusting smells on earth. I have come out of a store-shed where it was stowed, or a steamer's hold in which the barrels lay reeking in musty heat, almost choked, and certainly very faint, and this was after becoming fairly used to sickening things in Africa. These barrels of semi-plastic white or greenish paste are shipped to the United Kingdom in hundreds, direct as a rule, although a little is occasionally landed on the Gold Coast, for reasons the traders do not care to explain. Probably it finally reaches its destination as the dearer product of Accra.

In addition to the juice of the *Landolphia ovariensis*, or trailer, I have been shown a black rubber obtained from a tree which the natives say grows in many places; but this, although of fair quality, does not seem to be largely worked. The supply is apparently ample, but occasionally difficult of access, and with improvident recklessness the forests are being devastated near the coast. Thus, as the gatherers are forced to go farther and farther into the bush, the cost is steadily increased. A proportion of the rubber that goes out over Lagos Bar could probably be carried by a nearer route down-stream to the delta, but the ways of the native trader are occasionally mysterious. For instance, there is a certain commerce in tusks which come up overland from somewhere south of the German Cameroons, or at least they used to do so, and are then carried down the Niger and bartered away in one of the markets about Onitsha and Asaba. After this they disappear again, and where they eventually reach the sea no European knows. The curious thing is that there are excellent markets at the mouth of every river they cross on the weary journey, and yet the bearer-trains plod on league after league through forest and swamp round an immense half-circle, and in the end the ivory cannot bring a better price. Also, as we have seen, half the loads of the great camel-trains journeying from the Upper Niger to Morocco would be gladly purchased by white men who have tried to intercept them in the West Sahara; but the owners grimly refuse, and travel on through a sun-scorched wilderness to ship the goods across the Mediterranean at what must be a very heavy extra cost. There are many similar instances for which no explanation can be given; but a fortune awaits the adventurer who, running the risk of starvation or murder, can bring about a change.

Perhaps nowhere in the world is there at present such a field for the daring cool-headed man of enterprise, who, disregarding established customs, seeks a new outlet for his energies, as in Western Africa. Such a one must, however, be well versed in what is known of its geography, understand its natives, and be prepared to carry his life in his hands; for in the regular trade channels competition is keen enough. The old order of things has changed, but man is still the same, and we have not yet seen the end of romance. There are to-day far more adventurous Britons doing heroic things in the remote corners of the earth, and laying the foundations of future greatness, than ever there were in the days when England first awoke to claim the supremacy of the seas. Instead of the caravela's lateen they use the screw-propeller; and in place of plundering the Spanish treasure-ships or sacking the cities of the Gulf, they are hewing roads through the malaria swamps of the tropics, surveying waggon-trails down the thundering cañons of the North, floundering with aneroid and triangulation amid the snows of hitherto untrodden peaks, or driving the breaker-plough through wastes of lonely prairie. We have lost the old feudal love of empty glory, which is perhaps not altogether a pity, for a good deal of purposeless slaughter was perpetrated in its name. Now quiet determined men — Government engineer, survey packer, homestead pre-emptor, and free-lance trader — undertake hazardous enterprises because it is fitting they should be done; or, crowded out of the over-filled homeland, wring a sustenance for their children out of virgin soil, and future generations shall profit by their toil. All this is, of course, a diversion; but it is occasionally well that those who dwell at home should turn their eyes across the seas, and seeing, understand.

I remember one or two disease-stricken traders telling me a little story in a factory beside a muddy Niger creek, which may serve to illustrate what the seeker after new openings has occasionally to face.

There had been trouble in the bush, where the naked Jakkeries or Sobos had gone out to raid and murder one another in a periodical outbreak of discontent, and the trade of the factories in that district fell away. Agent Johnson moodily watched his receipts grow smaller week by week, and then remembering he had heard the black traders speak of a wealth of rubber-vines somewhere among the inland creeks, determined to attempt the foundation of a profitable industry. Those waterways had lately been placed under the ban of the Ju-Ju, and even before that the Government officials rarely ventured into the forests surrounding them without a strong detachment of Yorubas at their side. But, like others of the same stamp, Johnson made the attempt with neither bodyguard of sable soldiers nor machine-guns. He took with him a rusty revolver, with which a certain lady passenger afterwards nearly took a good missionary's life when aiming at a porpoise, and a dozen Krooboy paddlers, who, having been freely regaled on Hamburg gin, were not quite in a condition to know where they were bound, or they assuredly would not have gone. So he started in a big cotton-wood canoe loaded with rolls of cloth and cases of gin intended as "dash" to propitiate the black headmen, and slid away in the early dawn, lest the vice-consul should place a veto on the expedition.

When the Krooboys became sufficiently sober to understand matters the most part bolted at night, taking, as usual, as much as they could carry with them; and about a week after he started Johnson found himself sitting in the half-empty canoe in pouring rain, endeavouring to persuade the two who had not run away to continue the adventurous journey up a creek of very doubtful reputation. By-and-by a big headman's steward, or some other kind of slave in authority, came along with a handful of retainers carrying flintlock guns, and wanted to lead the rash European before his master a prisoner bound with ti-ti. Johnson objected, and explaining that he came as a guest, enforced his arguments by gestures with the revolver; and when the body-guard had dragged the canoe ashore and placed the remnant of his possessions upon their woolly heads, marched behind them towards a native village, feeling sorry he had come.

A burly headman, attired principally in a red tennis-jacket, received him suspiciously, and the usual palaver followed, which the trader's partial knowledge of the Jakkery and kindred tongues enabled him to understand. He explained his intentions as unconcernedly as he could, and submitting a case of gin and a few rolls of cloth for the headman's approval, asked for fresh carriers and permission to depart. This was refused, and the sable ruler, who was doubtless unwilling to let so rich a prize slip through his fingers, and yet hesitated to attempt violence, knowing that the death of a European would probably be followed by the visit of an inquisitive and heavily armed launch, took counsel with his subordinates. After this he replied that there were very bad people in the bush who shot strangers from ambush, and therefore he would take care of the white man until he could order up a further assortment from the factory, when they could arrange some business together.

Johnson, however, could read between the lines, and the message a naked bushman took downstream in a canoe was not directed finally to the factory assistant, but to the vice-consul, asking for help at once, and he felt he had done wisely when he found himself virtually a prisoner in the headman's house. The "palace" was a low mud-walled affair roofed with palm-thatch, and, as usual among some Jakkery tribes, entered by a passage half-underground. It was also alive with biting insects, and insufferably foul and hot, while for a week the trader and his Krooboys were never permitted to cross its threshold. Johnson insisted upon keeping his retainers with him for safety's sake. Then one night another scantily attired potentate marched into the village with a strong band of armed followers, and listening in the doorway, the trader made out that this one claimed some kind of authority over the other, and wanted to take him away.

His original host seemed to object vigorously, and when presently a big palaver was held, enlivened by the last of the trader's gin, both sides were soon in a state of semi-intoxication, and on the point of coming to blows. Johnson knew that general chaos and the random burning of huts would follow the first nervous letting off of a flintlock gun, and retiring into the interior of his prison, set his wits to work. It was, as is generally the case, half-full of gin-cases, kegs of trade-powder, and other barbaric treasures, including a number of Snider rifles, which had no business there, and the reverse of a nice place to be made fast in should a fire break out. Neither did the trader desire to be taken farther away from the coast, the only point from which he could expect help, and, as he afterwards said, he did not like the way things were going at all.

One of the Krooboys solved the difficulty, and with matchet and gun-butt the prisoners attacked the wall desperately, their exertions quickened by the angry yells which entered the passage. At last the rammed earth gave way, and crawling through the opening, they found themselves in the cool night air, and, slipping unobserved amid the bananas to the river, launched a canoe and paddled for their lives. Johnson safely reached the settlement, and was censured by the Government officer for his rashness, and later on the trade of the factory improved with more peaceful news from the bush. And this is one narrative of a kind common enough on the fringe of every scantily known district, where such adventures receive very little comment because they are by no means unusual. It is also repeated, as nearly as I can remember, in the trader's undemonstrative style. Some day—so the principal actor said—he intends to make another attempt to get out that rubber, and he will probably succeed.

When he does he will not only have hardly earned a little for himself, but every pound of produce he sends down will be so much work and wages for his countrymen at home, and we may wish him and his kind God-speed.

CHAPTER XXVII.

FAREWELL TO THE NIGER.

AT last, one misty day, I stood on board a deep-loaded mail-boat hauling out from Warri wharf. The winches clanged and hammered as they heaved on the tight-strung wire, and a roaring jet of vapour swept aloft from the escape-pipe overhead. Now and then a blackened face streaked with grime and perspiration rose up above the fiddley gratings, and its owner, gulping in a breath of comparatively cool air, disappeared again into the sweltering depths below, for firing in the tropics is man-killing work. But the dripping, panting stokers had their hearts in their task that day, and a long trail of dingy smoke streaming across the forest told that they were toiling with a will.

The mail-boat was filled to the hatches with palm-oil and kernels. Her decks swarmed with Krooboys, wildly excited and vociferous, for they were returning to their "we country"; while the second mate and bos'n were hard at work passing green cases of gin, cotton cloth, and matchets which the sable factory hands had received in return for twelve months' labour, down the half-opened hatch. This was a precautionary measure, because when the Krooboy has imbibed a sufficiency of Hamburg gin he sometimes becomes difficult to handle, and has been known to turn a steamer's decks into a respectable battle-field over disputes about the ownership of cloth. Meanwhile a squad of big Yorubas and other fighting men from the north, going back after serving the White Queen to a region far off in the wilds of the hinterland, leaned quiet and grim against the bulwarks, holding themselves contemptuously apart from the noisy heathen around.

Twice the boom of the whistle went ringing across the cotton-woods, and still the canoes came off, one bringing a sickly youth looking forward eagerly to the home he was never to reach alive, another with an invalided agent, while trader and Government official were climbing up the ladder or hurrying about the decks. There were packets to be delivered, or bundles of curios and kindly messages to those they loved at home; while high up at the foremast-head the Portuguese ensign fluttered out on the sultry breeze as a token that the steamer was bound north and west *viâ* Madeira for the land they served so well. Then the anchor rose grinding to the bows, and as the stern-warp splashed into the river we felt that the last link binding us to Africa was gone. When next that rope ran out through its port the end would touch British soil. Then there was a fresh shouting from the Krooboys, a grasping of hands between friends, some of whom would never look into each other's eyes again, a short bidding of farewells, "Good-bye," one "God bless you," "You'll tell them all I'm well," and the crash of the big brass mail-gun rang through the listless air.

Then a hoarse cheer rose up, the engines commenced to throb, and as the oil-tank gathered way a group of yellow-faced traders stood on the trodden bank, watching her slide down the river with their hearts in their eyes. She was bound to an island where was neither heat nor fever, and they were left behind to toil on in the steam of Africa until, too probably, the breath of the malaria brought them their last discharge.

The burning afternoon was fading into dusk as we steamed forth through the muddy white-crested ridges that sweep Forcados bar. The long swell ran blood-red to the westward, and a silent group stood aft upon the poop watching the last of the Niger forests that loomed up fainter and fainter against the darkening east. All of them had suffered many evils there, and one or two would carry painful mementoes of the fever-land with them all their lives. Soon the tall palms and cotton-woods became blurred and indistinct, the creaming surf on the hammered shoals merged into the dusky sea, then gathering wreaths of night-damp hid the forest from our sight. With a jest which had more of a sigh than mirth in it, one man, whose death-warrant was written upon his face, turned away, and the little group broke up. Slowly they straggled forward towards the tall bridge-deck, where the pure breath of the Southern Ocean swept humming beneath the awnings as with whirling screw the big oil-tank drove out to the westwards, heading for open sea.

Next morning she dropped her anchor in the tumbling Lagos Roads, and here a branch-boat brought us the usual contingent of broken-down humanity. Few of those who came off in her could have dragged themselves on board, and were swung aloft through mid-air in a sawn-off tub beneath the rattling crane. Willing hands helped the sickly wretches out upon the deck, found them easy lounges in chairs of Madeira work, or carried them away below, while, as we steamed again to the westward, Government surgeon and mail-boat doctor held anxious consultations beneath the throbbing poop. It was no business of the former. He had already done his part in Africa, and was now going home to gather strength, and rest; but he could not fold his hands while men lay sick about him. Besides, his skill was clearly of a higher order than that of the steamship doctor, though the latter was a conscientious man, and all the way to the "roaring trades," in spite of personal weakness, that surgeon did noble work. In too many cases, however, neither patient watchfulness nor the wisdom of long experience might avail, for the grip of the malaria was stronger than human skill. So every now and then at the changing of the watch a group of bareheaded men stood silently about the gangway, where a shapeless roll of canvas lay beneath the crimson folds of the ensign upon a grating at the rail. Then for a space there was no movement or sound about the ship save the throbbing of the screw and the roar beneath the bows, while the bronzed skipper, balancing himself against the heave of the deck, read reverently from the open book in his hand. Presently he beckoned to a watcher at the skylights, and the monotonous song of the engines died away, while through the sudden stillness that followed, the words, "We therefore commit his body to the deep . . . in the sure and certain hope," rang clearly across the drowsy gurgle of water along the bends. Some one cut a lashing, and a seaman laid his hand on the flag; the grating tilted sharply, and there was a hollow splash in the sea. Then the engines recommenced their pounding, and the rolling steamer went on her way again, leaving one who had wrecked his health in Africa to sleep in the green depths of the ocean until—there shall be no more sea.

If I remember correctly, there were six such funerals before we reached "the trades"; but this was not unusual, for it must be borne in mind that the majority of both Government officers and traders are very determined men. They have been sick so often that they accept fever as a matter of course, and if it comes upon them when trade is brisk at the factory or there is trouble brewing in the bush, hold on grimly, trusting they may overcome the weakness as they have done before. Thus many of them only yield too late, even if they yield at all, and are carried in lurching hammocks through the bush to the nearest beach, or slide down the muddy rivers in canoes, worn-out skeletons, or, as sometimes happens, raving mad. This explains part of the mortality at the coastwise settlements or on shipboard; and turning over consular papers in the Government offices at Freetown, I saw that two previous steamers had buried respectively eleven and thirteen men. There was also a big Belgian mail-boat came up astern of us homeward bound from the Congo, and her course for a thousand miles was marked by the rolls of weighted canvas that went overboard. "They died with us all the way like rotten sheep," so her officers said.

Then if any one ask the question, "Is it, after all, worth while?" the answer can be only "Yes."

Fortunately as a nation we have little fear of death, and deep in the hearts of the people there is an instinctive recognition that a man's part is not to shirk the hardships or escape from the sorrows of life. As it has been written, "The English are a dumb people. They can do great acts, but not describe them"; and again: "The life of all gods figures itself to us as a sublime sadness—earnestness of infinite battle against infinite labour. Our highest religion is named the worship of sorrow. For the son of man there is no noble crown, but a crown of thorns."

Further, the sacrifice is needed, and we should be thankful there are men who do not hesitate to make it. Looking at the matter superficially, it is a mere earning of a pittance by the collection of revenue or the shipping of palm-oil by those who, it may be, can earn their bread in no other way. But to understanding eyes it means much more than this. In the first place, we have laid our hands upon a wide tract of Western Africa, and there is a moral obligation upon us to govern it, protect the weak, do something to relieve the seething misery, and let in the light of civilisation. If we abandoned our hold upon it, in less than twelve months the land would sink into darkness and a chaos of bloodshed. As many Governments have found, it is easier to enter in than to march out with honour again, for once a work of this kind is undertaken there can be no turning back.

Also, the teeming population of our islands depends for sustenance to a great measure on commerce over the seas. Whether the dream of some, that in a time of evenly distributed wealth the land would feed even a greatly increased people, will ever be realised the future alone can show. Such hopes, however, savour too much of the millennium; for from the expulsion from Eden onward the majority of men have won their daily food in anguish of mind as well as by the sweat of their brow. Meanwhile, when there is a constant struggle to find orders for the busy mills and work for the myriad hands, when hostile tariffs year by year strike hard at our foreign trade, it is of the utmost importance to find new outlets for our energies and fresh markets for our goods. Think of what one steamer does alone when she sails for the feverland with endless rolls of cotton, hardware, and metal goods. Men have been housed and fed for standing beside the looms or filling the moulds in the foundry; clerks, railway hands, stevedores, and porters have been paid to put those goods on board. The palm-oil and rubber she brings back give work directly or indirectly to several thousand men, and there is not an ounce of merchandise that goes in and out across the smoking river-bars but contributes its own quota to find our people bread.

Then there is the drastic training of our men. Smooth things have seldom been good for any nation since the beginning of history; for when comfort developed to luxury, and men grew afraid of hardship or physical pain, the end was drawing near. Thus the reckless adventurer who sets up his rickety factory on unknown creeks in defiance of the fetiche taboo, or, heeding neither hunger, thirst, nor fever, presses on into the wastes of the hinterland, is doing far more than finding a sale for so many rolls of cloth. Where he has opened a way many will follow after, and the hardihood and resolution that such hazards teach is probably worth more to the nation than the trade that soon flows in. The grim struggle against almost insurmountable difficulties, the necessity for a dogged purpose and relentless holding on in the face of many perils, will set its own stamp upon those who embark therein, for it is things like these make men. Further, the hopes of harassed merchants and manufacturers go with him, as well as those of factory hand and fitter who starve on half-time at home. Too many of these have found to their sorrow that British goods cannot be sold against a duty of 50 per cent, and they at least can realise the urgent need of a field for fresh extension. And such a field lies ready waiting, in the great basin of the Niger, 2000 odd miles from the mountains of Kong to Lokoja camp.

After all, so far we have but set our foot on the fringe of Western Africa. Throughout the greater portion of its length our real dominion scarcely reaches 100 miles from the seaboard, in some parts barely ten. And yet, in spite of lack of harbours along the thundering beach, the obstacles to transport in the shape of quaking swamp and creeper-choked forest, the trade of that region is already very great, and advances by leaps and bounds. Thus far we have gone with everything against us—natural difficulties enough to daunt the bravest, hostile tribe, and deadly climate—and beyond there lies a vast and goodly land. Here, as we have shown, instead of degraded fetiche-worshippers, dwell a people trained in industrial arts, trading even across the ends of the desert, and organised in arms. Instead of the fever-swamps, there is a dry land of plume-grass, dotted with the small white cattle or checkered by fields of grain. The clusters of rickety hovels give place to strong walled towns with mosques raised high to Allah; and here the camel-trains come in on the one hand from Morocco, on the other from the Nile. Also the possibilities of this region are enormous: it became great twice already, and there is a highway through all its length in the Niger or Joliba.

Of late the eyes of many traders have been turned expectantly north. Already the cry has been raised for the construction of light railways from Sierra Leone, from the Gold Coast, from Lagos, all converging on the basin of the Niger, and if the Government do not help them the traders will do the work themselves. Many men will perish before the last spike is driven and the narrow-gauge steel highways connect the land of the Northern Moslem with the Guinea shore. But that spike will be surely driven, and then there will be a sudden change in the map of Africa.

Now, with the exception of one or two short-length tracks, salt and cloth filter northward from stockaded town to town on slave carriers' heads, each bush headman claiming a lion's share for toll, until all that comes out of the forest has increased in value perhaps five-hundred-fold. Now the expeditions march north for weary weeks, wading or hewing through steamy forest and swamp. Then our goods will be whirled through intact, unbroken, in a few short days, and the men who sicken or perish as they grope a way across the fever-belt may travel safe and whole. One locomotive would do more in a day than a legion of woolly-haired carriers could, if they were willing, accomplish in a month, while the steam-engine neither tires nor mutinies; and when, as usual, the Empire follows the adventurer, another great dominion will lie sheltered beneath the flag. In those days there will be no Chartered Company, for the work of such organisations is but to lay foundations; and when that is done a stronger power takes hold, which labours, though sometimes blindly, for the general good of mankind as well as extension of trade. The steamer will follow the railroad, not only on the slow Niger reaches below Lokoja but throughout all the network of muddy waterways, and the result will be very startling to those who do not know Africa.

It is neither a dream nor a fancy. Far-seeing men have been steadily working with this one object in view. Some have died of fever or broken down their constitutions seeking a gateway through the swamps. Others, at regular intervals, have spoken plain words in the ears of her Majesty's Ministers. Come it will; and when a vast region greedily receives our products and sends us in return the riches of the hinterland—precious woods, spices, dyes, feathers, and dust of gold, with unnumbered tons of cheaper merchandise—they will know that their labour has not been thrown away. Whether Christianity will extend its beneficent influence over the whole of this region, or for a while at least, and until the time is ripe, we shall rule over an intelligent people still staunch to the Moslem faith, who is there can tell? As the sturdy Haussa private says when he sets forth on some perilous march through the forest, the end will be "sa Allah ya yerde"—"as God shall will."

Meantime shall not our sympathies go out to

those who labour in the steam of the forest—trader, missionary, or official — as they grimly clear the way, bidding them be strong and of a good courage, and quit themselves like men? And the nameless rank and file, who perish and are forgotten? They, also, have done their part, and gained a hard-won rest; and, after all, it is such as these who have made the nation great.

INDEX.

Accra, 57.
Aggri beads, 230.
Akassa, 78.
Alligators, 238.
Ants, 240.
Arab invasion, 121.
Arabs and their ways, 184.
Axim, 55.

Barwood, 307.
Benin, New, 179, 193.
" Old, 198.
Bishop Crowther, 286.
Black trader, 300.
Bonny, 277.
Brass men, 91.
Brass river, 243.
Brohemie, 206.

Camel caravans, 5, 118.
Camwood, 307.
Cape Coast Castle, 54.
Characteristics of negro, 301.
Chief Dore, 195.
Chopping oil, 305.
Clapperton, 9.
Clerks at the factories, 19, 185.
Coffee, 307.
Cotton, 307.
Country cloth, 308.
Court in Niger country, 146.
Crawford, Major, 145.
Cross river, 277.
Crowther, Bishop, 286.

Current of African rivers, 234.

Dahomey, 62.
Diseases, 85, 203, 329.
Domestic slavery, 174.
Dore, Chief, 195.
Dwarfs, 61.
Dyes, 307, 308, 309.

Early history, 1.
Elmina, 56.
European residence, 84.

Factory building, 182.
Fascination of the tropics, 228.
Fetiche. See Ju-Ju.
Fever, 85, 203, 259, 329.
Forcados, 126.
Freetown, 21.
Fulah race, 123.
Funeral, West African, 254.

Gin trade, 81.
Gold Coast, 54.
Guinea-worm, 85.
Gums, 306.
Gunboats, patrol, 248.
Gun-cases, new use of, 221.

Harbours, 52.
Haussa constabulary, 59.
Hindoostan, hulk, 231.
Historical, 1.

Y

INDEX.

Ibo tribes, 294.
Igara tribes, 295.
Inland reaches, 115.

Jakkery tribes. See Benin, Warri, Sapelli.
Jigger insect, 86.
Ju-Ju feasts, 236.
　,,　house, 158, 237.
　,,　system, 165.
　,,　treasure, 198.
Justice, administration of, 146.

Kernels, 151, 244.
Kola-nuts, 309.
Konno tribe, 30, 291.
Kroo country, 47.
Kroomen, 45.
Kuranko tribe, 291.

Lagos, 66, 327.
Lander, 10, 75.
Leopard men, 27.
Liberia, 43.
Limba tribe, 291.
Lokoja, 296.

Mail, 136.
Major Crawford, 145.
Mangroves, 139.
Mendi tribe, 290.
Missionary influence, 264, 285.
Monrovia, 43.
Moslem conquests, 6, 292.
Mosquitoes, 217.
Mouths of Niger, 70.
Mungo Park, 8.

Nana, 205.
Negro characteristics, 301.
　,,　trader, 300.
New Benin, 179, 193.
Nun river, 72.

Onitsha, 295.
Opobo, 282.

Othman, Sheik, 124.

Palm-kernels, 151, 244.
　,,　oil, 151.
Park, Mungo, 8.
Piece of cloth, 227.
Pine-apples, 221.
Portuguese, 7, 199.
Protectorate of Niger Coast, 10, and throughout.
　,,　Sierra Leone, 288.
Puncheon of oil, 303.

Raiding of Akassa, 91.
Retail trading, 227.
River-bar, 73, 278.
Royal Niger Company, 10, 75, &c.
　,,　Constabulary, 297.
Rubber, 311.

Sahara coast, 119.
Salt, 78.
Samori, 29.
Sapelli, 217, 231.
Segu, 121.
Sharks, 219.
Sierra Leone, 21, 288.
Slavery, domestic, 174.
Slave-trade, 170, 295.
Sofa tribe, 30, 291.
Sokoto empire, 124.
Songhay empire, 122.
Source of Niger, 290.
Surf, 53, 58.

Teneriffe, 15.
Timbuktu, 118.
Tornados, 41.
Trading clerks, 19, 185.
Transport of goods, 51, 289.
Treaty of Brussels, 154.

Warri, 138, 150.
Weima, battle of, 29.

Yoruba troops, 83.

PRINTED BY WILLIAM BLACKWOOD AND SONS.

MESSRS WILLIAM BLACKWOOD & SONS' NEW BOOKS.

ANNALS OF A PUBLISHING HOUSE. Vol. III.—JOHN BLACKWOOD. By his Daughter, MRS GERALD PORTER. With Two Portraits and View of Strathtyrum. Demy 8vo, 21s.

WITH KITCHENER TO KHARTUM. By G. W. STEEVENS, Author of 'Egypt in 1898,' 'The Land of the Dollar,' 'With the Conquering Turk,' &c. Eighth Edition. With 8 Maps and Plans. Crown 8vo, 6s.

"Mr G. W. Steevens' description of the battle of Omdurman reaches, we do not hesitate to say, the high-water mark of literature. Sir William Napier might have known more about the details of the battle, but even he could not have brought the blood of the reader to his forehead in a more exciting way."—*Spectator.*

"Mr Steevens has given us a notable work, which deserves to be widely read."—*Daily Telegraph.*

EGYPT IN 1898. By the Same Author. With Illustrations. Crown 8vo, 6s.

"All persons bound East should provide themselves with this book. It is full of information. Those who stay at home will get from it a better idea of the country and its people than from half-a-dozen more pretentious works."—*Westminster Gazette.*

SOLDIER AND TRAVELLER: BEING THE MEMOIRS OF ALEX-ANDER GARDNER, Colonel of Artillery in the service of Maharaja Ranjit Singh. Edited by MAJOR HUGH PEARSE, 2nd Battalion the East Surrey Regiment. With an Introduction by the Right Hon. Sir RICHARD TEMPLE, Bart., G.C.S.I. With Two Portraits and Two Maps. Demy 8vo, 15s.

"We have rarely come across a volume of better reading than these memoirs of Colonel Alexander Gardner....... As the Colonel had a bright, effective, straightforward style, the very ideal for a life of adventure, the form of his memoirs is as good as the substance, and it would be difficult to say more than that."—*St James's Gazette.*

"You could hardly get a more vivid or faithful picture of Europe in the Dark Ages than Colonel Alexander Gardner saw while in the service of one or other of the Afghan chiefs, and, I may add, you could hardly find in any picturesque historian a more vivid or vigorous record of these thrilling experiences than that given in the Colonel's own words."—*Truth.*

Dedicated by Special Permission to H.R.H. the Duke of York.

RETRIEVERS, AND HOW TO BREAK THEM. By Lieut.-Colonel SIR HENRY SMITH, K.C.B. With an Introduction by Mr SHIRLEY of Ettington, President of the Kennel Club. With Illustrations. Crown 8vo, 5s.

"In sympathetic analysis of canine nature, born of close intimacies and lifelong acquaintanceship, we have read nothing so good of the sort since Sir Edward Hamley wrote 'Our Poor Relations.' The style is free, racy, and frank, and here it is evidently the man himself. Even those who have never owned, and never hope to own, a retriever, must nevertheless find the book delightful reading....... The course of schooling he suggests is admirable, from curbing youthful impetuosity to the perfection of cool and finished retrieving."—*Times.*

WILLIAM BLACKWOOD & SONS, EDINBURGH AND LONDON.

NEW NOVELS.

WINDYHAUGH. By GRAHAM TRAVERS, Author of 'Mona Maclean' and 'Fellow Travellers.' Crown 8vo, 6s.

MR AND MRS NEVILL TYSON. By MAY SINCLAIR, Author of 'Audrey Craven,' &c. Crown 8vo, 3s. 6d.

JOHN SPLENDID. THE TALE OF A POOR GENTLEMAN AND THE LITTLE WARS OF LORN. By NEIL MUNRO, Author of 'The Lost Pibroch.' Third Edition. Crown 8vo, 6s.

"Neil Munro's latest work shows what a Scotch romance can be—of what interest, what stirring excitement, and with what a fascinating *mise-en-scène*.......The interest never flags, the mind never wearies."—*Daily Telegraph.*

THE ADVENTURES OF THE COMTE DE LA MUETTE DURING THE REIGN OF TERROR. By BERNARD CAPES, Author of 'The Mill of Silence,' 'The Lake of Wine,' &c. Crown 8vo, 6s.

"A brilliant series of imaginary episodes during the Reign of Terror.......The faculty of invention which the author displays is not less remarkable than his command of an ornate but genuinely picturesque style, and he is to be congratulated on the choice of a theme so excellently adapted alike to his vivid—and at times somewhat lurid—imagination and his equipment as an artist in decorative diction."—*Spectator.*

A CROWNED QUEEN: THE ROMANCE OF A MINISTER OF STATE. By SYDNEY C. GRIER. Crown 8vo, 6s.

"This fine romance.......The complications of the high game of political intrigues are subordinated to the appeal of a moving and tragic love-story."—*Daily News.*

LIFE IS LIFE, AND OTHER TALES AND EPISODES. By ZACK. Second Edition. Crown 8vo, 6s.

"Take them altogether, they are the best things of the sort we have had since Mr Kipling came to the front—powerful, vivid, direct, and admirably written.......It is a remarkable book, and shows that we have a new writer of short stories of uncommon strength."—*Standard.*

THE IMPEDIMENT. By DOROTHEA GERARD (Madame Longard DE LONGGARDE), Author of 'Lady Baby,' 'A Spotless Reputation;' and Joint-Author of 'Reata,' &c. Crown 8vo, 6s.

"The author holds our interest as she lays scene after scene before us, and she keeps the final issue well hidden till the end comes."—*Manchester Guardian.*
"An excellent story by Dorothea Gerard, a tale full of cleverly conceived situations, and remarkable for the ability displayed in the portrayal of the leading characters."—*Scotsman.*

WILLIAM BLACKWOOD & SONS, EDINBURGH AND LONDON.

www.ingramcontent.com/pod-product-compliance
Lightning Source LLC
Chambersburg PA
CBHW030305240426
43673CB00040B/1069